The 33rd

Editor-In-Chief	Scott Stein
Senior Editors	Albert DiBartolomeo
	Kathleen Volk Miller
Layout Editor	William Rees
Graphic Design	Krissy Beck
	Lauren Beltramo
Editorial Co-ops	Ari Melman
	Francisco Santoni
Design Co-op	Lindsey Fratz
Student Interns	Anna Clay
	Anne Most
	Brittany MacLean
	Brooke Segarra
	Danielle Goddard
	Dori Molozanov
	Kaitlyn Benesch
	Makane George
	Margo Jones
	Michael Benesch
	Michelyve Petit
	Nichole Hulse
	Olivia DiPasquale
	Renee Daggett
	Zack Ssebatindira

Sponsors

Drexel University
The College of Arts and Sciences at Drexel University
The Department of English and Philosophy at Drexel University

Dr. Donna M. Murasko, Dean, College of Arts and Sciences,
Drexel University
Dr. Abioseh Michael Porter, Department Head, English and Philosophy,
Drexel University

The 33rd Volume 5
Drexel University
Department of English and Philosophy
3141 Chestnut Street
Philadelphia, PA 19104
www.drexelpublishing.org

Cover photo by Richard Quindry Photography

Copies of this volume are available for $10 by writing to the above address.

ISBN 978-0-9820717-4-8

Thank you, thank you, thank you and thank you to: Dr. Donna M. Murasko; Dr. Abioseh Michael Porter; all the judges from the Drexel Publishing Group Essay Contest, the Week of Writing Contest, and the Freshman Writing Contest (Genevieve Betts, Ken Bingham, Valerie Booth, Ingrid Daemmrich, Blythe Davenport, Albert DiBartolomeo, Anne Erickson, Robert Finegan, Alexander Friedlander, Robert Gilmore, Casey Hirsch, Maria Hnaraki, Monica Ilies, Rebecca Ingalls, Henry Israeli, Karen Kabnick, Miriam N. Kotzin, Lynn Levin, Michael Leone, Deirdre McMahon, Kathleen McNamee, Anne-Marie Obajtek-Kirkwood, Emilie Passow, Rakhmiel Peltz, Lydia Pyne, Donna Rondolone, Don Riggs, Patricia Henry Russell, Eric Schmutz, Jonathan Seitz, Fred Siegel, Eva Thury, Monica Togna, Brigita Urbanc, Marshall Warfield, Kathleen Volk Miller, Scott Warnock); Department of English and Philosophy, especially Mary Beth Beyer, Eileen Brennen, and Nicole Kline; contest participants; Drexel Publishing Group staff.

Distributed by the Drexel Publishing Group
The fonts used within this publication are Archer and Avenir

Credits:

Barclay, Scott. "Has the Tide Turned on Marriage Equality: From the Controversial to the Mundane, From the Unusual to the Routine" originally published in Mobilizing Ideas, 2012. <http://mobilizingideas.wordpress.com/>

Betts, Genevieve. "Pest Vignettes" originally published in OVS Magazine, 2011.

Cohen, Paula Marantz. "The Meanings of Forgery" originally published in the Southwest Review, 97, 1 (2012).

Daemmrich, Ingrid. "From Erasmus to Twitter: Parody as Medium for Local and Global Social Networking" originally published in International Society of the Study of Humor, 2011.

Dilworth, Richard. "Does Political Reform Exist" previously published in Pennsylvania Legacies, vol III, No. 2, November 2011, pp. 40-41. Pennsylvania Legacies is a publication of The Historical Society of Pennsylvania.

Fox, Valerie. "Incorruptible" originally published in Hanging Loose, 2011.

Herbert, James, and Richard E. Redding. "When the Shrinks Ignore Science, Sue Them" originally published in Skeptical Inquirer, 2011.

Israeli, Henry. "A Canticle with Dashes of Remorse" originally published in Zocalo Public Square.

Kotzin, Miriam N. "How to Write A Sustainable Poem" originally published in The Flea, XIII, February, 2011. Web.

Kotzin, Miriam N. "How to Write A Sustainable Love Poem" originally published in The Flea, XIII, February, 2011. Web.

Leone, Michael. "From the Terrace of the Hollywood Hotel" originally published in The Saranac Review.

Levin, Lynn. "How to Eat a Pet: A Gastronomic Adventure in the Andes" originally published in Alimentum: The Literature of Food, 2006.

Rosen, Gail D. "Worthwhile Waiting for Superman Doesn't Explore Reasons for Failing Schools" originally published in When Falls the Coliseum. <whenfallsthecoliseum.com>

Rutberg, Donald. "Home of the Road Warriors" originally published in Lehigh Valley Literature Review.

Sandapen, Sheila. "The Spider Princess" originally published in GrowSeeds.com.

Shure, Myrna. "Anger, Oh Those Tantrums!" originally published in Thinking Parent, Thinking Child, 2005.

Volk Miller, Kathleen. "Too Close for Comfort" originally published as "Parenting Secrets of a College Professor" in Salon, 2012.

Warnock, Scott. "Warning: Your Child May be a Carrier of Adverbs" originally published in When Falls the Coliseum, 2012. <whenfallsthecoliseum.com>

Welcome

The 33rd anthology is a visible expression of the College of Arts and Sciences' commitment to interdisciplinary scholarship and writing excellence. Within its pages is an eclectic mix of short stories, essays and scientific articles written by students and faculty from fields across the University, from engineering to nursing to English. This volume demonstrates the incred ible diversity of Drexel scholarship: we are one institution composed of diverse perspectives. These unique perspectives enhance our community and have the power to inspire others to new insights and innovations, whether that's writing the next best-selling novel or discovering a new molecule. But powerful stories and miraculous discoveries are nothing without the skills of communication. These skills allow us to share our ideas, our research, our vision, with the world.

Whether you dream of being an author, an architect, or an environmental scientist, your training starts here, with the tools of communication.

Donna M. Murasko, Ph.D.
Dean
College of Arts and Sciences

Preface

As is often noted, the Department of English and Philosophy has established a well-deserved reputation not only as a place where instructors of all ranks are passionate about teaching and learning—derived from classroom and other such experiences—but also as the one locale at Drexel where excellent writing is seen as a daily, achievable goal. Because our ultimate objective is to make excellent writing a defining characteristic of a Drexel education, we will continue to help our students understand that a fine blend of traditional literary skills and modern thought and practice will help to make them excellent, even outstanding, writers. We, the faculty in our department, have therefore set as our primary goals the achievement of the highest academic standards, the creation of a congenial atmosphere for our students, and a dynamic teaching and scholarly environment.

It is thus with immense pleasure that we present the fifth volume of this yearly anthology. In *The 33rd* 2012, we aim to encourage our students to fuse insights derived from their varied experiences and knowledge to create a document that truly should impress readers because of the complex web of writing the authors present, even with an occasional undergraduate self-consciousness.

Using varying approaches that, even in these early stages, reveal the complexity, density of texture and meaning, and the richness of vision and artistry that often characterize good quality writing, the students—guided by their very able instructors—have carefully demonstrated in print some famous words of wisdom by Diane Stanley, author and illustrator: "Good writing is clear thinking." What I now hope the students, again with guidance from all of us, will continue to do from this point on is to apply the other half of Ms. Stanley's statement: "Reading is how you learn what good writing sounds like."

We are particularly heartened by the efforts reflected here because scarcely a false note is struck in this volume. The pieces in the anthology—though varied—continue to demonstrate the relevance and importance of high quality writing and good reading habits. Taken together, the contributions by both students and faculty reveal that literary and cultural exchanges between these two symbiotic groups continue to develop and improve.

My personal congratulations—as well as those of the whole department—go to all who participated in this laudable and practically useful project. To those whose selections were published, I would like to conclude by offering some more words by the writer Enrique Jardiel Poncela: "When something can be read without effort, great effort has gone into its writing." Bravo!

Abioseh Michael Porter, Ph.D.
Department Head
Department of English and Philosophy

Table of Contents

Contributors

Freshman
Writing

Introduction

The thousands of compositions written by students enrolled in the Freshman Writing Program at Drexel represent their extraordinary experiences and perspectives. Composed over weeks of reading, research, discussion, contemplation, and revision, these compositions are a reflection of how students are learning to use writing as a tool for creative, complex inquiry, and are making their writing matter beyond the boundaries of the classroom: in the development of the self, in the crafting of proposals for change, in the building of ideas that lead to innovation.

The Freshman Writing Award offers a showcase of some of the most excellent student work from this year. After a competitive multi-stage process of evaluating and narrowing down the submissions, the winners and honorable mentions are announced, and the awards are given at the English Awards Ceremony in the spring. I can say with confidence that these students, who hail from all corners of this institution, have made us proud not just as instructors and as a program, but also as a university that aims to create a culture of writing across the disciplines. We hope that these texts will serve as evidence to our writers and readers that—no matter what field you have decided to pursue—writing will be a critical tool for your exploration and success.

I want to thank the generosity of FWP faculty member Ingrid Daemmrich, sponsor of the FWP Writing Contest, and the hardworking Drexel Publishing Group for bringing this book into being. I also want to extend my deepest gratitude to Department Head Dr. Abioseh Porter, Dean Donna Murasko, and Provost Mark Greenberg for their enduring support of writing pedagogy, innovation, and assessment. Finally, I want to especially thank our many beloved, wise faculty who continue to devote tireless inspired hours to make this program stronger each year.

Rebecca Ingalls, Ph.D.
Director, Freshman Writing Program

Casey Condon

Pixels, Primates and a Pipe Dream

An aged, weathered gorilla slowly cranks a phonograph which plays a simple, yet memorable melody. As the tune quickens and the bass starts to pound within the television's speakers, a much more athletic-looking ape, sporting a snazzy red tie and clutching a vine in one hand and a stereo in the other, dramatically swings into view. A childish chimpanzee donning a red baseball cap is not far behind and joins his burly primate buddy, and the two jam out to the now rock-and-roll inspired tune. The scene shifts and the duo of adventurous simians are dashing through the jungle, collecting bananas, leaping across chasms, and stomping on troublesome crocodiles. On the other side of the glass that separates this fantastical world from one a bit more familiar is a six-year-old boy in his pajamas staring intently at the screen, clutching tightly the only connection he has to this new, exciting world: a purple and gray Super Nintendo controller.

As this conglomeration of bleeps, bloops, bits, and bytes called *Donkey Kong Country* entrances me more, my parents and relatives give my sisters and me other video games for holidays and birthdays. I sit silent with my large eyes transfixed to the television set, brimming with excitement that there are so many new worlds and experiences waiting for me through this medium. I curiously ponder the origin of these worlds. It is not until a crisp November day when I, sitting in the living room on an ugly blue couch in triumph over a particularly difficult mine-cart level of *Donkey Kong Country*, realize that someone, not God, but some man, had created these worlds.

As I enter the large, gothic building that will house the next eight years of my education and exploration, the next "level" in my life begins. A red 98% stares up from a sterile white sheet tainted by my heavy pencil marks, and instead of smiling in satisfaction at my achievement, I watch the clock intently, feet tapping, wanting nothing more than to escape that room and explore. My saddle shoes make hollow "clacks" as I walk slowly down labyrinthine corridors, examining each large marble block in the wall with great scrutiny, my spirit yearning for the one that would lead to some secret treasure. Similarly, my heart races as I sit on the cold radiator in the limestone-encrusted basement boy's bathroom awaiting a specter who I have no doubt lives there. I am Donkey Kong, or Mario, or Link, obligated by fate to accomplish these tasks. Although these excursions yield no concrete results (except for the occasional discovery of an unused room), they set my imagination ablaze. I am enthralled by the sense of mystery and discovery contained within these walls, and my small hands draw basic levels and characters based on these adventures.

An impatient teacher in her ruffled blouse and orthopedic shoes looks over my shoulder, annoyed that the margins of my marbled composition book are littered with stick figures and the monsters in my imagination. At home I hear "Casey! Get off the Nintendo right now!" through clenched teeth. My mother takes out the garbage again because I'm too busy flinging the pesky King Bowser into the spiked bombs surrounding the floating arena. My mom may be upset but Princess Peach is forever grateful for being rescued by my quick wit and even quicker twitch reflexes. I am certainly not wasting my time by trying to complete every single side quest in *The Legend of Zelda: Ocarina of Time* or by doodling relentlessly on every vocab list and math test that comes my way, but I am instead preparing for my future as a video game designer.

When I'm in fourth grade, a family friend messes up my hair and blabs about how cute I am. She then asks, in an accent with no t's and few spaces, "So Casey, whaddo ya wannabe when ya grow up?"

"A video game designer..." I answer reluctantly, having already predicted her response.

"Well, izzunt that cute!" she retorts, humoring me with a polite smile and generic words of encouragement. In the meantime, my uncorked creativity continues to spill onto my marble notebooks and several pages of Microsoft Word. Lacking any sophisticated software, I draw a small mound using the line tool, then some bridges and doors, and then a whale in a small pool of water. I press the 3d button, adjust the percentages, and suddenly a vast mountainscape towering above the clouds sits before my eyes. This and other crude-looking creations are huge steps toward reaching my dreams. My still very miniature hands click away at the computer, exploring the corporate sites of companies like Nintendo, Sony, EA, Square Enix, and the like. I could almost feel the cold aluminum in my hands as I imagined adjusting the little metal plaque sitting proudly on my desk reading, "Casey Condon: Game Designer."

The innocent years of grade school come to a close and Scranton Prep is an immense, intimidating castle in the distance, literally. Determined to keep my grades up I sit hunched over at my desk, doing algebra with my feet woven into the framework of my IKEA office chair. Although a calculator occupies my hand that yearns instead for a Wii controller, I must reject the allure of the newest Donkey Kong game. In my few free hours I read about the industry, getting to know all of the most influential figures. Sigeru Miyamoto,

Koji Igarashi, Keiji Inafune, and Michel Ancel are all people I seek to emulate, even though in my research I am confronted with stories of the many trials of game development. The fatigue and stress I feel in AP Chemistry are probably nothing compared to that of those whose lives depend on the public's opinion of some polygons and a few lines of code. Despite this information, the passion for game design still burns inside of me, and I speed through my informational PowerPoint in freshman computer class and spend the rest of my time linking pictures of haunted houses together to create a point-and-click style adventure game.

During one summer in high school, I procure an internship at my Uncle's web design and development company. As the ancient scanners and copiers click and buzz, completing their assigned task with the urgency of one approaching his execution, I peer around the office, watching as whole websites and applications are constructed from scratch. Feeling especially inspired and restless, I finally decide to take action, stop dreaming, and actually make something tangible. The sterile interface of my free trial of Adobe Flash stretches out before me, complex yet full of potential, and I start following a basic tutorial to create my very first video game.

I immediately start to veer from the path the tutorial so plainly laid out for me by creating my own objects and backgrounds to populate my digital space rather than the ones provided for me. I stray even further by adding slight physics to the on-screen avatar, a floating pencil, so that even when a button was no longer pushed down, the pencil still has some momentum to carry it a tiny bit further. As enemies, erasers with tacks and paperclips for facial features, invade the blue-and-yellow skies, purple mountains, and stone citadels drawn into the background of the first stage, the game suddenly poses a challenge to the player. As the constant trial and error of learning something new continues over the length of my internship, I feel increasingly satisfied. My dream is materializing right in front of me, and now there is no monkey with a phonograph, but a pencil that can shoot graphite, and the creator is not some aloof corporation far away, but a seventeen-year-old who is beginning to fulfill a childhood fantasy.

It is the fall of my senior year. I am standing in a huge atrium; my eyes dart quickly from the grand staircase to the ornate busts and headless angel to the smooth, sexy arches on the upper floors. The whole room has a golden, ethereal glow. A group of other seniors and I make our way upstairs and into an art gallery where we are bombarded with information about Drexel University. The information presented is the usual "look at how great we are" spiel presented with a blue and gold flair. Although impressed in general, one fact I had been ignorant to prior really stands out—Drexel University is third in the country for game design. How could I have not known this before?! Not only is this the perfect place to master my craft, but after a tour I can honestly see myself walking the streets of University City among all of my fellow dragons. "And with our VIP application you can apply for free!" I hear a thin, platinum blond woman in admissions brag. Later that week I sit at my computer, spell-checking my essay and praying that I haven't made any stupid mistakes. Then, with a hesitant click of my USB mouse, I officially apply to Drexel University.

It is a few months before I go off to Drexel and I am able to occupy a bit of my summer with what I love to do. A very crisp-looking gorilla with realistic fur and incredibly smooth movement swings across my plasma television. His classic red tie sways realistically with the breeze and his gargantuan footsteps are given weight as they echo through the surround sound speakers with a definitive thud. The world around him comes to life in the form of waves crashing gently in the background and thin trees swaying as the gorilla dashes past them on the run to collect more bananas. He adventures through the now fully polygonal worlds of beaches, jungles, cliffs, and factories with no less zeal than he did when his matter was pixels. As I, an 18-year-old 6-year-old, stare into the screen smiling, clutching the Wii controller and watching as the world of *Donkey Kong Country Returns* unfolds in front of me, I know I am on the right track.

Works Cited

Donkey Kong Country. Rareware Games. Nintendo, Inc. 1994. Super Nintendo Entertainment System.

John Quagliariello

Winter Starts in October, Right?

Halloween is a day on which people of all ages dress up in costumes in celebration. Upon the arrival of dusk, children traverse throughout their respective neighborhoods in search of candy and other various goodies. Halloween epitomizes the season of autumn, so naturally, this past Halloween was marked with three inches of snow on the ground and sub-freezing temperatures in the city of Philadelphia. It was "perfect" Halloween weather.

In the final two sentences of my first paragraph, I was being sarcastic. I underwent a major debate in my mind with regards to how I should word each sentence, and then, subsequently, type each sentence. Several options included using italics, but they might have caused confusion, for italics are usually employed when stating a title of a book or possibly showing the voice of a ghostly spirit. The next option included putting an asterisk next to the word perfect[*], but then I thought of my educated readers who, like myself, would assume that an asterisk would lead to a footnote at the bottom of the page. My third option was to just write the sentence without any punctuation, but this, too, would cause problems. Without any punctuation, a reader might assume that I did believe snow was normal weather on Halloween, and then could either be interested in the statement and continue reading my paper, or think that I was unintelligent and I would lose any and all credibility in the eyes of my reader. By exhausting all of my options with punctuation, I was left with no choice but to employ quotation marks around the word "perfect." Although this was not my ideal choice, I needed to ensure that the reader could detect my use of sarcasm. However, this caused me to undergo a small "moral dilemma," for as any frequent user of sarcasm would know, sarcasm is most effective when others are unsure of your true intentions.

The topic of written sarcasm has always proved to be a difficult challenge in my own personal writing ventures. These challenges can be directly attributed to the basic nature of sarcasm, which is defined as "[a] form of irony in which apparent praise conceals another, scornful meaning" (Sarcasm). "Irony," in turn, can be explained as "expressions in which the intended meaning of the words is different from or the direct opposite of their usual sense" (Cheang 366). Therefore, sarcasm is intended to be a contradiction, and will only prove to be effective if both the user and the intended audience are educated in the proper employment and detection of sarcasm within basic societal interactions. As it turns out, this education begins at the elementary level, for sarcasm can first be detected at the age of six (Glenwright 430). At this tender age, children cannot actually distinguish direct sarcasm, but rather the subtleties associated with it. They will notice that a statement is untruthful, changes in facial expressions, and changes in vocal tone (Glenwright 430).

Tone plays an especially important role in sarcasm. In a study conducted by Patricia Rockwell, a professor of communications at the University of Louisiana, Rockwell randomly selected 24 individuals and then randomly assigned each individual to read a phrase with either sarcasm or sincerity. The acoustics were then recorded and analyzed, and the conclusion drawn was that sarcasm induces vocal cues that are of "slower tempo, lower pitch level, and greater intensity" when compared to the same phrases said in a non-sarcastic manner and that "listeners can decode posed sarcasm from vocal cues alone" (Rockwell 492). Similarly, the same conclusion was drawn in a separate research endeavor conducted by Henry S. Cheang and colleagues, researchers at the McGill University School of Communication Sciences and Disorders. A random sample of native English speakers were selected to read a phrase four times, with sarcasm, humor, sincerity, and neutrality being used respectively. The acoustical variances between the four different readings were then subsequently analyzed. Cheang concluded that "acoustic changes... therefore, could be interpreted as prosodic cues which are most important to the expression of sarcasm" (Cheang 375).

Facial expressions, unlike tonal cues, do not play a major role in the use of sarcasm, but still can provide a user's audience with clues in detecting sarcasm. According to the Encyclopaedic Dictionary of Psychology, "facial gestures...communicate rapidly changing states in the communicator" (Non-verbal communication (NVC)), meaning that when sarcasm is spoken, subtle differences can be noticed in the facial expressions of the speaker. Some of the most common gestures include a rolling of the eyes, movement within the lips, and the raising of the eyebrows, all of which can be used as identifiers for the audience.

Returning to the education in the recognition of sarcasm, children must learn to properly recognize and identify the changes in vocal acoustics and facial gestures. In addition to using the visual and vocal identifiers, children must also grasp the concept of how sarcasm differs between the sexes. Men are much more direct in their use of sarcasm, and will use expressions such as, "Nice going, Einstein." Women, on the other hand, are more likely to use the practice of exclusion. For example, "It's great that a woman your age isn't pushed aside for younger, fresher talent," excludes the receiver from the benefit of being "younger and fresher" (Bennett). It must also be noted that men are much more likely to use sarcasm in everyday conversation whereas women tend to save sarcastic remarks for moments of extreme scathing (Bennett). By the age of 10, all of these skills will have been naturally obtained and understood by most individuals, and they, in turn, will have successfully learned how to detect, interpret, and implement sarcasm into their own social interactions (Glenwright 447).

With tonal speech patterns playing such an important role in identifying and distinguishing sarcasm from other speech patterns, my initial problem is once again brought to attention, for how can sarcasm be successfully employed in written communication? Unfortunately, at the present moment, a foolproof method does not exist, but several techniques can be used in order to increase the probability of success.

The first such method is a two-step process, which first involves an identification of the author's gender. As previously discussed, gender is important due to how each sex uses sarcasm in interactions (Bennett). By identifying the author's gender, the passage in question can then be analyzed to determine if it fits the description for how each gender tends to employ sarcasm.

Another method involves the use of symbols and emotions within textual situations. First introduced in 1982 by Scott Fahlman, a professor at Carnegie Mellon School of Computer Science, an emoticon can be characterized as "a facial expression represented by a short combination of letters and other characters you can enter on your keyboard" (Goldsborough). Some examples include J and L, which can be typed as :) and : (respectively. Abbreviations can also be used to show emotion, with the most popular textual emotional abbreviation being "LOL", which is short for "Laugh Out Loud" (Goldsborough). It should be noted, however, that "both female and male users are equally likely to use emoticons...In addition, females were found to use emoticons mostly for humor, whereas males tended to use emoticons to express teasing and sarcasm," so it is imperative that a reader recognizes and identifies the author (Lancaster).

A third, and innovative, method of showing sarcasm in print media can be attributed to Sarcasm Inc. This small Chicago-based company created and patented a new symbol known as the sarcasm mark. This piece of punctuation, as seen below, is used in the same manner as any type of ending punctuation, and marks a statement as sarcasm (Gordon).

Before using any of these methods, however, the formality and genre of the writing must first be taken into consideration. In most colloquial instances, such as instant messaging and text messaging, the use of symbols and abbreviations in order to overcome the informalities associated with such media is acceptable (Goldsborough). In more formal situations, however, these types of communication are no longer appropriate, so authors must rely on other methods to convey sarcasm. Currently, the sarcastic mark is an unfeasible method due to its current copyright restrictions, so authors must directly use sarcasm within their writing (Gordon). Such is the case in satirical writing, such as "A Modest Proposal," by Jonathan Swift, who proposed a solution to Ireland's population and famine problems; the Irish should simply eat its newborns. Most instances of satirical writing, however, are not as blatant, so authors must rely on readers to grasp and comprehend any intended sarcasm.

Revisiting my first paragraph, I now have the confidence to write the final two sentences without any further indicators.

Halloween epitomizes the season of autumn, so naturally, this past Halloween was marked with three inches of snow on the ground and sub-freezing temperatures in the city of Philadelphia. It was perfect Halloween weather.

If you as a reader are still having trouble understanding my true intentions, then I wish you the best of luck in curing the common cold.

Works Cited

Bennett, Samantha. "Study claims sarcasm is mostly a 'man thing'." *Pittsburgh Post-Gazette* 26 Feb. 2006. Web.

Cheang, Henry, and Marc Pell. "The Sound of Sarcasm." *Speech Communication* 2007: 366-381. Web.

Glenwright, Melanie, and Penny Pexman. "Development of Children's Ability to Distinguish Sarcasm and Verbal Irony*." *Journal of child language* 2010: 429-51. ProQuest.

Goldsborough, Reid. "Punctuation on the Internet Is Fanciful and Practical." *Community College Week* 13 Dec. 2010. Web.

Gordon, Andrea. "When LOL won't cut it, try sarcastic punctuation." *Toronto Star* 10 Jan. 2010. Web.

Rockwell, Patricia. "Lower, Slower, Louder: Vocal Cues of Sarcasm." *Journal of Psycholinguistic Research*. 483-495.

---

[*] Here is a footnote for all of my educated readers.

"Non-verbal communication (NVC)." *Encyclopaedic Dictionary of Psychology.*
    Abingdon: Hodder Education, 2006. *Credo Reference.* Web.

"Sarcasm." *The New Dictionary of Cultural Literacy, Houghton Mifflin.* Boston: Houghton
    Mifflin, 2002. *Credo Reference.* 16 Apr. 2003. Web.

Stephen Zachariah

Euthanasia: A Controversial Exploration

"Sure, we are granted life, liberty, and the pursuit of happiness, but what about the right to die?" inquired Dr. Michael Howley, my section instructor for "Clashing Views in Health and Society." We were briefly discussing prevalent, controversial medical issues facing today's culture when someone brought up "Dr. Death"—Dr. Jack Kevorkian, a champion of euthanasia (physician-assisted [or physician-directed] suicide).

Professor Howley then introduced a scenario and posed a question to the class. A 52-year-old man is diagnosed with incurable amyotrophic lateral sclerosis (also known as Lou Gehrig's disease). His muscles degenerate to a point where he has virtually no control over his limbs, he suffers from acute physical pain, and he frequently chokes on his own saliva due to his severe breathing difficulty. His family cannot even bear to see him in so much pain. Does this man have the right to end his life by means of Kevorkian's lethal injection, or must he suffer through the remainder of his life without hope for recovery? Professor Howley's situation really set my mind in motion. I remembered the pain I endured when my wisdom teeth were removed. Not only did I have infinitely less agony than this man did, but I also knew that I would eventually get better and the pain was only momentary. At the same time, I also saw that my professor's argument was heavily one-sided; the answer to his question seemed to be a no-brainer. I began to wonder how society, law, and the professionals in the medical field saw the question. I pondered to myself, *what makes the topic of euthanasia so contentious?*

I wanted to begin my exploration with a search for Jack Kevorkian, the name that prompted my professor to provide the class with the scenario. Faintly aware of controversial interviews with this Dr. Death, I decided to look for these transcripts or for the videos themselves. One of Google's search results took me to *www.cbsnews.com*, where Mike Wallace of CBS sits down with Dr. Jack Kevorkian in 1998 as part of a *60 Minutes* special. It was through this interview that I learned that the situation Professor Howley presented to the class was not hypothetical. The man with Lou Gehrig's disease was Thomas Youk. In the interview, Dr. Kevorkian plays a video of his administration of a series of lethal injections to Youk, including the moment of his death.

The reason that he decided to show the clip to the public was to force the American justice system to arrest him and place him on trial for murder. As the doctor who supposedly helped over 130 people commit suicide (earning him his famous nickname), Kevorkian wanted the court to finally make a concrete decision about the issue. He was acquitted three times when he *assisted* the suicide of a patient (when the patient was the one who flipped the switch that sent the lethal fluids into his or her bloodstream). In this case, Kevorkian *directly* administered the lethal injections because Thomas Youk's disease prevented him from taking part in his own euthanasia. Kevorkian declared, "Either they go, or I go. If I am acquitted, they go because they know that they will never convict me. If I am convicted...I will go. This issue has to be raised to the level where it is finally decided."

I found this interview and the clip of Youk's euthanasia very powerful. It was fairly surprising that Dr. Kevorkian had to present it in such a manner in order to get the attention of the legal system. Equally surprising was the time (four months) it took for a verdict to be made about his actions. Clearly, even the court system was in some way caught up and hindered by this controversy before they even indicted him. Jack Kevorkian was eventually found guilty of second-degree murder. Based on his previous three acquittals, I deduced that the court seemed to draw the line this time because this act of euthanasia was more of an act of physician-directed suicide rather than an act of physician-assisted suicide.

Here, I think the issue was one of autonomy. The decision to end a life is not a light one. If a patient on his or her own directs or initiates the process of euthanasia, it is much more certain that he or she truly wanted the procedure to be done than if this were not the case. Extending this point further to both physician-assisted and physician-directed suicide, I understood that this point of contention centered on the patient. Even though the patient provides his or her consent, can it ever be known that his or her *genuine* wish is to be euthanized without any external pressures from family, society, or the hospital? In such a scenario, there will always be the pressure of being less of a burden to one's family, the pressure of a financially burdened family desperately needing inheritance, the pressure to be an organ donor, and the pressure of not overusing the resources of the hospital. I was beginning to scratch the surface; now I wanted to uncover a firsthand view of this procedure from a medical standpoint.

I immediately turned to a mother of one of my close friends, registered nurse Alice Koshy. Nurse Koshy currently works at Staten Island University Hospital. During much of her 30-year career as a nurse, she has worked closely with cancer patients. I conducted an e-mail interview with her and inquired about her views on euthanasia based on her experience. Even though she did not have direct experience with euthanasia, she did have a lot to say about it. Nurse Koshy wrote, "Almost all the terminal patients I have cared for have always so strongly held on to whatever was left of their lives...My work in these hospitals has really showed me how far medicine has come. Terminal patients really do have a range of treatment options. We can do much better than offering these patients an escape." She ended her e-mail response with a discussion of two major potential ramifications that may occur if euthanasia is readily available to terminally ill patients: diagnosis of a terminal illness can develop an "implied" expectation for a patient (who may really want to live) to choose euthanasia, and research in the area of terminal illnesses will decline if most patients opt for euthanasia instead of treatment—preventing possible cures for these diseases in the future.

I was somewhat disappointed but not too surprised that Nurse Koshy's experience did not overlap with any cases of euthanasia. What did catch me off guard, though, was her opinion of it. This made me see that the idea of euthanasia itself seriously belittles the progress of modern medicine. In the twentieth century alone, it has cured (or at least properly treated) numerous diseases that were once fatal—malaria, tetanus, some forms of cancer, whooping cough, smallpox, polio, and many more. Also, with the advent of anesthesia and other medications, physical agony can be reduced a great deal as well. For these reasons, I do not find her optimism unfounded. Still, I do believe that doctors and caregivers must not delude themselves. They must face the fact that there are some cases where additional treatment may not always be effective or palliative. Thomas Youk's story from the *60 Minutes* interview really brought this into light. Nurse Koshy's next point about the "implied" expectation was strikingly similar to the pressures affecting autonomy that I previously described. Her final thoughts formed a very interesting and convincing argument regarding the research of terminal illnesses. How could any conclusive tests be performed on a disease if most of its victims chose to die? Moreover, who would even fund such research? These questions most definitely promote the provocative nature of euthanasia. From here, I wanted to hear from scholars and academics about the euthanasia controversy.

A quick search for "Euthanasia Ethics" restricted to scholarly, peer-reviewed publications on the Summon toolbar of Drexel's libraries website led me to "End Games: Euthanasia Under Interminable Scrutiny." In this article, Dr. Malcolm Parker of London's Imperial College Cancer Medicine Department challenges the rational capacity of a terminally ill patient's mind from his own experiences and studies: "Unrelievable pain is seldom the motive for requests for assisted death. Clinical depression motivates some requests... Treating depression leads to a change of mind concerning the desire to die in some patients. Not many terminally ill patients have a clear and persisting wish to die" (530). In light of his experiences with terminally diseased patients,

Dr. Parker calls for more holistic studies in this area. He believes that there are other factors besides depression that may negatively affect the mind of the terminally ill. He then finishes his piece by describing methods for empirically studying the minds of these patients (531-36).

The very fact that someone is suffering from a terminal illness may impact his or her judgment. This possibility stunned me: people who requested and received euthanasia may not have really done so had they been aware of the depression or other impairing condition that impacted their judgment. I completely agree with Dr. Parker's demand for more studies pertaining to this possibility. However, I am not in favor of the highly technical nature of the studies he plans on implementing in this field. I do not think that any set of numbers will ever be able to define a patient or his or her condition. From my vantage point, psychiatrist-conducted case studies would be much more effective. Nonetheless, Dr. Parker does present a potent fuel for the euthanasia dispute—the possibly impaired mental and judgmental capacity of the terminally ill. Wondering if any other shocking arguments were out there, I forged on in the realms of Drexel's library database.

I returned to my previous Summon search and skimmed through about five pages of entries until my eyes stopped at Michael Clark's "Euthanasia and the Slippery Slope." I was quite familiar with what the phrase "slippery slope" meant—one action leading to the next, progressively getting worse and ultimately ending up far from what was initially intended. I wanted to see how Professor Clark of the University of Nottingham's Philosophy Department related this argument to euthanasia in his publication in the *Journal of Applied Philosophy*. He references a previous study to form the peak of this slope: "Witness a survey by Mansoon of 570 university students, 326 of whom said they would approve of 'mercy killing' of the unfit if a population explosion could not be averted through education and contraception" (252). From here, Clark goes on to say that Nazi Germany ignored warning signs such as these before they started a mass genocide of those also deemed "unfit." He does not see any country escalating that far. On the other hand, he does use the Netherlands (which made voluntary euthanasia legal in 1984) as an example of this "slippery slope" argument. Since euthanasia legalization, the Netherlands has become a country where involuntary euthanasia (without patient permission) is regularly performed by hospital staff members who claim that they know what is best for the patient and the facility. Also, this country is where babies with certain disabilities or deformities are regularly terminated. Clark also believes that the Netherlands may continue down this path (or slope) and worries for the future of countries that adopt the same policy (251-57).

This article was almost as shocking as the article by Dr. Parker. The conclusion that Professor Clark jumps to after citing a small survey seems to be a bit too dire, along with his attempt to parallel this with the social climate of Nazi Germany. However, I did find his profile of the Netherlands to be very relevant and strong. It is hard not to be appalled by the way that nation has descended the "slippery slope." The legalization of euthanasia that was enacted to honor a patient's autonomous choice has very much led to the opposite: hospitals making life-or-death decisions on behalf of patients. This raises a series of questions. What else will become implicitly accepted along with euthanasia practices? How will regulatory measures seek to restrict euthanasia? Will they be effective? This host of inquiries leads me to believe that the "slippery slope" is certainly another controversial implication associated with euthanasia.

After exploring these points of contention, I was curious to see the levels of general public opinion regarding this topic in recent years. Returning one more time to Drexel's library website, I entered "Euthanasia Public Opinion" in the Summon search toolbar. Only after scrolling through several pages of search results did I find a publication found in the *Journal of Medical Ethics* that seemed too perfectly fitting to be true: "Trends in Public Approval of Euthanasia and Suicide in the US, 1947-2003," by O. Duncan (Professor of Sociology at the University of California Santa Barbara) and L. Parmelee (Editor of *Public Opinion Pros*). This heavily detailed article is based primarily on statistical analysis and survey presentation (that frankly was well above me in terms of comprehension). In the midst of this methodical description, the authors present the results of a public approval survey (conducted from 1977 to 2002 with a total of nearly 40,000 participants) concerning euthanasia and suicide for an individual with a terminal illness. The questions presented in this survey were, "When a person has a disease that cannot be cured, do you think doctors should be allowed by law to end the patient's life by some painless means if the patient and his family request it?" and, "Do you think a person has a right to end his or her own life if this person has an incurable disease?" The percentage of participants who answered "yes" to each question was plotted on the y-axis and time (by year) was plotted on the x-axis. This produced two curves: one for the first question and another for the second question. Finally, two trend lines were drawn, depicting a steadily, clearly rising number of people answering "yes" to the two questions every year (Duncan & Parmelee 266-72).

The gradually increasing trend of this graph comes as no shock to me. I (surely along with many others) strongly sense the direction of cultural advancement towards acceptance, understanding, freedom, and individualism. This underlying attitude seems to be applied to many other concerns of society (such as gay marriage and medical marijuana use). I could not help but wonder if this increase in public approval really was rooted in an understanding of its contentious associations and repercussions. This is not to take a stance against euthanasia. I do not disagree with an increase in approval if those who do approve accept the implications. However, it is unlikely that this is the case. I do not expect anyone to have such a level of understanding about euthanasia without thorough research.

Even at this point, my exploration is not finished. There are definitely more points that form the backbone of the controversy associated with euthanasia than the ones outlined in this research composition. Clearly, this study can be extended even further. Just exploring autonomy, curative research, terminal patients' mental condition, and the "slippery slope" argument were enough to show me how much euthanasia is a hotly contested issue. In terms of public opinion, it really cannot be known for sure whether the trend of increased approval is from an informed or blindly accepting standpoint. Regardless, what I see now is that much more than just the patient's wishes must be considered in any situation of this kind. Revisiting Professor Howley's scenario at this point, I realize that the answer is clearly not a no-brainer. I am left without a concrete response to that situation. I now understand from this exploration a sense of the intricately woven complications that are involved with the option of euthanasia.

Works Cited

Clark, Michael. "Euthanasia and the Slippery Slope." *Journal of Applied Philosophy* 1998: 251-57. Print.

Duncan, O. D., and L. F. Parmelee. "Trends in Public Approval of Euthanasia and Suicide in the US, 1947-2003." *Journal of Medical Ethics* 2006: 266-72. Print.

Kevorkian, Jack. *60 Minutes*. Interview by Mike Wallace. 1998. Web.

Koshy, Alice. Personal interview. 9 Nov. 2011.

Parker, Malcolm. "End Games: Euthanasia Under Interminable Scrutiny." *Bioethics* 19.5-19.6 2005: 523-36. Print.

Justin Roczniak

The First Crush: A Retrospective Analysis

I have been told in the past that high school is not about learning knowledge; it is really about learning how to socialize. It is everyone's first great social experiment: through trial and error, you develop your first real friends in high school, you learn how to work as a team in classes, you learn about camaraderie on your sports team, and you learn how to develop romantic relationships with members of the opposite sex.

These trials go better for some people than for others, but I think one trial in particular stands out for everyone as being one of the ones with the most error: the first crush.

It started with a simple suggestion.

"Justin," said my good friend Chris, in his characteristic Southern drawl, "Don't you think Madeline is hot?"

Chris and I, to this day, disagree on almost every subject, except for high-speed rail, which we both agree is necessary for the United States to remain competitive in the world economy. This, I think, will ultimately cost him the 2024 Republican presidential nomination, though he maintains that he will be the ideal candidate. But I digress. This was one of the few times when we agreed on a matter of importance.

"Yes, Chris, now that you mention it…" I said.

This was a dangerous thought to place in the head of a high-school sophomore with no previous romantic experience. Yes, Madeline was quite pretty.

Madeline was a short girl with brown hair and a pretty face whose primary occupation was coxswain of the second men's varsity eight on my high school's rowing team. This essentially entailed yelling at eight sweaty guys (including myself) to row faster for two hours a day. When off the water, she didn't yell as much, and mostly hung out and teased the guys who were in her boat. Outside of rowing, we shared a math class together and occasionally saw each other at lunch, but she was in a completely different social circle than I was, so this did not occur very frequently.

She also had large breasts, which were usually displayed as prominently as Catholic school attire allowed for. I cannot pretend that this was not a factor in my attraction to her.

I made the assumption, based on my total lack of self-confidence, that Madeline was out of my league. A lot of people, I think, would have taken the sensible route here, and given up. However, I saw an obvious solution to this problem: move to a higher league. So began the quest to climb the social ladder. It started with a rap battle during Spirit Week.

I am not a rapper, I never intend to become a rapper. I do not listen to rap music. So for me to enter the Spirit Week rap battle was outrageous and without precedent. They called people up from the cafeteria to participate. I went up to the stage, the only person in the school who had managed to forget to dress out of uniform for "Hip-Hop Day." In short, I was a white person. They asked me for my rapper name. I said I didn't have a rapper name. They came up with one for me, and dubbed me "The White Wizard." I could tell this was going to end poorly. I've forgotten who the other guy was up there whom I was rap-battling (is that the correct way to phrase that?), but he certainly looked the part a lot better than I did.

However, despite my out-of-character appearance, I had done some minimal and basic research on how to perform in rap battles beforehand. As it turned out, the other guy hadn't. So I started with

> *"Yo Justin's my name*
> *And rappin' ain't my game*
> *And I didn't have the time*
> *To think of any rhymes*
> *But I know that my rap*
> *Is better than your crap!"*

He expertly countered with a blank stare, frankly aghast that I had managed to say anything at all. I was declared the winner amid thunderous applause from the audience, and I essentially ran the school for several weeks afterwards.

In hindsight, this would have been the ideal time to ask Madeline on a date. However, I hadn't the nerve at the time, and furthermore, I was waiting for some undefined "perfect moment" in which to ask her, and then presumably we'd have lovely times on dates and going for walks in the park and going to nice restaurants together and picnics and horse-drawn carriage rides and all those other wonderful things that couples do.

So I procrastinated, and I overthought things, and I procrastinated. While procrastinating, I tried to maintain my newfound social status in ever more grandiose public stunts: every school presentation I made was a riotous laugh for the audience, I would antagonize our crazy cat lady biology teacher at every opportunity, I entered the school talent show with a stand-up comedy act. (They didn't allow it. Enough people wanted to see it, though, that the driver's ed. teacher lent me his room so I could perform there. It was standing-room only. I felt pretty smug after that.)

One day a few members of the rowing team, including myself and Madeline, were holed up in the boathouse for several hours while the rest of the team was out practicing, due to a boat shortage. We ended up sitting in a circle in one of the many purposeless rooms that made up the building. Conversation progressed naturally through subjects pertinent to teenagers: hating on teachers, hating on fat kids, hating on losers, hating on homework, hating on the Catholic Church, how much asbestos was in this building, and so forth. Then, the conversation moved to the subject of "Who was your first crush?"

The inevitable happened.

When my turn came up, I said something along the lines of "It's you."

Many years of conditioning have forced the next ten minutes out of my memory entirely. I remember clearly that the answer was "no." I remember clearly that she said I wasn't her type. One of my friends helped me remember years afterward that he immediately left the room and burst out laughing in disbelief at the incident, which, I think, was the only valid response to witnessing something like what happened. My other friend who also witnessed the incident maintains that had I owned a Porsche 911 at the time, the outcome would have been entirely different. (He was very insistent that only a Porsche 911 would have done the trick.)

It was, in short, highly embarrassing.

Later that day, on the bus home, listening to "Sittin' on Top of the World" by Cream, I dealt with the emotional fallout. It wasn't as terrible as I had thought it was going to be, though it lasted longer than I had hoped it would.

Over the short term, I learned several valuable lessons, which I shall enumerate here:

> 1. Don't wait so long to ask a girl out that you become emotionally involved before it even begins.

2. Things don't always turn out like a fairytale romance.

3. Eric Clapton makes the best feel-bad music.

However, over the long term, I realize that the experience changed me. Before the first crush, I was a bookish, dull, and generally extremely pedestrian student with no special talents and no interest in developing any, and my grades were poor, to boot. After going through all I did to attract Madeline's attention, I was left with a lifelong affinity for public speaking, a razor-sharp wit, a considerably heightened social status at the high school, and my grades were still poor. (But the teachers liked me better, except for my biology teacher.) It changed me for the better, in short. Given an opportunity to wipe the whole incident from my memory, I'd have to decline, as embarrassing as it was.

And if you're curious, Madeline and I were back on friendly terms by the end of the week, and we're still friends to this day.

Kenneth Wittwer

Oscar Wilde and the Dangers of Extremes

I was raised in two considerably conservative communities, and as a result I had an incredibly difficult time coming to terms with my sexuality. While my parents have always been open and supportive, the surrounding environment has not usually been as receptive. After several years of questioning my identity and wondering where I fit in the complex web of twenty-first century social constructs, I came out of the closet midway through my junior year. My decision to openly express my true sexual identity was well-received by most of my family members and close friends, but for many students (and some faculty members) of Kingsway Regional High School, I became a target. Hate mail, verbal harassment, physical harassment, and even fake Kenny Wittwer profiles on Facebook became somewhat routine for the last two years of my high-school career. While I was not expecting the entire universe to accept me for who I am, I had no idea that my high school community was locked in the mindset of a Billy Graham telethon.

Since my school had no LGBTQ curricula, I decided to do some research on my own time. I wanted to find how different cultures accepted or condemned homosexuality, and I wanted to find notable LGBT people from history and explore how their sexual orientation positively or negatively affected their public reception. I came across dozens of historical figures whom I had heard of before but might not have known were gay or bisexual, including Walt Whitman, Neil Patrick Harris, President James Buchanan, and even Alexander the Great (however, there is still some speculation about the last two names). Despite all of my independent research, I discovered the most fascinating LGBT historical figure in my senior year AP Literature class: an innovative and eccentric writer with a *carpe diem* life stance named Oscar Wilde.

I first stumbled upon Wilde when I was given my senior research paper assignment. The class was provided with six or seven different classic novels, and we had to pick one about which to develop our own thesis. We were not asked a universal question or given a topic to explore; our only requirements were that we analyzed a classic novel through a critical lens in at least eight pages and utilized at least five sources, and the rest (which was a lot) was left for us to decide. I picked up Wilde's *The Picture of Dorian Gray* upon recommendation from my literature teacher, and my brother had previously told me that I would love it. The novel quickly became one of my favorite books of all time, and I wanted to learn everything I possibly could about the life of Oscar Wilde.

Oscar Fingal O'Flahertie Wills Wilde was born in the mid 1850s to a notable physician father and a poet mother. Wilde was a highly motivated student who was granted scholarships to Trinity College and Oxford, where he commenced his obsession with Aestheticism. He published his first collection of poems in 1881 and married Constance Lloyd three years later, eventually having two children with her. Throughout the 1880s and early 1890s, Wilde published numerous poems, plays, essays, and aphorisms that became wildly popular, and his fame matched that of his words as he gained a reputation for being eccentric and flamboyant. His eccentricity became more than just a personality trait as it became clear that he was a gay man, despite his marriage.

When I first dove into the world of Oscar Wilde, I prematurely stopped my research into his personal life. In hindsight it seems so foolish to be unaware of his downward spiral, but I was so fascinated with his writing that I didn't notice my ignorance. While I have never viewed anyone as a heroic figure or idol, I gained enormous respect for Oscar Wilde for (eventually) being so openly flamboyant. As an atheist, I found his seize-the-moment philosophy invigorating and inspiring, and I found his collection of aphorisms, "Phrases and Philosophies for the Use of the Young," to be both intriguing and highly quotable. It wasn't until I delved into other authors' analyses of his life and finished reading *The Picture of Dorian Gray* that I realized that Oscar Wilde was deeply flawed.

While he was married and had two sons with his wife, Wilde gained a reputation for having affairs with young undergraduate men. Lionel Johnson, one of Wilde's poet friends, introduced him to a young Oxford student named Lord Anthony Douglas. The two quickly become romantically involved, and Douglas lured Wilde to the shady world of underground gay prostitution. Wilde had several affairs with young male prostitutes in addition to his relationship with Douglas, and once Douglas's father, the Marquess of Queensberry, found out about the affair he accused Wilde of being a sodomite. Wilde was offended by the accusation; although it was true, sodomy was a felony in that time, and Wilde was insulted that he was accused of being a felon. Wilde privately sued Queensberry for libel, and Queensberry avoided the lawsuit by proving that his accusation was justified. Wilde was then arrested for sodomy, gross indecency, and other charges related to homosexuality. Wilde chose to stay in England rather than flee the country to avoid a trial, and he was eventually sentenced to a brief but horrendous term in prison. He was released from prison into a society that wanted nothing to do with him, and he lived in poverty until his death three years later (Stade ix-xli).

While I initially admired Wilde for his *carpe diem* philosophy, I eventually realized his lifestyle was pure hedonism. His life can be efficiently summarized in his epigram, "I can resist everything except temptation." Wilde took the concept of self-gratification to exponential proportions and abandoned any sense of morals. While his wife was pregnant with their second child, Wilde began an affair with Robert Ross. Ross was known for being openly gay and unaffected by the Victorian attitudes against homosexuality, and he was only seventeen years old when he and Wilde became romantically involved. Despite the numerous affairs he had with minors, undergraduates, and prostitutes, Wilde remained married until 1898. Prolonging the marriage while he obviously was not remaining loyal to his wife demonstrates Wilde's shallow desire to be viewed favorably by the conservative Victorian community and illustrates his lack of respect for his own wife and the institution of marriage as a whole.

When I first began my research on LGBT historical figures, I was looking for a role model who was open about his sexuality and left a positive impression of the queer community in his time period. Wilde may have increased the visibility of the Victorian queer community, but making him the spokesperson for LGBT rights would be a grave mistake. Harvard professor Michael Hattersley suggests that Wilde's openness about his sexuality did more harm than good for the LGBT community. After the media circus surrounding his sodomy trial, people associated homosexuality with affairs and prostitution rather than stable same-sex relationships. Hattersley argues that Wilde is the source of modern-day stereotypes of gay men: feminine flamboyancy, emotional instability, and sexual promiscuity. The LGBT rights movement did not commence until the late 1960s, and Hattersley believes that the movement could have been ignited sooner if Wilde had set a better precedent and had not made homosexuality synonymous with hedonism (Hattersley, "Did Oscar Wilde Set Back Gay Rights?").

Wilde's tragic downfall initially left me to wonder what is acceptable in our society and how I should properly behave. Wilde revealed who he really was as a person and ultimately hid no aspects of his personal life. As a result he was sent to prison and lived his last few years in impoverished exile. If I live without restraining any aspects of my personality, should I expect such negativity? I realize that our society is far more accepting of LGBTQ people than London in the Victorian era, but there are still significant segments of the population who view homosexuality as a sin and gays as immoral hedonists who should have fewer rights than everyone else. Should gay, bisexual, and transgender people act "straight" in order to be viewed more favorably by social conservatives?

Wilde's fate conflicts with the belief that it is best to be yourself, a basic yet profound moral that Americans highly value to a certain extent. Our nation is gradually accepting and embracing diversity in all aspects of personal and cultural identity, and children are now taught to embrace what makes them different from their peers. But if embracing your unique identity can result in exile (and possibly imprisonment), then is it worth it? Should we compromise our identities and yield to the parameters of convention for the sake of maintaining our place in the socioeconomic hierarchy? Wilde's life illustrates that conformity is the best choice, and for a brief period of time I agreed with this conclusion. His fate temporarily scared me into submission, and although I had already come out of the closet, I continued to act in a heteronormative manner in order to avoid social rejection.

I eventually realized the foolishness of my behavior and fully came out of the closet, revealing my true self as a gay man who does not respect traditional gender roles and exhibits some feminine characteristics while identifying as male. I also realized that all aspects of Wilde's life—his relationships, his attitudes, his fate—were extremes. There is no need for me to be as wildly eccentric as Wilde or harshly narrow-minded as the society in which he lived; there is a happy medium in which gays can be accepted by their community and live in peace. I also learned that it was foolish to view Wilde strictly as either a hero or a villain; while he did create a negative reception of LGBT people, he nevertheless brought the queer community into the spotlight and demonstrated the foolishness of overreliance on morals in society. When people view their moral beliefs as the only answer, acceptance of diversity becomes impossible. However, if people abandon all of their morals, as Wilde would advocate, our society would spiral downward into decadence and chaos.

The turbulence of Wilde's life and the rigid conservatism of his time period exemplify the dangers of extremes; whether it be abstinence or polygamy, Puritanism or hedonism, infatuation or exile, or hero or villain, extremes are to be avoided at all costs. No aspect of life can be explained in a dichotomous system; there always must be willingness to examine the gray areas.

It is in the absence of extremes and acceptance of variation that true identities can flourish. Wilde led an incredibly hedonistic life in a time period of strict conservatism, and as a result he was rendered incompatible with his society and essentially erased from it. The society in which I live is increasingly progressive and embraces diversity, and if I live honestly and modestly (without surrendering my identity) then I can avoid a similar fate.

Works Cited

Hattersley, Michael. "Did Oscar Wilde Set Back Gay Rights?" *The Gay & Lesbian Review Worldwide* 2006: Web. 26 Oct 2011.

Stade, George. *The Collected Oscar Wilde*. New York: Barnes & Noble Classics, 2007. Print.

Siara Johnson

Personal Writing: Lines: Words:: Writing: Me (Personal Writing: Lines are to Words as Writing is to Me)

Author's Note:

My purpose in writing these journal entries is to explore the reasons behind my personal writing. I have examined the psychological effects of this activity. I wrote this piece for people who also take part in personal writing so that they may come to understand themselves and their habits as an outcome of their writing. It is also directed towards people who do not take part in personal writing to show them the logical benefits I have found in doing so.

November 4, 2011

Why am I writing? Technically writing in here is me talking to myself; which I can much easier do in my head… So why do I feel so compelled to take the time and energy to write down my thoughts? Actually, I am doing the very thing I am questioning by writing this entry. I feel like writing opens my mind to new perspectives, because if I did not write I certainly would not be asking myself these questions and analyzing my actions. I have done personal writing for years now and I cannot remember when or why I started, but I do know that I have a writing fixation. It seems to be therapeutic, but so are hot baths and I almost never take those. What is the secret behind my desire to write? I think I am going to see what other people have to say about personal writing, and maybe their thoughts will send me in the right direction.

November 6, 2011

In reference to my question from the other day, I stumbled upon the concept of constructivism by Lev Vygotsky, which helps me in understanding my writing. In Hirtle's article "Coming to Terms," constructivism is defined as: "a way of building knowledge about self,… everyday experience, and society through reflection and meaning making" (1996, p. 91). I feel as if my personal writing is a form of constructivism; I write about myself, the things I go through, and the people around me. When I write about these things I am able to make connections between myself, events, and people so that I can build mental representations for every aspect of my life. Now, I am not only narrating—I am asking questions and being insightful. I am learning through writing because as Vygotsky believed, "external, social speech is gradually internalized to become a semiotic resources that [I] can use for problem solving and thinking through the medium of inner speech" (Hirtle, 1996). Therefore, the act of writing is simply a representation of my 'inner speech' that I put within my visual field. I can physically interact with my thoughts and experiences to build knowledge as my mind makes associations with the words on the page before me.

It is great that I write to facilitate my thought processes; even Hirtle states that this 'constructive' approach is a way to "open boundaries through inquiry, not through unquestioned acceptance of prevailing knowledge. It is the realization that knowledge is never neutral, that the ways in which knowledge is mediated and created are as dynamic and important as the knowledge itself" (1996, p. 91). What I took from his idea was that instead of only thinking about things, I challenge myself to put my thoughts into writing, and by looking at my ideas internally and externally I am viewing them from different angles. By actively seeking to learn, through writing as thinking, about the situations I encounter, I am able to overcome inaccurate impressions and gain true understanding. I can also use previous insights to aid my dissection of current events.

November 9, 2011

I came upon empirical evidence that my writing is beneficial for me. It assists what is known as my working memory by, in essence, cleaning out the unnecessary crud from my consciousness (Klein & Boals, 2001). Working memory is my fixed workspace that deals with higher-level thinking and anything in my awareness (Klein & Boals, 2001): so basically, my ability to focus. Klein and Boals discuss how the limited size of the working memory is inhibited by negative experiences that invade my mind and reduce my ability to give attention to productive thinking, such as problem solving. They have investigated the belief that expressively writing about stressful situations will free working memory space and enable me to think about current tasks (Klein & Boals, 2001). This idea makes complete sense in that I am incapable of thinking productively when a negative stimulus is tugging at my mind. Therefore, the way to clear my mind is to give all of my attention to bad experiences by writing about them to aid in gathering my memory of events into concise, less painful forms that are easier to ignore (Klein & Boals, 2001). This is relevant because before I began writing expressively, I became overwhelmed as a child—with issues concerning my mother's lack of mood control—and now I see that it affected my ability to focus in school.

In second grade, I talked continuously in class. At one point, my desk was moved beside the teacher's. I could not focus on assignments, so I would talk to my nearest friends for distraction. I did not talk much at home out of discomfort; I just thought to myself. In school I wanted to get away from thinking, so I talked. Although I was closest with my dad, I lived across the country from him because my mom and stepfather moved away from Texas. We did move back the summer before fourth grade. I split my time between my mother's and father's houses, but one morning I found my dad dead. He died in his sleep as I slept next to him. I felt even more lost. My emotions were all over the place.

When I started fourth grade, I was assigned to write a poem about something meaningful. This was the beginning of my personal writing. My poem was to my dad in heaven; I asked him all sorts of questions and told him how I felt about his death. Surprisingly, I felt a sense of peace. Writing the poem gave me a sense of accomplishment, and I realized that schoolwork was not that bad. After this experience, I did not make the conscious decision to write expressively; it just happened. I began to write angry poems whenever my mother had an episode and upset me. I also began to stabilize my thoughts and emotions, and got more involved with academics. I stopped talking at inappropriate times, and was excited to work and think. Somehow I unconsciously understood that writing about the negative things crowding my mind gave me control. I was no longer overwhelmed because I had the power to manage my attention. I was able to clear my working memory and focus on classwork, instead of talking to get my mind away from invading thoughts. I developed the compulsion to write in order to relieve internal tension.

Klein and Boals found that students who write expressively increased their working memory, ability to write coherently about negative experiences, reduction of pervasive thoughts, psychological and physical health, and GPAs. Mental health was enhanced because people who can control stressful thoughts are able to cope efficiently. I demonstrated these findings when I was overwhelmed by bad experiences before I began writing. I felt suppressed from talking at home and was incapable of focusing in school. As for increased GPAs, when the working memory is free there is "improvement in the ability to store and transform information" (Klein & Boals, 2001, p. 252), which can be applied to academic functioning. I demonstrated this when I gained the capability of giving my full attention in class, and I began to do better the more involved I became. Expressive writing forced me to stop avoiding bad experiences and to examine them. As a result, I developed coherence in my writing and thoughts.

November 11, 2011

I have the most amazing answer to my question... autobiographical memory: "self-referenced memory of personal experiences in the service of short-term and long-term goals that define identity" (Fivush, 2011, p. 562). An exclusive aspect of autobiographical memory is autonoetic awareness: "the conscious experience of self as recalling the past" (Fivush, 2011, p. 561).

I explicitly demonstrate autonoetic awareness as I write about experiences which over time form my behavior and attitudes as a result of my knowledge gained from my personal history (autobiographical memory) (Fivush, 2011). Fivush explains that "although language clearly does not determine thought, it facilitates certain forms of thought over others" (2011, p. 564), which illuminates why I seem to be able to think differently about things when I am writing them, versus solely thinking about them. I think that it is fantastic that human character is basically formed by our interactions and perceptions of situations, and the idea that writing about those things is merely an enhancement of what the mind already unconsciously does. I have physically taken action on the formation of my identity through writing.

Going a step further, Fivush adds that "coherent narratives move beyond a simple sequence to provide an explanatory framework for understanding how and why events unfolded as they did. The framework includes intentions, motivations, thoughts and emotions that create a human texture and content for events" (2011, p. 564). In essence, repetitive writing betters my ability to write and consequently organizes my comprehension of experiences, which facilitates self-growth (Fivush, 2011). Practice improves any skill, so the more I wrote, the better I got and the more I found solace in it. I have certainly developed a much clearer idea of who I am. I believe that my writing reflects this since it changes with me. I began with emotional poems, then diaries and now journals where I write my thoughts as they come to mind to no specific audience. I also write down quotes (song lyrics, phrases in books, inspirational statements, snippets of conversations) for sources of motivation and personal connection.

November 12, 2011

Yesterday I did not introduce the three functions of autobiographical memory. Researcher Bluck discusses the importance of these functions in relation to modern or postmodern society, in which change, not continuity, is the norm, and there is an imperative for the individual to forge a unique identity based on a unique life history that will allow them to explore and predict their future role in an ever-changing world. The individual has the freedom and the burden of creating a unique life story to serve their own needs for self-continuity and to present themselves to others (2003, p. 10-11).

The three functions he is implying in these statements are self, social, and directive. These categories are a way of organizing autobiographic memory into understandable sections (Bluck, 2003).

The most involved function is the self; this concept supports the growth and stability of identity as a person experiences life (Bluck, 2003). Bluck mentions how "self-continuity through adulthood is maintained by the interdependent relation of self and autobiographical memory... autobiographical knowledge may be especially important when the self is in adverse conditions requiring self-change" (Bluck, 2003, p. 5-6). I believe that as a child, when I wrote expressive poems about my mother's conduct and my father's death I was able to organize these experiences in the form of writing. As I learned how to cope, I evaluated how to behave, edited my beliefs of effective communication, and questioned my and other's actions, overall building self-understanding. Removing myself from the events through writing, I examined behaviors, outcomes, and implications that ultimately altered my mental representations and clarified the way I viewed myself. I started to learn more about myself and developed opinions as my pen scribbled across dozens of pages. Almost an adult, I am continuing my method of personal writing because it is my space for constructing and maintaining the identity I associate myself with, which, in turn, supports my internal functioning (sanity).

I agree with Bluck's reference to Wilson and Ross's idea that memory allows us to say "'I am the same person as I was before—but better'... people self-enhance past selves as inferior to their current one" (2003, p. 12). As I wrote, I improved my thoughts and behaviors, and built self-confidence; hence, I became a better person than I was. Further research discusses how people control their memories to benefit self-continuity by temporarily storing away negative experiences and images of self, while promoting positive ones (Bluck, 2003). I separate myself from negative experiences by writing and can then store them. After years of privately writing about my mother and father, I have come to the point where I can publicly write about them. I can distance myself emotionally, and wish to find answers to questions by interacting with others.

I wrote a research paper on the effects of bipolar parents on children, a college application essay on the effects of my father's death on my self-motivation and academic achievement, and an English paper that caused me to realize my dad's death led me to another inspirational figure, and these journal entries of self-analysis! The more I read and write about these experiences, the more connections I make and strengthen my concept of self. Olson voiced my realization when he said, "Writing enables us to say and think things we could not. Or at least have not, said or thought without writing" (1995, p. 288). I had never publicly narrated those experiences. In writing them, I learned more about those situations as well as myself. Other research describes how repeated narrations of painful memories toughen a person's emotional regulation for those events (Bluck, 2003). This explains why I cried when I read my paper about the day my dad died to my class, but now, after multiple occasions, I can calmly discuss it. Additionally, my powerful memories are relatively easy to put into writing for excellent responses to prompts—benefiting my academic success and further reinforcing my self-image.

Did I unconsciously discover the importance of autobiographical memory and form an internal drive that influences me to write? Have my writings changed over time to reflect my changing self-perceptions and growth?

November 13, 2011

The second function of autobiographical memory is social: memories enrich conversations, enable empathy, and aid in supporting and building relationships (Bluck, 2003). As a child, instead of turning to other people and discussing my thoughts, I used writing to create a conversation with myself. I describe experiences, then question, reflect, and analyze them just like I interact with others. Maybe the reason I handwrite such exploratory narratives is because of an intimate connection with myself—as if there is my consciousness that I embody as my physical self, and the 'other' is my unconscious self represented by my written words. The more I write, the more self-secure I become, and this results in self-intimacy in handling stressful experiences. A major aspect of the social function is what Bluck refers to as parental influence:

> Parents influence children's developing self-concept
> through the way that they engage in emotional past talk
> with them. They also influence the way that the child
> sees him or herself in relation to others, and how they
> see motion as an integral part of social relations. Finally,
> another function is to teach and inform, or socialize
> children about how to express, and maybe even how
> to experience, or cope with their own emotions (i.e. to
> regulate emotion) (2003, p. 16).

Since I lived across the country from my father, I was not able to interact with him before he passed away—limited to short phone calls and a two-week visit in the summer—and I was emotionally detached from my mother. I did not have the opportunity to do what Bluck described. I believe that instead of suffering from a lack of interaction, I adapted and used writing in the place of parental interaction. The previous quote highlights the importance of verbal exchange as a child. I wonder if writing took the place of parental influence on self-guidance and emotion regulation. Before I began to write, I did not fully understand society's norms for behavior (my disruptive talking), talk about emotional problems, have a good idea of self-identity, or know how to handle my feelings (I would have brief episodes of emotional distress and attempt to push away/ignore stressors). Now after writing for years, I can effectively manage all of these. Once I became open with myself and understood how to articulate and control my thoughts, I was able to transfer those abilities to social relationships and finally build close friendships and connections with my family. Perhaps this partially explains my fascination with psychology;

now that I have developed an understanding of myself and my behaviors, I have the desire to learn about others and aid them in achieving self-continuity.

November 14, 2011

Directive is the last function of autobiographical memory: used to solve problems, guide future behavior, and foresee future situations (Bluck, 2003). This aspect helps people understand the world and discover how to act by enduring and analyzing experiences (life history) (Bluck, 2003). Bluck quotes Katherine Nelson, who said that "memory is a knowledge structure that is 'not about the past but about the future'" (2003, p. 9), because every person uses their past to build schemas about situations, people, problems, and all other aspects of life, and use those mental representations as guidance for things that are going to happen. I write my experiences, what I learn, the associations I make and what to do next—my written autobiography. Marlin Killen, one of my psychology professors, stated that "the more ways in which people put a piece of information into their brain, the more places it is stored in the brain and the easier it is to recall and utilize that information." I think, write, and talk about an experience; it gets engraved in my memory and I can unconsciously/consciously employ that knowledge in future situations. Writing enriches my pool of knowledge from which to draw.

Bluck notes that in today's world, "there is an imperative for the *individual* to forge a unique identity based on a unique life history that will allow them to explain and predict their future role in an ever-changing world" (2003, p. 10). Maybe I felt this societal pressure and because of my lack of external aid with personal issues, I turned to writing in an effort to find and develop myself in order to succeed. I have taken my technique of synthesizing and analyzing information and applied it to academics and self-organization. I write to increase my memory and analysis of events, and I write notes to increase my memory and analysis of information for a test. Writing is a tool for learning and achievement; I write experiences for personal remembrance, and to learn from the tests within life.

November 15, 2011

Who would have thought that the simple act of writing would have had a massive influence on who I have become? I have discovered that writing my thoughts shapes my beliefs, skills, behavior, and personality. Bluck mentioned William James's statement that "were an individual to awake one morning with all personal memories erased, he or she would essentially be a different person" (2003, p. 12). Such insight I would never have come up with on my own, but now, after exploring myself and the work of others, I believe in James's idea because I understand the huge impact that past experience has on a person. I wonder if autobiographical memory was something that I have always had and it just needs to be found, or if I did indeed build it through my personal writing.

Writing these entries shows growth in my sense of self. Now that I am relatively self-stable, my writing is a resource for modification, and I am willing to be more open with others, versus when I was in the process of building my self-concept and I kept everything to myself. Personal writing is technically introverted, but it has influenced my social interactions because the formation of my identity resulted from past experiences and my comprehension of those events. I use writing to shape myself—I am the result of my writing.

Works Cited

Bluck, S. (2003). Autobiographical memory: Exploring its functions in everyday life. *Memory*, 11(2), 113-123.

Fivush, R. (2011). The development of autobiographical memory. *Annual Review of Psychology*, 62(1), 559-582.

Hirtle, J. (1996). Social constructivism (coming to terms). *English Journal*, 85(1), 91-92.

Klein, K., & Boals, A. (2001). Expressive writing can increase working memory capacity *Journal of Experimental Psychology*: General, 130(3), 520-533.

Killen, M. (November 23, 2011). Memory Encoding. *General Pre-Professional Psychology Lecture*. Drexel University, Philadelphia, PA.

Olson, D. R. (1995). Conceptualizing the written word: An intellectual autobiography. *Written Communication*, 12(3), 277-297.

Aaron Hartmann

A Class Divided: Philadelphia

The Problem

Supreme Court judge Louis Brandeis once said, "We may either have democracy in this country or we may have great wealth concentrated in the hands of a few, but we can't have both" (Brandeis). In Philadelphia, it only takes a walk through Center City to notice the alarming population of homeless and poor citizens. Ironically, on that same walk one will see luxury automobiles, investment bankers wearing designer suits, and a number of gourmet restaurants reserved for the wealthy. Citizens of lower socioeconomic status in Philadelphia are at a distinct disadvantage when compared to their wealthy counterparts. The issue of income inequality is not novel; it is rather a battle that this country and this city have been fighting since they were founded. For example, Thomas Jefferson wrote about "some dissatisfaction in the army at not being paid off before they were disbanded, and a very trifling mutiny of 200 soldiers in Philadelphia," in a letter to the Marquis de Chastellux on January 16, 1784. There has been a serious disconnect between the mindset of the wealthy and the general population. In America and in Philadelphia, the struggles of the average citizen have been overlooked and denounced by the upper class.

Part I

"According to the United States Department of Housing and Urban Development, a person is considered homeless if he/she is sleeping in a place not meant for human habitation or in an emergency shelter or transitional/ supportive housing. A person who is homeless does not have a fixed, regular and adequate nighttime residence" (A Portrait of Homelessness). Philadelphia has approximately 6,500 people out of its 1,526,006 residents homeless on any one given night (A Portrait of Homelessness). This ranks among the top in the nation when compared to other major cities. Perhaps even more disheartening than having one of the largest homelessness rates in the nation is that families comprise 47% of the homeless population in Philadelphia and 93% of these families are single-parent families (A Portrait of Homelessness).

Often the inner-city poor are perceived as a lesser, uneducated group of degenerates. They tend to be stereotyped as lazy "moochers" who do nothing but take advantage of the social systems America has to offer. But can a family of four that has an income of a mere 24,000 dollars a year embrace a life which could be considered being worth "mooching" for? It was not more than a year ago that the top wage earners in the nation were distraught about the "Bush era tax cuts" not being extended because they might not be able to receive *as much* money as they already were. "By the time I feed my family, I have maybe $400,000 left over," stated John Fleming in an interview he was featured in during September of 2011 (Benen). It is safe to say if Mr. Fleming feared living on "just" 400,000 dollars a year, he would have a serious problem living the life of these homeless "moochers."

Homelessness just begins to describe the wealth inequality issue which plagues Philadelphia. The national poverty line is currently set at $22,350 for a family of four and a mere $10,890 for an individual resident (USDHHS). Thirty-three percent of Philadelphians are living at or below the national poverty line (Census, Philadelphia, Pennsylvania). Approximately 25% of the population in Philadelphia does not have financial access to adequate nutrition (Greater Philadelphia Coalition Against Hunger). An estimated 33% of Philadelphians struggle to pay off medical debt (Barth). This is not just the 160,000 citizens who are uninsured, but also citizens with insurance who struggle to pay their medical bills (Philadelphia City Planning Commission).

These statistics may create the image that Philadelphia is an overly impoverished city, but it was reported by CNN Money as having one of the largest numbers of jobs which pay more than $100,000 in the nation. How is it possible to have these two polarized extremes within the same city lines? For the most part, the issue of income inequality is hidden from the general public, ignored by the top wage earners, and covered up by Philadelphia's government. According to the Brookings Institution, "only 18% of Philadelphia adults hold a college degree, one of the lowest levels among large U.S. cities. Indeed, below-average rates of educational attainment cut across racial and ethnic lines in Philadelphia, affecting whites, blacks, and Hispanics." Without the ability to think critically and analytically, the population is forced to believe whatever is told to them without recourse. As more public officials who advocate decreased government spending are elected into office, resources for education will be cut even more, moving the inner city school system further into an intellectual wasteland. This process cyclically puts those citizens of Philadelphia at a disadvantage compared to the people already on top of the monetary food chain.

Part II

When warning his old business partner about the enormous strength of Standard Oil, John D. Rockefeller said, "I have ways of making money you know nothing about" (Rockefeller Biography 146-47). This statement is still true for the vast majority of millionaires around the globe 100 years after Rockefeller first said it. As previously stated, one-third of Philadelphia's population lives below the national poverty line, yet 12% of the population makes above 100,000 dollars per year (Census, Philadelphia, Pennsylvania). In 2005, Philadelphia was listed as being one of the richest cities in the world when ranked by GDP. It only fell behind major financial trading cities such as Tokyo, New York, Los Angeles, Chicago, and London (City Mayors). Philadelphia, also home to the best graduate school for business in the world, Wharton at the University of Pennsylvania, produces some of the wealthiest people in the nation, including Donald Trump, the Chairman and President of the *Trump Organizations*, Warren Buffet founder and CEO of Berkshire Hathaway, Brian Roberts, CEO of Comcast, and former fraudulent bond trader Michael Milken. The aspiration for wealth accumulation is embedded in the history and the minds of Philadelphians.

It is difficult for average citizens to fully comprehend the different lifestyle which the rich are able to inhabit. Twenty-six of the most successful billionaires in the world have lived in Philadelphia at some point in their lives. A billion dollars is a monetary figure which is difficult for the masses to fathom actually having. Dave Johnson published an article to explain just how much money one billion dollars actually is. This is an excerpt from said article:

> Let's Go Shopping. So you say to yourself, "I want me some of that. I'd like to place the following order, please."
>
> • One Maybach Landaulet (one of the finest of all luxury automobiles) for $1 million to drive around in. (Actually to be *driven* around in.)
>
> • One Le Grand Bleu yacht for when I want to get seasick. Le Grand Bleu is one of the largest private yachts in the world at 104 m (341 ft.) in length. And retails for a mere 100 million dollars.
>
> • One Gulfstream G550 private jet for $40 million.
>
> • One private island for $24.5 million (medieval castle included) for when I want to escape the masses. Dark Island, a prominent feature of the St. Lawrence Seaway, is located in the lower (eastern) Thousand Islands region, near Chippewa Bay.

- One $8 million estate for when I have to go ashore and mingle with the masses (but not *too* close.) Located in Atherton, CA.

- One $5 million watch so I can have one.

- **Total: $178.5 million.**

  My change after paying with a billion-dollar bill is a meager **$821.5 million left over**. I might be hard up for cash after my spending spree, but I can still stay in a $20,000 room every night for 112 years.

  So, as you see, $1 billion is more than enough to really live it up. People today are amassing *multiples* of billions, paying very little in taxes and using it in ways that harm the rest of us (Johnson).

Johnson makes it very clear how much money billionaires actually have at their disposal. Remember, Philadelphia produced 26 of the most successful *billionaires* in 2011, according to Forbes magazine. These people have accumulated multiples of billions of dollars per year.

With that being said, not all wealthy people are billionaires, especially not in Philadelphia. This, however, does not mean there is a shortage of wealth within the city. Philadelphia is home to some of the world's most renowned five-star restaurants such as Morimotos, Le Bec Fin, and Davio's Steakhouse. It also hosts large investment firms like Barclays International, Haverford Investment, and Blackrock Financial. All of these firms handle billions of dollars of assets per year and generally only cater to the extremely wealthy. A difference in Philadelphia, when compared to other large American cities, is its excessive amount of luxury automobiles. While walking through Center City Philadelphia, one is likely to encounter a rather hefty amount of high-end Ferraris, Audis, and Maseratis on almost every street. Philadelphia has been noted as a great place for the rich to live; the culture, shops, and fine dining allow those with the highest incomes in America to live luxurious and exciting lives. With the right amount of disposable income, one's every desire can be accessed within the city limits.

Part III

Why is there a distinct separation between the rich and the poor? In America, we are taught to believe that we all have an equal chance to succeed, that we are all created equally, and that there is no legitimate excuse as to why someone cannot be successful. However, this equality of opportunity is not a realistic assurance to the entire population. Children who grow up in low-income neighborhoods, such as Mantua in West Philadelphia, are more exposed to criminal behavior and receive small amounts of funding for education while high-income neighborhoods, like Chestnut Hill, have low "blue collar" crime rates and more funding for their school systems. A larger proportion of the poor population's income will go to bills, food, and taxes than those in higher tax brackets (Reich). This means that the poor have less money at their disposal to save for the future or a "college savings account" for their children. Citizens who derive from higher socioeconomic status have different, unequal, and unabridged opportunities to financial success in America and in Philadelphia.

What keeps this separation in place? In Philadelphia, the monetary hierarchy keeps those individuals who derive from a certain status, be it rich or poor, to continue to stay in their positions. It is almost impossible for someone of the lowest income levels to obtain large amounts of wealth in Philadelphia. Simply growing up in a crime-infested area creates a more likely chance of being involved in crime or dying at a young age. Of the entire incarcerated population in Philadelphia, "approximately 55% are high school dropouts...60% cannot find a job after being released" (Mayes). It would not be fair to say that people who go to jail are not created equally; their choices throughout life made their opportunities limited. However, a study produced by the Justice Policy Institute showed that the chances of being incarcerated have increased in low-income areas as nationwide crime rates have dropped. This means that children growing up in low-income areas are significantly more likely to be incarcerated in their lifetime than go to college or to even receive a high school diploma.

Funding for public education in America is primarily financed through property taxes. This means a community of 3,000 households whose average property value is only $50,000, where the property tax is .94%, will receive $1,410,000 in education funding. Meanwhile, a community of 3,000 households whose average property value is $400,000 with the same property tax will receive $11,280,000. That is $9,870,000 more that the higher-income community has to spend on better quality teachers, more advanced technology, and other school supplies. Also, as a government becomes more focused on the needs for businesses to succeed so that their wealth will somehow "trickle down," state funding for education will also fall. This reduces resources for the low-income school systems even further. As students become less educated due to unavailable or inadequate resources, they will become more susceptible to beliefs and policies which actually act against their self-interest. Lower education levels also drastically reduce the chance of a citizen increasing their current economic situation or leaving the low-income area which keeps them trapped underneath the wealth hierarchy.

Part IV

How to combat this issue? It is important not to remove the capitalist society which is the basis of America's economy. This system has given rise to the advancement of healthcare, vast amounts of technology, and an overall improvement in the quality of life. Capitalism is not the root issue of income inequality. Capitalism is an economic principle powered primarily through the human instinct to look for one's own self-interest. We are all driven by the opportunity to obtain some sort of wealth. For capitalism to truly work, a free market is optimal. A free market is not synonymous with an unregulated market, however. In many cases and many industries, oligopolies are present, preventing a consumer-driven price option. Slight regulation and an increase of scrutiny for the wealthy will help resolve the issue of income inequality.

The capital gains tax is currently set at 15%, no matter how much money is being generated. This means that money invested in the markets will only be taxed at a rate of 15%. A hedge fund manager making income from capital gains payments is most likely paying less in taxes than the average American because his or her income is not actually being taxed as income. The removal of the capital gains tax, which would result in having the money generated through investment taxed as regular income, would be a first step in developing a more equal wealth distribution. Secondly, people who are under the poverty line should not pay income tax because such a large proportion of their income goes to taxes and bills so that almost no income is left to stimulate businesses in the economy. Further, most of the social services used by those under the poverty line are funded by taxes. Tax restructuring is just one step in conquering the issue of wealth inequality in America.

As mentioned previously, many markets are not purely competitive. Small general stores have to face the vast economy of scale which Wal-Mart offers. In this situation Wal-Mart is known as a price setter. Other companies in the same industry have to follow suit with how they set prices in the market. The issue with this is that it does not allow for small businesses to grow due to the fact they do not have the large amount of resources that Wal-Mart has. Companies that are already large will go to towns that have smaller businesses and either buy them out or wait for them to die, but how does this affect income inequality? Before large corporations and conglomerates were established, wealth was able to be dispersed more evenly among businesses. Currently, income is dominated primarily through which company can hold enough market-share to set prices, allowing that particular company or the top companies in the industry to generate an unheard of amount of wealth. As the people who are already on top begin to receive more of the population's money, the gap between those who are paying for the goods they offer and those who are selling said goods grows larger. The unregulated markets which allow for businesses to obtain a majority of the market share in a particular industry provide inadequate competition for pure capitalism to be obtainable. The first steps to closing the gap between the rich and poor are to close the gaps that allow the wealthy to avoid paying the correct amount of taxes or to collectively gain an illegal amount of market share.

Conclusion

The income gap in Philadelphia is an issue which affects not just the extremely poor or extremely wealthy. Income inequality affects all citizens. A member of the Occupy Philadelphia movement, Nahur Suleimun, explained that the people of Philadelphia are upset: "They think we are all ignorant, they think we aren't aware of the situation they put us in" (Suleimun). Not just the homeless, not just the poor, not just the hungry, but the people of Philadelphia are upset with their current situation. This is a situation which keeps certain members of the population of Philadelphia unfed, unclothed, homeless, and unemployed. The Constitution of the United States reads, "We the People of the United States, in Order to form a more perfect Union, establish Justice, insure domestic Tranquility, provide for the common defense, promote the general Welfare, and secure the Blessings of Liberty to ourselves and our Posterity, do ordain and establish this Constitution for the United States of America." It does not say we the people with money, we the wealthy, rather it clearly states, "We the people." A strong city, a strong government, and a strong nation must reflect the will of the people, not address those who fund its officials. Closing the gap between the wealthy and impoverished will not be an easy task, but neither was breaking the oppression of Great Britain. In this city, a city which is known for being the home of the American Revolution, it may be time to break free from the reign of tyranny yet again. Philadelphia: A Class Divided, will soon be restored to a home of liberty and equality.

Works Cited

"A Portrait of Homelessness." *Trevor's Campaign for the Homeless.* Web. 31 Oct. 2011.
    <http://trevorscampaign.org/index.php?option=comcontent&view=article&id=
    2:2007-homeless-statistics&catid=1:all-news&Itemid=7>.

Barth, Kerry. "Mayor Nutter discusses Philadelphia's 'Renaissance.'" *The Quad,* the
    student newspaper of West Chester University. Web. 20 Nov. 2011. <http://www.
    wcuquad.com/news/mayor-nutter-discusses-philadelphia-s-renaissance-1.2556015#.
    Tskt5WPQdnm>.

Benen, Steve. "Political Animal—Hint for wealthy lawmakers: don't seek pity from voters." *The Washington Monthly*. Web. 20 Nov. 2011. <http://www. washingtonmonthly.com/political- animal/2011_ 09/hint_ for_ wealthy_ lawmakers>.

Brandeis, Louis. "Democracy Quotes: International Endowment for Democracy." International Endowment for Democracy. Web. 20 Nov. 2011. <http://www.iefd.org/ articles/democracy>.

"Brookings: Executive Summary—Philadelphia in Focus: A Profile from Census 2000." *Brookings* 1 Nov. 2003. Web. 31 Oct. 2011. <http://www.brookings.edu/reports /2003/11_livingcities_philadelphia.aspx>.

Census. "Philadelphia, Pennsylvania (PA) income, earnings, and wages data." City Data, 1 Jan. 2009. Web. 31 Oct. 2011. <http://www.city-data.com/income/income-Philadelphia-Pennsylvania.html>.

Chernow, Ron. *Titan: the Life of John D. Rockefeller*, Sr. New York: Random House, 1998 Print.

"City Mayors review the richest cities in the world in 2005." *City Mayors* 1 Jan. 2005. Web. 12 Nov. 2011. <http://www.citymayors.com/statistics/richest-cities-2005.html>.

Johnson, Dave. "Nine Pictures Of The Extreme Income/Wealth Gap." *OurFuture.org*. Web. 12 Nov. 2011. <http://www.ourfuture.org/blog-entry/2011020612/ understanding-extreme-incomewealth-gap>.

Fesseden, Ford, and Alan McLean. "Where the One Percent Fit in the Hierarchy of Income." *The New York Times* 28 Oct. 2011. Web. 31 Oct. 2011. <http://www.nytimes.com/ interactive/2011/10/30/nyregion/where-the-one-percent-fit-in-the-hierarchy-of-income.html?nl=todaysheadlines&emc=thab1>.

Mayes, Eric. "Successful ex-inmate reaches out to others." *PhillyTrib.com*. Web. 20 Nov. 2011. <http://www.phillytrib.com/cityandregionarticles/item/763-successful-ex-inmate-reaches-out-to-others.html>.

McCarty, Maggie. *Homelessness recent statistics, targeted federal programs, and recent legislation*. Washington, D.C.: Congressional Information Service, Library of Congress, 2005. Print.

"Penn Alumni: Home." *Penn Alumni*. Web. 20 Nov. 2011. <http://www.alumni.upenn.edu/>.

"Percent of People Below Poverty Level in the Past 12 Months (For Whom PovertyStatus is Determined)" *American FactFinder*, United States Census Bureau U.S. Census Bureau, 2009 American Community Survey. Retrieved 12 Aug. 2011.

"Percent of People 65 Years and Over Below Poverty Level in the Past 12 Months" *American FactFinder*, United States Census Bureau U.S. Census Bureau, 2009 American Community Survey. Retrieved 12 Aug. 2011.

"Percent of Children Under 18 Years Below Poverty Level in the Past 12 Months (For Whom Poverty Status is Determined)"*American FactFinder*, United States Census Bureau U.S. Census Bureau, 2009 American Community Survey. Retrieved 12 Aug. 2011.

Philadelphia City Planning Commission. City of Philadelphia Government. *Citywide Vision: Philadelphia 2035*. City of Philadelphia: Philadelphia City Planning Commission, June 2011. Print.

"Philadelphia County QuickFacts from the US Census Bureau." *State and County QuickFacts*. Web. 31 Oct. 2011. <http://quickfacts.census.gov/qfd/states/42/42101.html>.

"Press Release: 1 in 2 Philadelphia-District Households with Kids Can't Afford Enough." Greater Philadelphia Coalition Against Hunger. Web. 20 Nov. 2011. <http://www hungercoalition.org/news/news-release-1-2-philadelphia-district-households-children-can%E2%80%99t-afford-enough-food>.

"Project H.O.M.E.: Facts on Homelessness." *Project H.O.M.E.: Ending Homelessness in Philadelphia*. Project H.O.M.E, 1 Jan. 2011. Web. 31 Oct. 2011. <http://projecthome. org/advocacy/facts.php>.

"S1903. Median Income in the Past 12 Months (In 2009 Inflation-Adjusted Dollars)" American *FactFinder*, United States Census Bureau. U.S. Census Bureau, 2009 American Community Survey. Retrieved 12 Aug. 2011.

Sebelius, Kathleen. *Annual Update of the HHS Poverty Guidelines* (FR Doc. 2011-1237). Department of Health and Human Services. January 14, 2011. Print.

Suleimun, Nahur. Personal interview. 1 Nov. 2011.

Reich, Robert. "The seven biggest economic lies." Robert Reich. Web. 20 Nov. 2011. <http://robertreich.org/post/11329289>.

Sahadi, Jeanne. "Where the (best) 6-figure jobs are." *CNNMoney* 29 Sept. 2006. Web. 31 Oct. 2011. <http://money.cnn.com/2006/07/13/pf/six_fig_farthest/index.htm>.

Alex Fatemi

Superstition's Genesis

When I first went to Drexel University's Main Building, I found a bronze statue of a boy holding a bucket over his head as if to dump it on himself. What I found strange about this statue was that the boy's toe was a shiny, yellow color, unlike the rest of his body. The statue was accompanied by a plaque which explains that there is a belief that if students rub the toe, they'll have good luck on their exams. How could rubbing the toe of a bronze statue lead to one getting a higher-than-normal grade? Such a superstition simply doesn't make sense. What is most confusing about this superstition is how it even began. There are thousands of superstitions that make little or no sense, yet they still exist. One can't help but wonder, "How does a superstition like that start?" I looked at the statue in Main Building, known as "The Water Boy," confusedly and thought about rubbing its toe for good luck. I was so curious, I decided to look into how the superstition began. I thought, "Surely, something so bizarre would have a concrete beginning. It's just some old statue." However, after many days of looking at scattered bits and pieces of information, I found that the answer was rather surprising.

The first place I went for information on "The Water Boy" was the Internet. After many frustrating dead ends, I had found very little information about the statue. I did however, find the name and e-mail address of the curator who runs the Drexel Collection, of which "The Water Boy" is part. The collection is overseen by Jacqueline DeGroff. Ms. DeGroff responded to my questions about the statue with surprising speed. She knew a lot about the statue's history and confirmed a very important fact; "The Water Boy," or as it was originally known, "The Alsatian Vinter," was made by Frederic Bartholdi, the artist who designed the Statue of Liberty. As for how a statue from such a famous artist came to Drexel University, DeGroff explained and theorized that "Anthony Drexel was one of the major donors for the pedestal of the State of Liberty in the 1880s... Since [he] was a major donor for the pedestal, I suspect Drexel came to know Bartholdi during this fundraising." This theory makes sense and it would also explain how Drexel University has both "The Alsatian Vinter" and one of the few remaining original scale models of the Statue of Liberty. "The Alsatian Vinter" was sculpted, according to the date on its base, in 1869. It was on display at the Centennial Exposition of 1876 in Philadelphia alongside a few other pieces by Bartholdi, including the arm of the Statue of Liberty. So, interestingly, our "Water Boy" statue is very old and rather historic in some ways. This may have something to do with how it became a Drexel superstition. Back when it first came to the Drexel Institute of Technology, the statue's pedigree would have been a big deal. The statue was made by a famous and successful man, so perhaps the idea was that some of his success would rub off on students if they were to literally rub the statue. There is, however, a bit more to this superstition's history.

Unfortunately, Ms. DeGroff knew noticeably less about the toe-rubbing tradition than she did about the statue's past. She explained that the toe rubbing was something that began a long time ago and despite harming the precious statue, it is tolerated merely for the sake of tradition. She also didn't know when the statue actually came to Drexel University in the first place, as she had no record of it. The curator suggested that I try the Drexel archives in order to find more on the tradition. The people at the Drexel Archives quickly and kindly gathered up what materials they had on the statue and let me have a look at the information at Hagerty Library. Scattered about the library table were a variety of snippets of information. No one piece would solve the mystery on its own, but together, they gave a clear message.

The first big clue in my search through the archived documents was a picture from the 1955 Drexel Institute of Technology yearbook of a student rubbing the statue's toe. The caption below the picture explains the superstition of the toe bringing luck on exams and stated that the tradition of rubbing it was one they were proud of carrying on. This means that the toe rubbing was around before 1955, making it more than 56 years old. Since the tradition was seen as something to carry on, one can assume it was around for a long time before this yearbook. The caption also points out that, despite no one knowing if the superstition was true or not, students continued to do it because they wanted any help they could get on their exams. Did the students in the 1950s rub the statue's toe knowing that it was a Bartholdi statue? That fact is lost on many of today's students, but I wonder if back in the 1950s, the statue's history was equally unknown. If they did know the statue's past, that would support my theory that its history is why the superstition clung to it.

The only other important item from the archive was an article from Drexel's newspaper, *The Triangle*, from 1961. The article, written by Terry Degutis, brought one final bit of information to light which acted as the last nail in the coffin of my search. "The Alsatian Vinter" wasn't catalogued in the Drexel Archives (3). A strange mixture of excitement and peace came over me as I realized that this 50-year-old article had been searching for exactly what I was researching: when the tradition began. Unfortunately, Degutis had found all the same basic information on the past that I had. And, just as the article found itself at a dead end when even archives failed, so too did I.

After speaking with both the curator of the Drexel Collection and searching through the archives, I still have no idea when or how the superstitious idea that rubbing the statue's toe will give good luck in exams began. This may seem like a failed search, but in reality, it showed something I hadn't thought of. Superstitions like this, based on slightly more modern structures, seem as though they should have a start that someone could pinpoint, but the truth is that those beginnings were probably never recorded. The superstition of rubbing the statue's toe for good luck is well over 50 years old, and its beginning is unknown. The superstition around "The Alsatian Vinter" is something that has become a part of Drexel history without having a concrete starting point, as I assume many other superstitions have as well. Superstitions seem to be born from some circumstance or desire, such as wanting to do well on an exam, coinciding with something random like rubbing the toe of a statue. They're born by a want to have something help with success. Because of this want, there will always be superstitions like the toe of "The Alsatian Vinter" to make us feel better by helping us believe things will turn out better and we'll be lucky.

Works Cited

DeGroff, Jacqueline. Email interview. 21 Oct. 2011

Deguis, Terry. "Good Luck Charm In Halls, Water Boy's Toes Glisten." *The Drexel Triangle* 3 Feb. 1961: 3. Print.

Drexel Institute of Technology. *Drexel Lexerd* 1955. Philadelphia: Drexel Institute of Technology, 1955. 7. Print.

Abigail Harris

A Lesson Taken with Approximately One Cup of Salt

To say that August 31, 2009, the first day of my junior year of high school, was the beginning of an opportunity, would be a mistake. Not because some wonderful opportunities didn't surface during the year, but rather because the beginning was already well underway.

While most of my friends were dreading the return to school, I had been looking forward to it—most of it anyway. After a long summer of babysitting and trying to ice skate through an increasingly painful injury, I was ready for a change of pace. However, the looming college application process was more than daunting. As I drove from my house, past the blur of trees and over the stream I hardly noticed, I was inundated with a series of headache-causing questions: "Where is my life taking me? Where do I want my life to go? What do I think? And why is it suddenly so hard to make decisions?"

Too distracted to care that the sun was baking me against the black leather seats in my car, I spent the rest of my drive to school feeling sticky and trying to mentally bury the cycle of stress-provoking questions. I quieted my mind by reminding myself that college stuff was at least another year away. I was right in that I was a year and a half away from sending in a deposit, but I was naïve for believing that every step could be postponed for so long. In fact, by morning of the first day of junior year, I was already fully immersed in the very processes that I was dreading, and not even the bell could save me.

My first class of the day was called geo-environmental science. I wasn't sure what the class would be like, so I wasn't overly excited. However, I was told that I had the best teacher, Mr. Rowland. I tried to keep that in mind as I navigated through a hallway of obnoxiously squealing freshmen on the way to his classroom.

The room was big, but the three rows of six bulky rectangular lab benches filled up the space. Mr. Rowland had a large demonstration bench spanning almost the full length of the room and a desk off to the side. Like all teachers, Mr. Rowland had a white board and a SMART board. Instead of the usual "welcome" power point, Mr. Rowland's SMART board was streaming the Weather Channel.

The wall, positioned opposite the door, was filled with windows. Through them I could see the athletic fields and the tennis courts where my friends and I faked our way through gym class. I could see the walls of the stadium, which made me remember freezing cold football games and scalding hot chocolate. Even closer in view was the narrow meandering road, which connects the high school to one of the district's middle schools, and the parking lot where I eventually parked more often than not because I was always running late.

From the moment that I entered his room, it was clear that Mr. Rowland was not an ordinary teacher. He wasn't hiding behind his desk, or directing students to their assigned seats. As a matter of fact, he was sitting on top of a lab bench talking to some of my classmates when I walked into his room. He was a short, slender man with crazy, reddish-brown hair and a big smile.

Once the class arrived, he summoned everyone to a lab bench in the center of the room. There, he performed a demonstration on the properties of water density. He poured a cup of salt into a clear tennis ball container. Then, he dropped a golf ball on top of the salt mound. Just before adding water to the container, Mr. Rowland did what any science teacher would do. He polled the class, "Is the ball going to stay where it is, or is it going to float?" The response was typical. Some said stay, some said float, and those on the fence said nothing.

"Oh no!" Mr. Rowland blurted out with the raging enthusiasm of a game show host. "I guess we're going to have to find out." With a mischievous smile, be began to steadily, but slowly, pour the water into the container. The ball immediately began to shift, and Mr. Rowland encouraged our curiosity by repeatedly asking, "What's happening? What's happening?" Everyone huddled closer around the bench in order to have a better view of the container; the people in the back were standing on their toes. The ball wavered in the middle for a few seconds.

Then, the ball hit the salt mound with a thud, and Mr. Rowland was hit with about thirty different expressions of disbelief and disappointment. "No one said that we were done," explained Mr. Rowland, trying to reassure us that we didn't wake up at seven o'clock in the morning and trudge all the way to his classroom for nothing. He capped the container and motioned for everyone to lean further into the huddle.

In a soft whisper, as if the demonstration were a life or death situation, Mr. Rowland said, "Okay, when I say go, I'm going to hand this container to Andrew." Turning to face Andrew, Mr. Rowland continued with his instructions, "You're going to put a hand over the lid and shake the container as hard as you can until I say switch. When I say switch, you're going to give it to the person next to you, and so on."

By that point, Mr. Rowland had successfully managed to get our adrenaline rushing and our hearts pumping over a container of salty water. Though it seems juvenile now, everyone assumed a stance that was more determined than a sprinter in the Olympics. "Go!" Mr. Rowland shouted while tossing the container to Andrew, who instantly began shaking it. "Switch!" he shouted next.

I remember feeling like I was five years old playing hot potato. The container hastily made its way to everyone, splashing everyone in its path with the water that leaked from its lid. Finally, the container made its way back to the center lab bench. To everyone's amazement, the golf ball was actually floating at the top of the container.

In an instant, the giggling and excitement subsided to silent examination. As we stared at the golf ball suspended in water, Mr. Rowland remarked with true appreciation, "Isn't that amazing." Though the demonstration applies relatively simple principles, the ways in which two ordinary objects in nature, like salt and water, can interact truly is amazing.

After the demonstration, Mr. Rowland prompted a series of questions that forced us to think about how these principles apply to real life. We had to evaluate how even the smallest changes to the demonstration might affect the end result. As a class, we came to the conclusion that even a slight change to one material or step would disrupt the entire system, causing the demonstration to be unsuccessful. Again, encouraging us to elaborate, Mr. Rowland asked, "What about an ocean? If its salt content increases too much, or decreases too much, will it be 'successful'?"

Mr. Rowland was always pushing our class to see the bigger picture. He wanted us to realize that everything in the world, including us, is interdependent. With that realization comes a remarkable appreciation for the world in which we live, something that is very evident in Mr. Rowland. He is the type of person who can tear up at a sunrise or a hawk flying across the sky. He is the happiest person I know.

Happiness is something that everyone strives for in life. Therefore, as I began to plan my future, I was influenced by Mr. Rowland's beliefs because I admired the way he lived his life. I believe that his happiness comes from his ability to have faith in anything, but still be impressed by everything. He has faith that the seasons will change and that snow will fall, but when it does he looks at each flake as if he has never seen snow before. His ability to marvel at life is a quality that I can only hope to acquire.

By the end of the school year, I still looked out the window just as I did on the first day, but at some point, the view changed: past the fields and the stadium and roads, I saw mountains covered by trees and hidden by morning fog, and birds flew across the painted sky, illuminated by a rising, golden sun.

George Risi, Jr.

Global Applications of Scholastic Writing

"Opening: State the purpose of your writing. Give a clear and definitive thesis. Preview your main arguing points. Body paragraphs: Open with your subject. Present irrefutable evidence. Explain evidence. Repeat. Closing: Briefly recount your argument. Relate your argument to a larger context." Since the dawn of modern education, this has been the universal paradigm for writing the expository or persuasive essay. For educational purposes, these rules serve as an adequate template, but do they suffice as a standard for writing outside of school? Without courses specific to certain areas of writing (e.g. poetry, technical analysis, or fiction), are students getting enough exposure to variations on writing other than the standard book report or lab write-up?

Obviously, the same basic principles of grammar and sentence structure apply to all forms of writing, save, occasionally, poetry. Is that the extent of their overlap, though? In some cases, yes. According to a survey I conducted of roughly 100 freshman at Drexel University, a very high percentage employ little to no rhetoric in their daily writing. Moreover, many students claim that the primary media for their writing don't even require that they use punctuation, let alone "all that other stuff" they learn in the classroom. This result arouses the question, what skillset *is* needed for daily writing?

First, we will establish a baseline set of skills used in academic writing against which we will later compare the skills used in other forms of writing. William Strunk and E.B. White, in their book, *The Elements of Style*, detail the writing process from a technical standpoint. The body of the book consists of two sections with eighteen subsections. The first section concerns the rules of usage. The second section—the one in which we are more interested— discusses the principles of composition. The ten main principles, each with its own subsection, are as follows. 1) Make the paragraph the unit of composition: one paragraph to each topic. 2) As a rule begin each paragraph with a topic sentence: end it in conformity with the beginning. 3) Use the active voice. 4) Put statements in positive form. 5) Omit needless words. 6) Avoid succession of loose sentences. 7) Express co-ordinate ideas in similar form. 8) Keep related words together. 9) In summaries, keep to one tense. 10) Place the emphatic words of a sentence at the end. (Table of Contents). One step that is conspicuously absent from Strunk and White's model, according to most, is revision. In her article entitled "Revision Strategies of Student Writers and Experienced Adult writers," Nancy Sommers cites revision as one of the most crucial steps in composition. She then goes on to explain that student writers focus primarily on "deletion, substitution, addition, and reordering" (380-81) when they revise. From a technical standpoint, Strunk and White, and Sommer's stipulations, adequately represent the contents of most scholarly writing.

In the article "Writing Approaches of University Students," Ellen Lavelle and Nancy Zeurcher address the process of writing from a psychological standpoint. The two authors call the approach to writing described by Strunk and White a "procedural" approach.

The procedural approach involves a method-driven strategy based on strict adherence to the rules and a minimal amount of involvement... Such writers ask themselves, "Where can I put this information that I just came across?" The strategy is listing or providing a "sequence of ideas, an orderly arrangement"...

The procedural approach reflects wanting to please the teacher rather the intention to communicate or reflect. It is as though writing is to be managed and controlled toward that end...Perhaps the procedural emphasis on "control" in writing, not allowing for emergent factors such as voice and theme, keeps writers on task as limited by time demands. (377)

Described above is what I have found to be the critical difference between scholarly writing and casual writing—grades. Students' primary purpose in writing is to satisfy the requirements of the grader. Beyond this, most students could not care less about the quality and depth of their work. As long as their compositions obey the basic structure and are factually adequate, students receive satisfactory marks.

How does non-scholarly writing compare to what is discussed above? Do we still use the same methods and standards? According to my survey, academic and recreational writing share little common ground. I first asked my sample of students to categorize the things they had recently written. As expected, all of the subjects identified school/essay as one of the categories into which their work fit. Beyond this, the most popular categories were Facebook, email, instant message, and blog post—in that order. I then asked the survey-takers to consider those categories and say whether or not they formally and consciously revised what they wrote. The answer: a resounding "No." Seventy-eight percent of the students admitted to not revising the writing that they share with others. This invites the obvious question: would you be okay if somebody expected you to read their error-riddled work? I asked the survey takers to rate the importance of grammar, sentence structure, and overall writing quality on a scale from one to ten. The average rating was around 3.5.

To me, such a result is shockingly low. I am seemingly alone in the opinion that people should be able to easily read, understand, and critically evaluate the work of others. Disappointingly, I concluded that students apply few of the stylistic techniques they learn in English class outside of the classroom.

After recognizing that the age of artistic, terse, eloquent, or even grammatically correct writing might be a thing of the past, I reasoned that students must at least be using rhetoric to form and support arguments. When I polled the students, I found that I was correct. Seventy-one percent of the students reported using identifiable instances of rhetoric as defined in Drexel English 101. In a follow-up interview with Drexel freshman Tyler Ney-Smith, I asked him to elaborate on the rhetoric question. "It isn't that I consciously think, 'what logos could I use to back up my opinion?' more that, if you asked me to, I could identify the logos, ethos, and pathos in my argument" (Ney-Smith). This unconscious use of the rhetorical devices is an even greater victory for the academic community, which is, apparently, teaching students to immediately integrate what they have learned into their lives. During the interview, Ney-Smith also commented on the previously discussed topic of grammar and usage. He wished to discuss further the question where I asked the subjects to rate grammar importance on a scale from one to ten. "I personally would expect different levels of correctness in the different categories. Obviously, when you are reading somebody's Facebook status or a YouTube comment, you can expect it to be nearly gibberish, but blogs and emails are usually orders of magnitude better. Still, they probably wouldn't get a good grade as an English paper" (Ney-Smith). Indeed.

In an effort to incorporate a broader demographic, I extended my interviews beyond Drexel. I interviewed Zach Pasteris, a pre-med student at the University of Pennsylvania, whom I knew had recently spent some time at work with his father who holds an executive position at a large insurance company. Pasteris claimed, "The world of big business seems woefully devoid of lengthy writing. All of the high-level managers insisted that their subordinates submit reports and similar documents in bullet point form. The only full length texts were technical reports that I would need a dictionary to understand." He later explained that "all of the people in the office were obviously highly skilled writers. They must have been to reach such high level positions. However, they did not do much beyond basic communication that I witnessed" (Pasteris). In a similar interview conducted with my father, George Risi, Sr., he asserted, "When people send emails and submit reports, there is a general understanding that they will be grammatically correct. Beyond that, they do not have to sound very good, as long as they communicate the information with adequate detail." As a senior project manager at one of the top-ranked hospitals in the U.S., Risi does not receive many research papers or scholarly journal articles, so it is understandable that he is not concerned with the finer points of the writing. He did, however, add this at the end of the interview: "When it comes down to it, good writing will get you things you want in any industry. Somebody who writes well seems more deserving of a promotion or more funding than a person who writes poorly" (Risi). To summarize the interviews, we can conclude that, while technical knowledge of a certain field is more crucial to success, basic writing knowledge is a necessary starting point. Eugene Nida, author of "Sociolinguistic Implications of Academic Writing," agrees with this notion. In the very first sentence of his scholarly article, he summarizes his argument: "The language of academic journals tends to become so technical that only specialists are able to understand the unnecessarily complex features of vocabulary, syntax, discourse, and format" (477). This assessment seems to reaffirm my previous statement regarding technical knowledge of a subject being vital to success; one cannot understand such complex technical material with only knowledge of basic English.

Where does that leave us, then? Is school teaching useful writing practices? The answer, unequivocally, is yes. Of course, to be proficient in any single field, a student will have to venture beyond the discussion boards of English 101. But as far as the necessity of what we are learning is concerned, there is nothing more crucial than these basic writing practices. As a student who has continually scored within the top 1% of writers, it pleases me to see that fundamentally good writing has not lost its place in academia as social media would have us believe. Even in this modern world, where multimedia is continually becoming more accessible, I am confident that writing will continue to be a relevant form of communication and documentation.

Works Cited

Lavelle, Ellen, and Nancy Zeurcher. "The Writing Approaches of University Students." *HigherEducation.* 42 (2001): 373-91. Web. 29, Oct. 2011.

Ney Smith, Tyler. Personal Interview. 6 Nov. 2011

Nida, Eugene A. "Sociolinguistic Implications of Academic Writing." *Language in Society.* 21 (1992): 477-485. Web. 30 Oct. 2011

Pasteris. Zach. Personal Interview. 12 Nov. 2011

Risi, George Sr. Personal Interview. 12 Nov. 2011

Sommers, Nancy. "Revision Strategies of Student Writers and Experienced Adult Writers. "*College Composition and Communication.* 31 (1980): 378-88. Web. 9. Nov. 2011.

Strunk, William and E.B. White. *The Elements of Style.* Ithaca, New York: Pearson Education Company, 1959. Print.

Publishing Group
Essays

Introduction

Researching, thinking, and writing are at the core of the College of Arts and Sciences. No matter what field they're in, students must be able to research, to find and evaluate the best evidence and information on a topic. They must be able to think, to formulate original ideas and take a fresh approach to a problem or question. And, of course, they must be able to write—excellent research and thought must be communicated to others to have value. After all of their reading and thinking about the work of others, students must make their own contributions to the field by writing.

The constant exposure to accomplished works published in their field of study can intimidate students when they sit down to write. Or inspire them. It may do both as students struggle to bring their own vision to the subjects they study and find the right words. Fortunately, this struggle often yields remarkable writing. The following works, selected from student submissions to the fifth-annual Drexel Publishing Group writing contest, exemplify a firm grasp of subject matter and a facility with language.

The essays in this section of *The 33rd* cover a host of subjects from a range of disciplines in the arts and sciences, including the need for a name law in the United States, the causes of strong regional political parties, the value of online food criticism, and the use of technology to prevent fraud. The topics are as diverse as the students who wrote about them, but the essays all demonstrate originality and boldness as well as great skill in researching, thinking, and writing.

Ariel Pollak

Should America Pass a Name Law?

In 2007, a nine-year-old New Zealand girl sued her parents to change her name. The girl's lawyer explained to the court that the girl, Talula Does the Hula From Hawaii, was very distressed by her name and that her name caused her significant social problems. The court ruled to allow her to change her name against parental consent (McMahon), which was possible because of the name laws in New Zealand that prevent parents from giving their children socially unacceptable names. Laws like this exist in many countries: the Swedish Name Law prevented a couple from naming their son Brfxxccxxmnpcccclllmmnprxvclmnckssqlbb111163, pronounced "Albin" (Israel). There are no such laws in America, which is why two boys (from Michigan and Texas) are named ESPN, for the popular sports network ("Judge"), and one family named their children JoyceLynn Aryan Nation, Honszlynn Himmler Jeannie, and Adolf Hitler Campbell (Belkin). The name a child is given at birth can have long-reaching consequences in several areas and can be highly detrimental to the child, if the name is unique or inappropriate. The enactment of a name law would protect children from the many negative effects of highly unusual names.

Some parents who give their children unusual names believe that the names will help their children to stand out or feel special. This uniqueness frequently works against them, however, when their names are misspelled, mispronounced, misinterpreted, or mistaken for completely different names altogether. Often, parents are motivated by a desire to avoid negative personal connotations that common names may hold (Fabian), but highly unusual names may be just as off-putting. One study found that people with undesirable names were rated as less attractive than others when the name was the only information available (Samakow) and children with names that differ dramatically from the norm are popular targets for bullies. In retrospect, many parents would change their naming decisions: a study in Britain found that 20% of the surveyed parents regretted the unusual spelling of their child's name, 8% wished that the name was mispronounced less often, and 10% had lost their original affection for the name (Bryner).

The negative effects of odd names are more than simply social, however; some names can increase the risk of educational, behavioral, and psychological challenges. Boys who bear feminine names have more behavioral problems by middle school than their peers (Bryner), and adults who have extremely unusual or negative names have lower self-esteem, less educational achievement, and higher rates of smoking than the average. Children with names that are perceived as part of a lower socioeconomic class (such as those with nontraditional spellings, apostrophes, or uncommon letters like q or z) are considered less intelligent by the teachers, earn lower grades (Satran), and are more likely to be categorized as learning disabled than their more standard-named siblings (Birch). Spelling a name nontraditionally (as many parenting books suggest as an alternative to a unique name) is no better, as other research shows that children with unusually spelled names have reading and spelling delays (Bryner). "Special" names rarely have the effect intended by parents, causing instead frustration, negative judgments from others, and isolation.

The advantages of a national naming law would be significant. In a country where less than half of newborn children bear one of the fifty most common names (Satran), a law protecting children from the negative effects of highly unusual names could have a large impact. People might decry such a law as impinging on personal freedom; however, nearly all countries have laws that restrict perceived liberties to protect the rights of children. Laws to prevent parents from causing social, educational and/or psychological problems for their children already exist. While an awful name would not be categorized by most as child abuse, it would certainly not benefit the child during their schooling years, and is highly unlikely to be beneficial once the child matures. On the contrary, unique or odd names have a number of negative effects that have been previously outlined.

Additionally, naming laws are not without precedent: Since 1982, parents in Sweden have selected names for their children from a list or submitted their choices for a committee to determine whether or not the name is appropriate. The Naming Commission rejects names that they deem offensive or likely to cause discomfort for the child; in addition to preventing two parents from bestowing Brfxxccxxmnpcccclllmmnprxvclmnckssqlbb11116³ on their child, the commission also rejected Superman, Ikea, Elvis, and Metallica (Israel). New Zealand also has laws in place to prevent parents from giving their child a name that is offensive, a title or rank (like "Captain"), unreasonably long, or inappropriate as a name. In addition to the renaming of Talula Does the Hula From Hawaii (McMahon), another judge recently ruled against one family who wanted to name their son 4Real ("Judge."). Some countries, like Germany, Denmark, and Iceland, require names to be gender-specific to avoid confusion (Olsson).

Name laws can be easy ways to retain national identity and culture, like in Iceland, where names must be spelled with the Icelandic alphabet and fit the patronymic tradition. Other advantages of name laws include ease of digitalization, pronunciation, and spelling, as seen in the reasoning behind the name laws in China and Japan. Chinese parents must name their child using a character that can be represented on a computer, to prevent scanners from misreading ID cards, and Japanese parents must use a specific set of name kanji (characters) so that the child's name will be able to be easily read and written by others (Israel). Placing some form of restriction on what parents are allowed to name their children would not only help the children, but it would also streamline computerization and use of the name by others.

Countries that have implemented the laws have few negative results outside a few disgruntled parents who like to name their child "Sex Fruit," one name blocked by the New Zealand Naming Commission (McMahon), and they appear to be reasonable solutions to the problems that plague children who are christened with highly unusual names. I would suspect that in the next decade or so, as the children of the current unique-naming craze mature, the need for such a law will become far more apparent. The only perceivable negative of the enactment of a name law would be that Americans would have to stop gossiping about the off-the-wall names given to the children of celebrities, but I am confident in our ability to find something better to do with our time.

Works Cited

Belkin, Lisa. "Laws Against Baby Names." *NewYorkTimes.com*. 12 May 2009. Web. 9 March 2012.

Birch, B. A. "Bad Baby Names Can Hurt a Child's Education, Says Study." *Education News*. 14 January 2012. Web. 12 March 2012.

Bryner, Jeanna. "Good or Bad, Baby Names Have Long-lasting Effects." *Live Science*. 13 June 2010. Web. 10 March 2012.

Fabian, Karina. "On Naming Baby: Choosing Unusual Names." *Baby Zone*. Web. 10 March 2012.

Israel, David. "Oh no, you can't name your baby THAT!" *CNN.com*. 3 July 2010. Web. 11 March 2012.

"Judge Blocks Parents' Choice." *ABC News*. 23 June 2007. Web. 12 March 2012.

McMahon, Barbara. "Parents lose custody of girl for naming her Talula Does the Hula From Hawaii." *The Guardian*. 24 July 2008. Web. 13 March 2012.

Olsson, Juliana. "Legal Rules for Playing the Naming Game." *Rocket Lawyer.*
23 February 2011. Web. 10 March 2012.

Satran, Pamela Redmond. "Unusual Names: Why—and Why Not—To Name the Baby
Wyclef." *The Huffington Post.* 26 October 2009. Web. 12 March 2012.

Samakow, Jessica. "Bad Baby Name Leads to Insecurity, Less Education, More Smoking."
The Huffington Post. 6 January 2012. Web. 10 March 2012.

Ian Micir

William Blake's 'London'

At first glance, William Blake's "London" from the *Songs of Experience* collection appears to be about a man gazing and observing the streets of London through an overly grim and cynical perspective. But the image paired with "London" on the plates provided by the Blake Archive, as well as the choice of coloring of said plates, does more than simply coincide with Blake's words—it contributes critical meaning to the poem.

The general image on the "London" plates is that of a young boy and an old man on what we can assume from the context of the poem is a street in London. There is a stone wall behind the two of them, and the boy appears to be reaching out to his elder, guiding the old man into a doorway of some kind. The basic drawing is, more or less, the same on both plates; however, the difference in the choice of shading and coloring makes them far from duplicates, thus allowing the reader to interpret the meaning of the poem in a different way.

The variances of coloring and shading between the two plates bring about unique appeals to emotion and, potentially, some religious undertones. In Plate 1 (www.blakearchive.org/blake/images/songsie.aa.p46.100.jpg), behind the old man (bottom left corner of image), there is a dark shadow cutting along an angle in such a way that it suggests that the light is shining in a certain direction and that the boy is guiding the man along that path, which just so happens to be shining on the door. It's a bit of a stretch, but if the poem is expressing the speaker's inability to see anything but the negatives of his world, then the illuminated doorway could represent a higher power guiding him to an exit from the intolerable. The same concept can be applied to Plate 2 (www.blakearchive.org/blake/images/songsie.l.p51-46.100.jpg); however, the light appears directionless and the only shadow being cast falls directly on the door, which could indicate that the door isn't exactly leading to the most positive of places.

Oddly enough, considering the uniqueness of each plate, the most thought-provoking detail of the "London" plates has almost nothing to do with the vast spectrum of color. It is that the old man is the speaker in the poem, and he is blind. This fact may pass a reader by without viewing the original plates, proving the importance of the image that has been paired with the poem. In the 11 unique "London" plates, not one of them is drawn in a way to suggest that the old man's eyes are open; many of the sharper illustrations more accurately show them being closed. Now, a set of eyelids being shut is in no way proof of blindness, but for argument's sake, let's assume for a moment that the old man's eyes are indeed closed in the drawings, and that this is on purpose. It adds three new layers of meaning, specifically to Plate B.

The first and most obvious is that it identifies a speaker to whom we can assign the first-person perspective. It may appear, looking only at the text, that Blake himself is the narrator of the poem. But he is not. The creation of this character through which we experience the poem provides consistency with the rest of the *Songs of Innocence and of Experience* collection, as each poem creates a new character. It also offers further explanation of the role of the young boy in the picture. While the contrast between youth and age can still symbolize Blake's theme of innocence vs. experience, we can also assume that his body language (reaching out to the old man and seeming to open the door for him) portrays him helping to guide someone who's lost his way.

Secondly, the idea of color still applies to both plates. In Plate 2, the only part of the drawing that is colored is the old man's robe. The color chosen was a bluish grey, undeniably similar in shade to the eyes of someone with cataracts or glaucoma. So if the interpretation is that the color of his robe further supports the theory of blindness, then it could be said that the rest of the image is done in all black to illustrate the darkness of the old man's world.[1]

Third, and most importantly, the idea that the speaker is blind adds a whole new layer to the text itself. The pessimistic outlook of the speaker remains the same, but a close look reveals that nowhere in the poem does the speaker actually see anything. In the first stanza, he says, "I wander thro' each charter'd street,/Near where the charter'd Thames does flow" (Blake 94). The key words indicating his blindness are "wander" and "near." A word like "walked" or "strolled" would imply a movement with a more specific direction or purpose, but "wander" has the connotation of being lost or aimless. We also think of being *near* a river when we can see it, but the flowing of a river can be as much a form of auditory (or olfactory) imagery as it can be visual. The final two lines of the stanza are also careful to avoid any visual confirmation: "And mark in every face I meet/Marks of weakness, marks of woe" (Blake 94). Blake's choosing not to use the word "see" acknowledges that the speaker can't see what people look like, so with every person he meets, he has to fill

---

1 By that same rationale, the fuller, richer coloring of Plate 1 could represent the child's perception of the world. That is, of course, one of many ways to interpret the uniqueness of the plates, but this theory on the use of color on these two plates in particular correlates quite well with Blake's poetic representation of innocence vs. experience (though the darker, more mundane colors in Plate 2 feel more consistent with "London").

in a blank slate. In the case of the character's overwhelming depression and pessimism, he ends up filling the voids in his mind with images and traits he considers weak.

The second stanza is even more directly harping on the auditory imagery, as he only hears cries of men, infants, and other voices. It's not until the third stanza that any imagery is used, but the "blackning Church" and "blood [running] down Palace walls" are only his mental projections and are his mind's reactions to the sounds that he hears. They are his "mind-forg'd manacles"—he is imprisoned by his inability to see anything but the worst correlating images in his mind's eye (Blake 94).

The final stanza is a reflection of the speaker's early life and is the root of the psychological issue that has him incarcerated in negativity. He explains that above all, what pains him most, is overhearing young prostitutes having sex. This is the most painful for him because in his mind, the images are a reflection of self: a baby born blind because of a birth defect from a disease that his mother spread to his father, leaving him parentless, alone, and blind (Blake 94). This gives context to the image on the bottom right of the plates. The image shows a young boy on his knees holding his hands out to the fire (feeling for the warmth due to lack of sight). While not certain, it is likely that it's the blind man in his childhood: a young blind boy, alone and struggling to keep warm.

At last, the reader can grasp the final element of the speaker's cynicism. He's not a man who had acquired this gloomy perspective on life and then been stricken blind. Instead, he's a man whose cynicism is based upon getting an unfair shot at life. Now, as an old man, he sees himself and understands the roots of his hopeless emotions. With each harlot's moan, he hears the misery of his life repeating for some other unfortunate child until the child ends up with his own set of mind forg'd manacles, wandering the streets of London, somewhere within earshot of the River Thames.

Works Cited

Blake, William. "London." Image. *Blakearchive.org*. <http://www.blakearchive.org/blake/images/songsie.aa.p46.100.jpg>.

Blake, William. "London." *Blakearchive.org*. <http://www.blakearchive.org/blake/images/songsie.l.p51-46.100.jpg>.

Blake, William. "London." *The Norton Anthology of English Literature*. 8th Ed. M.H. Abrams and Stephen Greenblatt. New York: W.W. Norton & Company, 2006. 94. Print.

Arhama Rushdi

Regional Parties and Modernity: History of Political Development and Regionalism in France and Spain

When one thinks of political parties, one often thinks of national organizations with the purpose of influencing politics by nominating their members for political office. These organizations are usually formed through a mobilization of ideological beliefs and can be divided on a left-right spectrum. However, in many countries around the world political parties of a different nature also exist. Rather than forming through party realignments as a result of ideological shifts within the national population, these parties are formed to represent specific regions of a country that are often neglected by national parties. While a variety of different terms are used for such parties, including ethnoterritorial parties, subnational parties, and regional autonomy parties, for the purposes of this paper they will be collectively referred to as regional parties. Such parties look at politics from the vantage point of their specific regions (Crepaz & Steiner, 2011, p. 40).

In an era when the world has become a global village, when people have greater geographical mobility, when everyone has exposure to mass-media, when the notion of nationalism barely exists, one would think there would be no room for regionalism. However, in many countries around the world, regional parties are on the rise. In recent years, regional parties in Europe have actually increased. With so much modernity in Europe, one would expect the opposite. How come in some countries modernity has led to the weakening of regional parties while in others, with the same level of modernity, regional parties continue to flourish? Regional differences exist in almost all countries, so why do some have stronger regional parties than others?

France and Spain are examples of two such countries, with similar levels of modernity but very different party structures. There are over 59 regional parties in Spain, with multiple parties in the regions of Andalusia, Aragon, Asturias, Balearics, Basque Country, Canary Islands, Cantabria, Castilla Y' Leon, Catalonia, Extremadura, Galicia, Navarra, La Rioja, Valencia, and Ceuta and Melilla. In sharp contrast, only three regional parties in two regions of France, Brittany and Corsica, exist (Day, 1998).

This paper explores the political development of France and Spain to explain the differences that have led to the formation of strong regional parties in some countries but not others. The literature on the subject provides possible explanations for the causes of the formation of regional parties, including cultural, economic, post-material, institutional, and historical perspectives. It will be argued that in the case of France and Spain, a historical approach best explains these differences. The paper will then analyze the history of political development in each country to look at the differences in the development timeline as an explanation for why Spain currently has strong regional parties and France has relatively weak regional parties. Finally, it will be argued that a number of specific historical events have led to recent or latent grievances within regions, the formation of specific political frameworks, and low levels of transnational influence that allow for the formation of strong regional parties in Spain but not in France.

Plausible Explanations

The topic of regionalism, as it provides an interesting puzzle when coupled with globalization, is a widely discussed topic in literature. Political scientists have a variety of theories and explanations for the mobilization and formation of strong regional parties. One of the theories used to explain the formation of regional political parties takes a historical approach on the matter. Such scholars review the history of political development in each country to look at the differences in the development timeline as an explanation for why a certain country has or does not have strong regional parties. Such models are particularly useful because they allow for the use of various factors, in conjunction, to explain the strength or weakness of regional parties in a country. These factors include the level of cultural grievances, decentralization, and transnational forces.

Grabarkiewicz (2000) argues that successful regional parties form when latent regional grievances are embedded within the socioeconomic characteristics of the region, established parties are unreceptive to regional concerns, and political entrepreneurs organize and mobilize citizens by appealing to these grievances, as after recent suppression by an authoritarian regime. Furthermore, Tronconi (2006) argues that traditional identity and economic variables are not enough to explain electoral performances of regional parties. This is because such regional parties mobilize by appealing to the disappointed electorate.

Botella, Teruel, Barbera and Barrio (2010) argue that the type and duration of decentralization makes a difference on the careers of regional prime ministers. This study can be applied to regional parties as well. Fast and strong decentralization is usually bottom up and leads to grassroots politics, which supports regional prime ministers and parties. On the other hand, slow decentralization is usually weaker and top down; therefore, it is harder to mobilize the unhappy regional masses in support for a regional prime minister or party.

Tossutti (2002) also studied the factors that influence the success and failure of regional parties. He argues that transnational factors, like globalization, influence the success of regional parties. The study analyzed political parties across the world and found that parties catering to particularistic interests, like regional parties, are more likely to participate in ruling coalitions to support minority governments, or to serve as the official opposition in countries that have been relatively insulated from transnational forces. The research suggests that lower levels of globalization leads to the formation and success of stronger regional parties.

These theories fit into a historical approach because one must look at the history of political development in each country to analyze whether or not latent regional grievances exist within the population as well as the tradition of political power in relation to unitarianism, federalism, and transnational factors like globalization. Looking at the timeline of political development in France and Spain, one will find that the Spanish have more recent political grievances as a result of regional suppression than the French. Furthermore, Spain has a federalized political system while France's political system is still very centralized. Spain has also had a history of low levels of international diplomatic relations, resulting in less globalization in comparison to France. These theories provide a plausible explanation for the existence of strong regional parties in Spain and the lack of such parties in France. Furthermore, taking a historical-political development approach to explaining the formation and strength of regional parties can be generalized to most countries around the world, providing a useful model for further study.

Therefore, using the case of Spain and France, it will be argued that having strong regional identities alone is not enough cause for the mobilization of successful regional parties. In addition to the existence of strong regional identities, there must be a sense of recent or latent grievances within the region. These feelings, as it will be shown, are usually brought about by either identity suppression by a recent regime or a disappointed regional electorate who feels they have little political efficacy. Furthermore, these factors, coupled with a political framework of decentralization and low levels of globalization, prove to be a recipe for success of the formation of strong regional parties.

Franco's Lasting Legacy

Spain's first attempt at revolution started in 1868 and led to the creation of the first Spanish republic. However, its failure, considering the chaos that lasted during the one year of its fleeting existence, discredited republicanism in Spain for years to come (Ben-Ami, 1978, p. 1). Decades later, the second Spanish republic also proved to be a complete failure. Within five years of its start, a civil war broke out between the years of 1936 and 1939 (Amodia, 1977, p. 14). The Spanish Civil War ended in victory for General Francisco Franco's right-wing Nationalists, who executed, jailed, and exiled the leftist Republicans. The Spanish finally felt they were free from dictatorships, failed republics, and façade democracies. To the contrary, Franco's regime proved to be all of these things and more.

Franco's regime soon became a dictatorship and cut off all foreign diplomatic ties. Furthermore, Franco alienated himself and the government from the public who formed strong, lasting grievances towards the unreceptive political regime. Franco's regime was particularly good at suppressing regional identities. One of the most suppressed regions was the Basque Country. As a result, the militant Basque separatist group, Euskadi Ta Askatasuna (ETA), or Basque Fatherland and Freedom, was formed in 1959 with the aim of creating an independent Basque homeland, and went on to carry out a campaign of terrorist bombings and other illegal activities. (Freedom house, 2011)

Finally, after 36 years, Franco died, taking his authoritarian, suppressive regime with him. It wasn't then, in 1975, that Spain started its transition to a successful liberal democratic state. It wasn't until after the Spanish Constitution was drawn up in 1978, and the first government of the new democracy of the Spanish Socialist Workers' Party was elected in 1982, that the transition was completed.

Franco's regime's very recent suppression of regional identities has formed latent grievances, which explains the mobilization of numerous regional parties throughout Spain. Spain's transition to democracy only happened about thirty years ago. The majority of the voting population clearly remembers the suppression they faced under his regime. Soon after a liberal democratic state was established, political entrepreneurs organized and mobilized citizens who felt the government was unreceptive to their regional concerns and established successful regional parties by appealing to these grievances. It is no coincidence that the Basque Country in Spain, a region that was greatly suppressed during Franco's regime, now has the strongest regional party in Spain, the Basque Nationalist Party, with 6 seats in the National Parliament (EIU Spain, 2011).

France's Early Suppression

France, like many European countries including Spain, has had a long complicated history of political development. However, unlike Spain, France's transition to democracy started out much sooner. While the first French

Revolution of 1789 briefly allowed wide franchise, authoritarian rule soon returned. The second French Republic had universal male suffrage but was also quickly followed by the Second French Empire. Republics alternated with monarchist regimes until the creation of the Third Republic in 1871 after the Franco-Prussian War. The Fourth Republic was established after World War II, but it eventually fell victim to domestic political turbulence and a series of colonial setbacks. In 1958, Charles de Gaulle, France's wartime leader, returned to create the strong presidential system of the Fifth Republic, which still stands today (Freedom House, 2011). While French republics and empires constantly went back and forth, since the first French Revolution in 1789, there has not been a period of extended authoritarian and suppressive rule.

This timeline of political development could help explain the lack of regional parties in France in two ways. Firstly, as shown above, France has had a tradition of a wide franchise from as early as 1789; this meant there was little regional identity suppression and thus fewer grievances to use for support and mobilization of regional political parties by political entrepreneurs. The times when there was an authoritarian regime were either too short or too long ago to form strong enough grievances within specific regions to be able to mobilize entire political parties. This could explain the weak tradition of regional parties in France.

On the other hand, France's complicated history of political development may have prevented the formation of strong regional parties in another way. For almost 200 years, France constantly went back and forth between (somewhat) democratic republics and monarchial dictatorships. This caused the French to get used to the suppression of regional identities early on. Furthermore, this early suppression of regional identities led to the formation of a strong sense of nationalism and French identity. Thus, in modern times people have grown accustomed to having a national French identity rather than specific regional identities that were suppressed long ago. Therefore, present regional grievances are not strong enough to mobilize successful regional parties.

Transnational Forces

After studying regional parties in 21 countries around the world, Tossutti (2002) found that transnational factors, like globalization, influenced the success of regional parties. The study showed that those parties catering to particularistic interests, like regional parties, are more likely to participate in ruling coalitions to support minority governments, or to serve as the official opposition in countries that have been relatively insulated from transnational forces. Put simply, less globalization means stronger regional parties.

Looking at the history of political development in each country, one could use this theory to explain the existence and lack of regional parties in Spain and France respectively. Going back only thirty years in Spain's history, one can find examples of transnational factors, or the lack thereof, that can help explain the existence of strong regional parties in Spain. During Franco's long rule, many countries cut off diplomatic ties, and his regime was ostracized by the United Nations from 1946 to 1955 (Freedom House, 2011). This led to lower levels of transnational influence and less globalization. Therefore, according to the theory, and correctly, international insulation has allowed for the formation and existence of strong regional parties in Spain.

On the other hand, if we analyze the history of political development in France, there has been no similar situation, even within the century, where France has isolated itself from transnational forces. As a result, globalization swept through France with full speed. This could explain the lack of regional parties in France.

Effects of Decentralization

Political decentralization refers to a division of political authority among multiple levels of government, each with democratically elected officials and independent decision-making power (Brancati, 2007). A number of studies (Chhibber & Kollman, 1998, 2004, & Brancati, 2007) show a positive correlation between decentralization and the strength of regional parties. Data shows that in centralized systems 15% of the parties competing in national elections are regional parties while in decentralized systems regional parties make up 39% of the competing parties (Brancati, 2007).

While regional cleavages may form the basis for regional parties, regional cleavages do not automatically translate into party systems. There must be a decentralized political structure for the formation and success of strong regional parties. This is because decentralized governments have regional legislatures where it is easier for regional parties to gain seats compared to the national legislature. Therefore, regional parties have a greater opportunity to govern, making people more likely to vote for them, as they do not feel like they are wasting their votes (Brancati, 2007).

Looking back at the history of political development in Spain, we can see that the country has, many times, failed to form a successful regime under a strong national government. Therefore, starting with the constitution of 1979, and the creation of autonomous communities, Spain has made efforts to decentralize the political structure as much as possible (Gibbons, 1999, p. 13). In countries like Spain, that have regional autonomous governments with regional legislatures, it is no coincidence that regional parties are so successful. Furthermore, with every passing year more and more national powers are given to regional legislatures. This has increased support for regional parties that are growing with every election.

On the other hand, France has a unitary government with a very strong presidential system. France has always had a very centralized system. Until 1982 France was not considered decentralized because the sub-national level of government only had the power to administer decisions made at the national level. Contrary to its efforts to decentralize, due to the archaic nature of the present political structures, coupled with a tradition of ruling Paris elites, it has been unable to do so to the extent of other European countries (Wright, 1978, p. 206). France still remains one of the most centralized countries in the European Union (EIU France, 2011). This makes it very difficult for smaller parties at the local or regional level to mobilize support. Furthermore, the French are aware that even if elected, such parties will have little or no power, and thus do not want to waste their votes on them. This could explain why even though some French regions may have strong cleavages, they do not have strong regional parties.

Future of Regional Political Parties

As the case of France and Spain shows, having strong regional identities alone is not enough cause for the mobilization of strong regional parties. In addition to the existence of strong regional identities, there must be a sense of recent or latent grievances within the region brought about by either identity suppression by a recent regime or a disappointed regional electorate coupled with a political framework of decentralization or federalism that allows for the formation of regional parties.

According to the theory presented in the paper, one could predict that it is more likely that regional parties in Spain will dwindle than regional parties in France will strengthen. Looking at the future of Spain, it is likely that as time passes, the strong grievances the population of specific regions hold, as a result of Franco's suppressive regime, will weaken. Furthermore, in the future, Spain's diplomatic relations that were severed during Franco's regime are likely to improve, leading to greater levels of globalization. It is unlikely that the European Union, or even the current western political climate, would allow Spain to be suppressed under another dictator like Franco and reverse the process of its speedy decentralization. While increased decentralization in Spain may cause regional parties to strengthen at first, as mentioned before, decentralization alone is not sufficient enough a factor for the survival of strong regional parties. Therefore, taking all of these factors into consideration, despite increasing decentralization, one can say that in the future Spanish regional parties may weaken.

Along the same lines, one could argue that it is unlikely that strong regional parties will form in France. A dictator rule or any other factor that would lead to people of specific regions being suppressed, causing grievances on the scale of Franco's regime, seems unlikely. Furthermore, institutions like the European Union will only lead to more globalization, leaving little room for regionalism.

Works Cited

Ben-Ami, S. (1978). *The Origins of the Second Republic in Spain*. Oxford, UK: Oxford University Press.

Botella, J., Teruel, J.R., Barbera, O., & Barrio, A. (2010). "A New Political Elite in Western Europe? The Political Careers of Regional Prime Ministers in Newly Decentralized Countries." *French Politics*. 8, 42-61.

Brancati, A. (2007). *The Origins and Strengths of Regional Parties*. B.J.Pol.S. 38. 135-159.

Bryne, L. (2005). "Powered by Politics: Reforming Parties from the Inside." *Parliamentary Affairs*, 58 (3), 611-620.

Chhibber, P., & Kollman, K. (1998). "Party Aggregation and the Number of Parties in India and the United States." *American Political Science Review*, 92, 329–42;

Chhibber, P. & Kollman, K. (2004). *The Formation of National Party Systems: Federalism and Party Competition in Britain, Canada, India and the United States*. Princeton, NJ: Princeton University Press.

Crepaz, M.M.L., & Steiner, J. (2011). *European Democracies*. New York, NY: Pearson Education.

Dahl, R. A. (Eds.). (1966). *Political Oppositions in Western Democracies*. New Haven, CT: Yale University Press.

Davis, G.D. (2000). *The Rise and Fall of Regional Parties: The Reform Party of Canada, the Northern League of Italy, and the Western Canada Concept Party*. Ohio State University.

Day, A. J. (Eds.). (1988). *Political Parties of the World*. Chicago, IL: Longman Group.

EIU: Economist Intelligence Unit. (2011). *Country Forecast Spain*. New York, NY.

EIU: Economist Intelligence Unit. (2011). *Country Forecast France*. New York, NY.

Fournis, Y. & Pasquier, R. (2008). "Politicizing Regional Identities." *Journal of East West Comparative Studies.* 39(3). 37-53.

Freedom House. (2011). *Country Report: Spain.* Washington, DC.

Freedom House. (2011). *Country Report: France.* Washington, DC.

Gibbons, J. (1999). *Spanish Politics Today.* Manchester, UK: Manchester University Press.

Grabarkiewicz (2000). "The Rise and Fall of Regional Parties." *Ph.D. dissertation,* Ohio State University, OH.

Lipset, S. M., & Rokkan, S. (1967). *Cleavage Structures, Party Systems, and Voter Alignments: An Introduction.* New York, NY: The Free Press.

Spies-Butcher, B. & Vromen, A. (2010). "Suburban Affairs: Groups and Political Communities across Sydney." *Australian Journal of Political Science.* 45 (3). 437-455.

Tossutti, L. S. (2002). "How Transnational Factors Influence the Success of Ethnic, Religious, and Regional Parties in 21 States." *Party Politics.* 8 (1). 51-74.

Tronconi (2006). "Ethnic Identity and Party Competition: An Analysis of Ethnoregionalist Vote in Western Europe." *World Political Science Review.* 2 (2).

Wright, V. (1978). *The Government and Politics of France.* New York, NY: Holmes & Meier Publishers.

Devon Ikeler

Confessions of a "Facebook Whore"

Every girl has a little black book, pages filled with contact information from their BFFs, potential suitors, and connections to help them climb the social ladder. But, as of the 21st century, the little black book has become so last season. What's "in" style now? The little "blue" book—Facebook. Any girl who wants to be considered anyone has a Facebook, and if you don't, then, pardon *moi*, but who the hell are you? In girl world, it has become a social crime to not have a Facebook—it is our own personal tabloid of our lives and the people we know. I, myself, am one of those unfortunate females who have sold their soul to Mark Zuckerberg, the Facebook god, and have given into the supreme seduction of this social media outlet. I have become crazed, or if you must, a "Facebook whore," spending countless hours pouring my life out on the Web. Throughout my five years as a member of the site, I have mastered the skills of acceptable stalking, manipulating my reputation, and understanding the crazy tendencies us girls have become so well known for. Facebook has become our new life story and what we put on it affects our daily lives. This Facebook whore is so graciously letting you walk a mile in these highly fashionable heels since I've been around the block plenty of times, and these are my confessions.

I can guarantee that a girl will not leave the house unless she checks the mirror to make sure she looks okay. Facebook is my mirror. I wake up every morning to find my cellphone glued to my hand, and after checking my text messages, my finger is instantly attracted to the Facebook App (which has become extremely dangerous with the new iPhone technology). I obsessively scroll through my newsfeed, checking up on my friends' statuses, if anyone has written on my wall, who has commented on a post of mine, or if I have been tagged in a new picture. These notifications are my daily morning routine— just like makeup, they make my look complete. If I receive a new friend request, it feels just like wearing a brand new stylish outfit—it makes my day simply sparkle! Without receiving any new notifications after my beauty rest, I almost feel naked or as if I'm suffering from a bad hair day.

Now, you might ask why us girls spend as much time revolving our lives around Facebook as we do getting ready to go out on a date. As the social media chair for my sorority, I have found how important it is to update and share just the right information. Everything comes down to the simple notion of promotion:

girls use Facebook as a way to advertise who they are in order to gain some form of worth. If you post the wrong status or upload a scandalous photo, you can guarantee that your "friends" will catch this mistake and are already judging. In a recent study, a researcher at the University of Buffalo, Michael A. Stefanone, PhD, and his colleagues found that females who share more photos on social media sites tend to base their self worth on their image and appearance, using Facebook as a platform to compete for attention (Donovan).

Facebook is our first impression; it's a peek inside of our lives and who we are. Girls will manipulate their information, likes, what pictures they post, and how they overall act on the site as a way to gain a good reputation, to be seen as "cool," "attractive," or whatever else they desire. We want to be perceived well in order to make us feel better about ourselves, since there seems to be an everyday struggle with self-esteem issues among girls. So what do we do? We post an attractive picture of ourselves or a status worthy of bragging rights. The feedback that we receive from these updates boosts our attention morale, which we crave more than chocolate (hard to believe, I know). ("Facebook For Females" http://idontseedeadpeople.blogspot.com/2011/08/facebook-for-females.html).

Apart from Facebook being a cry for attention, us ladies have learned how to use this social media outlet in a productive manner. Our page has allowed us an easier way to advertise, network, and build relationships with our friends or, naturally, the opposite sex. For my sorority, I use my ever-so-important power to, in a way, control how the outside world perceives us. Anyone that likes our page instantly sees what we are about, what organizations we support, what our interests are, our philanthropy and recruitment information, as well as photos from various events to get a peek inside of our sisterhood. Advertising is an important tool in order to promote a cause or even yourself. Cindy Webster, CBS radio marketing director, claims: "Professionally, [Facebook] is god sent. I can simply make a status advertising the events I'm hosting, which all of my friends will be able to see and come out to support me. But that goes to say, as a public figure, you have to be careful if you have a private page. I get so many friend requests from people I don't know, all because they hear my name on the radio all the time. And as a woman, you have to be extra careful with who you accept and see your personal information. That's why these Fan Pages have become a great tool for promotion and even networking!" Cindy has recently been using Facebook to network with her old sorority chapter of Chi Omega: "It's been wonderful to reconnect with my sisters and rekindle our relationships. You never know what opportunities might pop up by keeping in contact with them and Facebook has made it simple to do such!"

Now, everyone knows that what comes with the good comes with the bad, and what comes with girls is drama, and Facebook is not exempt from the equation. Relationship issues tend to arise from the site simply because there is no "Facebook Official" title. "That's because to modern women, your Facebook relationship status is the equivalent of a high school promise ring. It's a public announcement that you've picked someone to stand by" (Mujic). There is also the other side to the story: the dreaded public announcement of a break up. Breaking up hurts, but changing your relationship status from "In A Relationship" to "Single" hurts even more—not even the little pink heart next to the horrible words can make you feel better. "Facebook prolongs the period it takes to get over someone, because you have an open window into their life, whether you want to or not," says Yianni Garcia of New York, a consultant who helps companies use social media (Bernstein).

Such hurt leads to the ever-so-popular passive-aggressive status updates. Us girls are known to make our hurt known—we wear our feelings on our sleeve, or in this case, our Facebook page. I cannot tell you how many times I have posted emotional lyrics or quotes as statuses hopelessly wishing "that boy" would see them and dig deep to the true meaning. For some reason, we think it's all right to post things we wouldn't normally say in person because we're hiding behind a computer screen, but in reality, what is posted on the Web always finds a way to come back around and haunt us (Bernstein).

Regardless of the petty drama and the obsession of living in a virtual world, I can't seem to escape social media. I don't mind stalking that hot piece of man in my class, updating those sad, attention-seeking statuses, or even posting my life through a million MUploads (mobile-uploads—get with the program), no, not at all. I enjoy indulging myself with the guilty pleasure that Facebook has become, regardless of the consequences or how it affects my life. In girl world, Facebook is our kingdom, and we are all the princesses. Now, if you don't mind, I'd like my shoes back so I can go out on a date with a boy who has been poking me, on Facebook that is.

Works Cited

Bernstein, Elizabeth. "How Facebook Can Ruin Your Friendships." *The Wall Street Journal—Heath & Fitness.* 25 Aug. 2009. Web. 12 Oct. 2011. <http://online.wsj.com/article/SB10001424052970204660604574370450465849142/html>.

Donovan, Patricia. "Study: Facebook Photo Sharing Reflects Focus on Female Appearance." University at Buffalo News Center. University at Buffalo, 7 Mar. 2011. Web. 12 Oct. 2011. <http://www.buffalo.edu/news/12339>.

Mujic, Marushka. "13 Ways Facebook Ruins Your Relationship." *MadeMan.* 1 May 2010. Web. 12 Oct. 2011. <http://www.mademan.com/13-ways-facebook-ruins-your-relationship/>.

Dana Formon

Bruises, Costumes, Auditions and Quick Changes— Dancers as a Subculture

They wear revealing clothes, use a different set of language terms that may not even be English, and have no problem exposing themselves with no modesty. They walk funny, sit funny, think too abstractly, and perform acts of self-mutilation. But for every bruise that's celebrated and every word that seems alien, dancers create spectacles that are attended and appreciated. Each aspect of a dancer's seemingly deviant behavior (masochistic tendencies and personal space, to name two) serves a purpose that has been carefully shaped both culturally and socially. Dancers may just be different, but they might also be uniquely their own entity, their own subculture. In order to determine subculture status, we will explore how space affects the one outlet that inspires and fuels why they do what they do: the performance.

1. Audition Space

Every performance starts with an audition. Whether it's an audition for an individual piece or for a company that will later perform many choreographic works in their repertoire, dance is as much about competition as is any testosterone-laden sport. Like sporting athletes, a dancer's body is the device by which they make their living, with thin and muscular figures being prized ever since the reinforcement by George Balanchine in the 1930s and '40s. Visual display of physical fitness is important regardless of what form of dance you are auditioning for, but two different schools of technique specifically choose to represent their bodies differently.

Ballet dancers wear skin-tight leotards, either halter-topped or spaghetti-strapped for the maximum amount of bare back to be shown; with the leotard is a pair of pink ballet tights, with a seam running down the back of each leg to elongate the dancer's lines. Opposite the ballet dancers are the modern dancers. Even though modern dancers have the same need for physical fitness, they show off their bodies by wearing what are known as "booty shorts" and a leotard or tight-fitted tank top. What's most important for a modern dancer is showing off their legs, arms, and back, so they can also be seen in unitards cut short in the leg.

Delaney and Kaspin stated, "[Clothes] express cultural meanings and identities and serve as markers of status, age, and gender as well as occupation activity..." (295). In this case, simply looking into an audition can give an observer many clues about the persons inside. Ballet companies are usually much better funded than modern companies and, therefore, may be regarded as being more respected artistically (a notion that will be discussed more in detail a little later), so jobs associated with a ballet-looking audition probably pay more and come with more benefits. If the dancers are in bare feet or socks, it can be assumed they are modern dancers, whereas pointe shoes are indicative of ballerinas. In either school of technique, the skintight and revealing clothing that these men and women are wearing can be considered a basic uniform for all dancers. A glimpse into cultural anthropology states that "modesty is a learned behavior" (Delaney and Kaspin 297), and although modesty is learned by almost everyone in the American population, dancers then need to learn that modesty may hinder their performance or career.

2. Rehearsal Space

Whereas auditions require dancers to bare all for the sake of getting cast, rehearsals are often incredibly lenient regarding what can and cannot be worn by dancers. Ballet dancers wear bright, fun colors and modern dancers often wear layers of clothing in rehearsals to protect their bodies since modern dance often requires more full-body contact with the floor. Wearing medical "red flags" like ankle/knee braces, wraps, hot patches, and joint supports are also acceptable in rehearsals, whereas they might not have been in auditions. As a dancer, you never want to give an auditioning choreographer a reason to doubt your physical ability; if you're injured, they might see you as an increase in medical insurance payments, not as a potential company member.

As previously mentioned, there is a large economic difference between modern companies and ballet companies. Although there are some very well-funded modern companies (Paul Taylor Dance Company, Parsons Dance, Merce Cunningham Dance Company, Alvin Ailey African American Dance Co.), there are many more ballet companies that run off of gracious donations (it's actually seen as a sign of wealth to become a top donor or benefactor to a ballet company). For example, Parsons Dance (a very well-known modern company) lists five donors that have contributed more than $25,000 in one season (parsonsdance.org); the American Ballet Theatre lists 18 donors (abt. org). In looking at dancer pay alone, Parsons Dance has 10 company members currently employed (parsonsdance.org); American Ballet Theatre has 28 dancers employed (abt.org), and the New York City Ballet lists a whopping 90 dancers in their company (nycballet.com)! Funds for paying the salaries of 90 dancers is substantially different from the amount needed to pay 10. Some companies (like the American Ballet Theatre, New York City Ballet, and Alvin

Ailey Dance Co.) are funded enough to have their own buildings constructed solely for their school and education programs, classes, and rehearsals. If a dancer gets the luxury of rehearsing in a private space solely for their company or piece, rehearsals may be a bit more relaxed, experimental, and exploratory since there is more time that can be used. Under-funded companies often have to pay for their rehearsal space and, in these cases specifically, "time is money" (Delaney and Kaspin 102).

What is arguably most disturbing about dancers (especially in the rehearsal process) is their obsession with battle scars. Ballet dancers en pointe (on pointe shoes) have ugly feet; it's a stereotype that is ridiculously true. Although they may cover up their feet in public, when among other dancers they use their feet as a conversation starter, comparing stories about how *this* bunion developed and the one time that *this* toenail fell off... Wearing pointe shoes in ballet is done to further elongate the lines of a dancer's legs and to give the appearance of floating across stage, but they are also a major source of pain and foot malformation. "Ballerina's toe" is a phrase used to describe the big toes of ballet dancers, which, after years of pointe work, actually point inwards instead of straight ahead. Pointe work can be similar in a way to Chinese foot binding (Delaney and Kaspin 323), being set in place by choreographers like George Balanchine and Marius Petipa (the-perfect-pointe.com). Pointe shoes (or rather, the mechanism by which dancers have their body weight stabilized entirely by their toes) were invented *by* a man (Charles Didelot) *for* women. Much like the medical ramifications of foot binding, excessive pointe work can lead to toe deformation, bone spurs, ankle injuries, and even later problems with the hips and knees. "For ballerinas today, pointe work is completely integrated with ballet technique. Even jazz and modern choreographers demand that women wear pointe shoes even though the steps are from a different idiom" (the-perfect-pointe.com). This practice may seem odd, damaging, and downright torturous, but pointe work by females is a "norm" or even an unspoken expectation of this subculture (Delaney and Kaspin 324).

Much the same goes for modern dancers; they roll, slide, dive, and fall (among other things, but those being some of the more extreme) across the stage for the sake of abstract and dynamic movement. Bruises, floor burns, blisters, and skin splits are common, and often worn around like badges, stars, and stripes on military jackets. The scars and calluses that are obtained serve as trading cards for stories, and although they aren't necessarily purposefully caused, dancers continue to put themselves in harm's way. Many ask, "But why?" Situations can often also arise when an injury is further stressed and becomes exacerbated, maybe even debilitating.

As seen in both modern and ballet dancers, many dancers might keep past or current injuries hidden to keep their status within a company or piece, for if a dancer has a severe-enough injury, the choreographer might swap them for an understudy, reducing their pay or exposure on stage. Normally it is only those with secured spots within major dance companies that take time off for injuries to heal. In cases such as this, it isn't just the rehearsal space that may aid in causing injuries and disparity between how a non-dancer and dancer view physical scarring, but it is the presentation of some injuries themselves that could prevent a dancer from even entering the rehearsal space.

When inside the rehearsal space, a choreographer's demands play a part in shaping the way dancers view ideas of personal space. There is arguably no such thing as personal space in dance, especially in partnering. Depending on the lift being executed, a dancer might find another dancer's groin in their face, or have to use their own hands as a cushion for another dancer to sit or stand on. What matters most in these situations is the overall aesthetic look of the final lift or pose; seldom does it matter how or what a dancer has to do in order to actually achieve the final image.

It's an unwritten rule (especially in heterosexual partner work) that no matter what, the male *cannot* allow his partner to touch the ground if a fall or slip-up were to occur. He is not allowed to drop his partner. This is enforced by the gendered idea of men being stronger than women; they do all the heavy lifting and are therefore liable if a woman is dropped—even if it is partially her fault! Whether he needs to place a hand across or on her chest, around her upper thigh, an arm between her legs, or throw himself onto the floor to cushion her fall, men are expected to go to extraordinary lengths to protect their female partners, and their female partners are expected, in turn, to be understanding of their methods for ensuring they do not hit the ground.

3. Tech Space

"Tech" is short for "technical rehearsal," the period between studio rehearsals and the actual performance when the dancers become acclimated to the space where they will be performing. Aspects of tech could include adjusting to any live music that might be danced to (in the case of some classic ballets), working with live animals, lighting the piece, working with props, and running technical and dress rehearsals. Dancers and even their choreographer cannot do all of this themselves; they need to hire outside help, they need theatre technicians to serve as stage managers, fly crew (those who control the flying in and out of the curtains and backdrops), light and music operators, and stage crew. Tech space is where the theatre "techie" meets the performer, and here two subcultures must alter their ways to function harmoniously within one space to produce one perfect performance.

What each subculture wears can be a distinct dividing feature in itself (Eckert 185). Never to be seen, techies wear "blacks," or black clothing from head to toe. Hard-toed shoes are also a must as equipment/props may be rolled over a foot during transport. During technical rehearsals, dancers can adopt one of two forms of dress. If they are just becoming accustomed to the space or setting/blocking light cues, they wear warm-up clothing and then perhaps some additional layers as well. Stages are often cold before dancing warms up the air, so dancers dress for warmth and comfort and act accordingly. When dressed in these baggy and restrictive warm-ups, dancers often walk through their pieces (or "mark" them); they rarely run a piece full-out. If they are not blocking a piece then they can be found running full-dress rehearsals (where they wear costumes, hair, and makeup as if they were performing the actual show).

The costumes dancers wear are often the exact opposite from their warm-up clothes, with one exception...they may still not serve a completely beneficiary function and might hinder movement. Classical-style tutus in ballet are often the primary cause of partner-work issues come full-dress rehearsals, with the tutu hitting the male partner in the eyes or face. Other aspects of costumes might be slippery, either in partnering or on a dancer's feet. Costumes might be loosely draped, putting the dancer at risk of tripping, or cut in a way that may expose the dancer if they move a certain way. Regardless of whether or not a costume might be at risk of hindering movement or falling off, they are not to mentally affect the dancer's performance—dancers need to perform full-out no matter how difficult movement may be. As the saying goes, "the show must go on."

4. Performance Space

On a communicative level, a dancer's language is affected by the space they occupy during a performance, whether they are in a dressing room or backstage. Dressing rooms are often relatively soundproof, so normal voices and laughter are permitted, as is joking and discussing topics that are unrelated to the performance at hand. Backstage areas (corridors) are for brief rehearsals before a dancer goes onstage, as well as warming up and discussion of non-dance topics, but verbal communication is kept to a low volume level. Although joking and group communication can happen backstage, dancers are respectful and mindful of others they are sharing their space with. Backstage can also be an area for mental preparation and pre-performance rituals—like prayer circles or "good luck" meetings between choreographers and their cast members—so dancers participating in conversations are acutely aware of what everyone is doing backstage as to not interrupt anyone else.

Directly backstage, in the "wings," is usually limited to piece-related conversation and also mental and physical preparation for the performance. If the music is loud, audience is clapping, or intermission is occurring, dancers can raise their voice. Nonverbal communication like pointing and marking of steps (perhaps a dancer's own method of sign language) is a means of answering questions that others may ask in regards to a specific dance. Since music can often impede hearing, many dancers backstage choose to sign questions or answers to each other instead of speaking.

Aside from the phenomena of dancer-generated sign language, one other impressive act worth mentioning that occurs backstage is the "quick change." A quick change may be one of the key causes for a dancer's lack of modesty and is exactly how it sounds: a quick change (of costuming). Some dancers may be in two pieces back-to-back that are independent of each other, and therefore have two different costumes, hair styles, and/or makeup applications—others might even need to change costumes during a piece! Arguably an art form in itself, a quick change often occurs between the dancer and a group of theatre technicians, usually on hair/makeup or costume crews; the goal is to get the dancer's clothing changed typically in a matter of seconds (definitely less than two minutes). Quick changes are often rehearsed with stopwatches, both during and before technical rehearsals, to ensure the dancer can get changed quickly enough and that all members of the changing team can effectively communicate with each other and with the dancer. A quick change can be just as choreographed as a dance piece.

During a quick change the changing team is in charge of the full removal of clothes and redressing of the dancer, while the dancer responds to touch and single-word cues that might signify them lifting an arm or a leg. In my experience, a double-tap on your toe means "pick up your foot, I'm putting your shoe on" and the word "up" meant "lift up your arms, I'm taking off/putting on your top." The word "go" is universal, it means you are finished being changed and to assume your place for the next piece.

The timing importance of a quick change is purely for the audience's benefit. The dreaded "dead space" is the term used to represent the length of time in between pieces that is too long, and audience members begin to get antsy or bored sitting in their seats waiting for the next piece. Usually, once a pause between pieces has exceeded forty-five seconds, you have entered "dead space." During a quick change, time is precious and certainly held to a higher value than usual; two seconds can make all the difference. In reference to Delaney and Kaspin's eloquent "poem" regarding the meaning of time, to realize the value of a second, ask a dancer during a quick change (82).

When a change occurs between pieces, time can become a bit lenient (which is where the maximum of two minutes may be found), but when a change must occur within a single piece, the music determines the amount of time a dancer has to change. When looking at quick changes, especially between two pieces, it's hard to ignore the disparity in the perception of time between dancers/crew and the audience. Forty-five seconds is a generous amount of time for a changing crew, but sitting in the dark and listening to rustling of programs in the audience can be pretty awkward and unnerving.

Whether dancers may seem immodest, disturbingly obsessed with bruises and scars, or otherwise different, it is important to remember that they are their own subculture. Subculture status, however, isn't just awarded because they are *different*; they follow their own sets of language rules, they have different appreciations for time, and their clothing (while following basic trends of form over function) (Delaney and Kaspin 297) is also created for specific purposes that have been developed through social and cultural shaping. The demands of the business create challenges that must be overcome to achieve success (like many other career paths in not *just* typical American society), and dancers create their personalities, their behaviors, their aspirations, and their lives based on this.

Works Cited

"ABT Dancers." *American Ballet Theatre*. Web. 05 Dec. 2011. <http://abt.org>.

"Company." *Parsons Dance*. Web. 05 Dec. 2011. <http://www.parsonsdance.org>.

"Dancers By Rank." *New York City Ballet*. Web. 05 Dec. 2011. <http://www.nycballet.com>.

Delaney, Carol, and Deborah Kaspin. *Investigating Culture: An Experimental Introduction to Anthropology*. 2nd ed. Southern Gate, Chichester, West Sussex: Wiley-Blackwell, 2011. Print.

Eckert, Penelope. "Symbols of Category Membership." *Jocks and Burnouts: Social Categories and Identity Within the High School*. New York: Teachers College Press, 1989. Print.

"Memberships and Support—The Chairman's Council." *American Ballet Theatre*. Web. 05 Dec. 2011. <http://abt.org>.

"Pointe History." *The Perfect Pointe*. Web. 05 Dec. 2011. <http://www.the-perfect-pointe.com>.

"Supporters." *Parsons Dance*. Web. 05 Dec. 2011. <http://www.parsonsdance.org>.

Christa Blumenthal

The Online Critic: A Guardian Angel for the Gluttonous Belly and the Gifted Chef

Hazy is the image of the poised food critic, painstakingly seated and served the chef's specialty in the chef's hopes of receiving a complimentary review. With the rise of online blogging and consumer review website yelp. com, anyone can be a food critic. With the click of a mouse, an account activation code, and a functioning keyboard, each and every restaurant-goer has the power to transform the public's mind, and consequently a restaurant's success, with their words. The influence of these online reviewers is undeniable; yet disagreement remains about whether their presence is positive or poisonous to a restaurant and its consumer base. The determining factor lies in the credibility of the reviews, and the relationship among them, the consumers, and the restaurateurs themselves. Credible Yelp reviews, as defined in the following paragraphs, aid consumers in their dining decisions and act as a powerful tool for the restaurant professional, boosting profitability or providing guidance for future improvement.

Online media rapidly replaces printed journals, newspapers, and novels, though the power of word-of-mouth remains poignant. Ask any restaurateur, and they will tout word-of-mouth as "one of the cheapest, yet most effective, promotions" (Shock 184). A friend or colleague's recommendations, and warnings, can influence an individual's decisions dramatically. Yet can a stranger's? Compared to professional restaurant critics with their crafty jargon, and professional guides such as Zagat or Michelin, Yelp.com carries the trophy of realism. According to the research of restaurant management expert Ioannis Pantelidis, consumers trust the words and opinions of other "real" people (484). Equality triumphs over expertise in the restaurant review field.

Ask the professionals, however, and you may hear a different story; at the University of Pennsylvania Food Summit this spring, seasoned critics and culinary experts themselves groaned when the topic of Yelp.com swept the discussion table. *Smitten Kitchen* food blogger Deb Perelman professed that she did not use the website, noting that "it's about a voice that you recognize." Drew Lazor, food critic for Philadelphia's *City Paper*, supported Deb's claim by gushing about Philly critic Craig Laban's influence: "That dude is a G!" The panelists further criticized Yelp, claiming it easily manipulated restaurants and could unnecessarily sink a dining establishment. Their views, though backed by their expertise in the culinary realm, contrast with popular opinion.

Yelp.com, with its twenty million reviews site-wide, determines the dining-out choices for over fifty-three million people a month, according to Yelp.com Local Business Outreach manager Luther Lowe (Cogsdon). Word-of-mouth may live on, but word-of-Yelper clearly has the bigger audience and influence. Such an influence means that the credibility of a review is crucial in positively affecting the review's viewers and restaurateurs alike. What factors, though, make a Yelp review credible or a crock?

To aid me in answering this question, I decided to put yelp.com to the test. Being an avid ethnic-food junkie, I searched Yelp.com's reviews for a variety of ethnic options. Over a weeklong period, I ate at three of the highest ranked cultural food stops in the University City neighborhood, comparing my restaurant experiences to those of the aforementioned yelp critics. Although the Indian eateries, Sitar and New Delhi, and the Thai restaurant Lemongrass all averaged four-star ratings, two of the three meals ended in disappointment. Confused by this inconsistency, I evaluated the individual reviews of each establishment, rather than simply judging by the overall number of stars that each had.

To an avid ethnic-food eater like myself, I found that certain reviews lacked credibility, clearly resulting in a skewed star rating on the restaurant's page. As expressed by Las Vegas chef Jet Tila: "[I]f a group of people who know nothing about food can jump on the Internet and become instant food critics just because they can form sentences, well screw it! ... A real food critic eats at least two to three times before beginning a review" (Tila). Below are some clear-cut examples that support the Yelp-criticizing population's viewpoint:

- The un-informed Yelper: Writes a review not only upon their first experience with the restaurant, but with the ethnic food itself. Such a Yelper reviews an Indian buffet scathingly (or positively, less commonly), claiming that the "chicken thing in the red sauce" or the "flat Indian pancake bread" (it's called naan!) was either delectable or disgusting. Inexperienced foodies simply can't be trusted—put their reviews aside.

- The overly boastful Yelper: Gushes praise to the extent of saying "BEST food I've ever eaten!" and "By far the greatest Indian buffet in the city!" Oh, really? Can you give me one reason to support your claim? The New York Time's article, "A Rave, a Pan, or Just a Fake?" identifies these reviewers as "a small, semi-underground group of entrepreneurs who, for a fee, will post a rave about your company" (Segal). Even if they're not paid, affiliation with or incentives from the restaurant appear to be a possibility.

• The scathing Yelper: Criticizes absolutely everything about the restaurant, either in a heavily descriptive "the rude, ugly waiter took hours to serve my bland, rubbery naan—everything about this place repels me" sort of way, or through a "worst meal ever! I will never return here so long as I live" dramatic, yet elusive, kind of statement. Certainly these reviews could be the shady work of a restaurateur's competitors. Despite this possibility, negative reviews are the minority.

Identifying the diversion caused by these unseasoned critics, I continued my exploratory research by creating my very own Yelp account. Yet before launching on a reviewing spree, I decided to figure out what it is that characterizes a review as credible. The most significant expectations of a customer, according to recent research studies, are (in order): "food, quality, price, greeting, and service" (Pantelidis 485). Especially in today's hard economic times, it is valuable for reviewers to include their value rating of the restaurant, of whether or not the food and quality is worthy of the price. Therefore, a credible review is one that highlights many qualities of a restaurant and a customer's experience there.

After revisiting two of the three restaurants multiple times apiece, I judged that I was well informed and able to conduct my first reviews. Using the guidelines of significance founded by Pantelidis, I rated the food in terms of taste and quality, comparing identical dishes to those in competing restaurants. Furthermore, I compared prices in determining a meal's value. Greeting and service, although mentioned in the review, were only briefly touched on; for to me, and backed by Pantelidis's study, "Food is king" (488). In the words of Francis Lam, Feature Editor for *Gilt Taste*, "[F]or the most part today, people read restaurant reviews because they want to know if they should eat there, what dishes are good, and how much it'll cost. If you just assembled a chart with that information on it, maybe with a dash of snark, most people would be perfectly happy with it." Yelpers take note: use these words as a guideline in accurately portraying restaurant experiences to the masses visiting Yelp.com.

In addition to the guidance that they provide to restaurant-goers, Yelpers can influence the profitability of a restaurant. According to research study done by Harvard Business School's Michael Luca on the Seattle restaurant scene, a one-star addition to an independent (non-chain) restaurant's Yelp profile boosts its revenue by 5 to 9% (2). Such numbers are substantial, influencing many restaurateurs to harness this effective marketing weapon to boost business. Furthermore, Yelp boasts its negative reviews as being a slim 15%; for this reason, the majority of restaurant owners are benefiting from Yelper's accounts (Cogsdon). One way that restaurants do so is by affiliating themselves with the site, establishing a few brownie points with Yelpers entering their doors (and maybe earning another star in the process!).

Restaurants proclaim their Yelp loyalty through a commonly seen red "Yelp loves us!" sticker; yet the effective marketing power of Yelp goes beyond a sticker on a glass door. Back on the computer screen, restaurateurs who keep track of their restaurants' online ratings and reviews regularly essentially see into the minds (and stomachs) of their patrons. Negative comments can highlight improvement needs for a restaurant. Ed Levine, owner of the San Francisco restaurant Tanglewood, upped the size of his plates after numerous Yelpers complained of the puny portions (McLaughlin). The ensuing positive reviews exemplified Yelp's vast power, and how the influence of a few Yelpers potentially halted a restaurant's decay.

In the past, successful restaurants had to carry out painstaking procedures to determine what customers valued. Customer advisory boards, exit surveys, group interviews, and customer satisfaction surveys were measurable steps taken by restaurants (Shock 42-46). With the convenience of Yelp.com, a customer's wants and needs are revealed with a simple search.

In addition, the occurrence of screen-to-screen interaction between patron and restaurateur is possible. Upon receiving a negative review, a restaurateur is capable of responding in order to "demonstrate how [they] are attempting to recover the service failure. This goes a long way in the feeling that the restaurateur cares about his or her reputation" (Pantelidis 488). Therefore, online restaurant reviews provide a means of interaction between customer and owner, an attempt on the owner's part to rectify problems and keep a customer's business.

Although the average online critics are no Craig Laban or French chef extraordinaire, they carry weight. In Lowe's words, "The whole reason someone is going to Yelp is that the consensus is more powerful than one writer or critic" (Cogsdon). This mass of critics, as long as credible reviews are offered, has the power to alter a restaurant's profitability and to mold consumer decisions and satisfaction when it comes to dining out. Despite complaints regarding the absurdity of some reviews and the increasing anxiety of criticized chefs, Yelp. com is a flashing sign, a pointer finger in a labyrinth of fare frenzy, where there are simply too many choices for consumers to make on their own. Yelp has the power to change what the average American eats, for what's positively rated may very well end up in a patron's stomach. Coming from food journalist of the renowned James Beard Foundation, Mitchell Davis, a review "generates discourse in the field of gastronomy that has the power to influence taste" (12). And taste, my friends, is what is needed in a city best known for Cheez-wiz splattered sandwiches and twisted pieces of dough.

Works Cited

Davis, Mitchell. "Let's Review." Introduction. *A Taste for New York: Restaurant Reviews, Food Discourse, and the Field of Gastronomy in America.* 11-12. New York University. Web. 22 Feb. 2012. <http://www.nyu.edu/ipk/files/docs/events/ Reviewing_part_1_-_Menus_in_the_Media.pdf>.

Luca, Michael. *Reviews, Reputation, and Revenue: The Case of Yelp.com.* Working paper no. 12-016. Harvard Business School, 16 Sept. 2011. Web. 22 Feb. 2012. <http://www. hbs.edu/research/pdf/12-016.pdf>.

Logsdon, Kay. "Yelp Versus the Restaurateur." *The Food Channel* Food Channel, LLC, 20 July 2011. Web. 21 Feb. 2012. <http://www.foodchannel.com/articles/article/yelp-versus-restaurateur/>.

McLaughlin, Katy. "The Price of a Four-Star Rating." *The Wall Street Journal* Dow Jones & Company, 06 Oct. 2007. Web. 22 Feb. 2012. <http://online.wsj.com/article/ SB119162341176250617.html?_requestid=219125>.

Pantelidis, Ioannis S. "Electronic Meal Experience: A Content Analysis of Online Restaurant Comments." *Cornell Hospitality Quarterly* 51.4 (2010): 483-91. *Sage Journals.* Sage Publications, 11 Aug. 2010. Web. 21 Feb. 2012. http://cqx.sagepub. com/content/51/4/483.full.pdf+html>.

Segal, David. "A Rave, a Pan, or Just a Fake?" *The New York Times* 22 May 2011, New York ed., BU sec.: 7. *The New York Times.* The New York Times Company, 22 May 2011. Web. 22 Feb. 2012. <http://www.nytimes.com/2011/05/22/your-money/22haggler.html?_r=3>.

Shock, Patti J., John T. Bowen, and John M. Stefanelli. *Restaurant Marketing for Owners and Managers.* Hoboken, NJ: J. Wiley & Sons, 2004. Print.

Tila, Jet. "A (Scathing) Critique of the Online Restaurant Critic." *Las Vegas Weekly* 14 Jan. 2010. Web. 22 Feb. 2012. <http://www.lasvegasweekly.com/blogs/jet-stream/2010/jan/14/critique-online-restaurant-critic/>.

Matthew Whitworth

Five Axis Diagnosis of a Clinically Depressed Patient

Patient is a middle-aged male who goes by his surname, Eeyore. He currently lives in a wooden house, address SE. Eeyore's Place, House 100, A Woods Boulevard. According to local developers in the area, the location is described as "Rather Boggy and Sad." He was admitted for consultation by his friends, Mr. W. Pooh, and Mr. C. Robin. Patient appears to have a gray demeanor and is often absentminded and lethargic. He often lashes out at himself verbally and was very sarcastic during the interview process. Patient's childhood is shrouded in mystery. However his primary support group is very strong; he seems to be surrounded by very happy and gregarious friends.

According to my preliminary conversation, I feel that the patient has a sound intellect. He can read, write, and teaches spelling to one of his compatriots. He is often critical of those in his primary support group. He is quoted as saying that his friends only have "grey fluff that's blown into their heads by mistake." His hobbies include writing poetry, cooking, and playing a social game called "Pooh-sticks," which he is quite good at.

The DSM-IV axis is as follows. Axis one: I would diagnose the patient with a Major Depressive Disorder Recurrent (296.3x); however, this does not stem from abuse or neglect in childhood. Axis two: Patient seems to have a mild form of Schizoid Personality Disorder. Yet, the patient is willing to be coerced into group activities when asked for help. Axis three: Patient might have some form of gastrointestinal problem, since his primary food intake is thistle. Axis four: Patient does not have problems with primary support group. Patient does not have problems related to the social environment. Patient does not have educational problems. Patient does have occupational problems, but appears to be unconcerned with finding employment. Patient has housing problems, since he is currently living in a condemned house, which is constantly falling down around him. Patient has relatively little wants, so therefore he has no real economic problems. Patient has no problems with access to healthcare services. He has no problems related to interaction with the legal system/crime, and lives in a very nice neighborhood. Axis five: I would place Eeyore at a 70 on the global assessment of functioning scale. His overall mood seems to be depressive on the surface, yet he functions well when coaxed out of his shell.

Mr. Pooh informed me of a case study where the patient received an empty honey pot and a popped balloon for his birthday. Instead of plunging into a deeper depression, Eeyore was overjoyed to receive something regardless. Due to this story and others provided by his support group, I would not prescribe any medication. Nevertheless, I would suggest that he take up residence elsewhere. I would also propose spending more time with his friends and relations. A roommate situation with Mr. Pooh would be ideal.

Marina Roscot

Preventing Fraud with Technology

In today's difficult economic times, fraud-related losses can rise dramatically and have negative consequences on communities and society in general. Cyber-attacks, skimming, altering payment terminals, installing malware within ATMs, and phishing for credit card and personal information are just some of the fraud threats impacting businesses and financial institutions around the globe. Internal fraud, from employee abuse of purchasing cards to large-scale fraud involving high-value contracts and breaches of controls, can have serious consequences for companies. Highly publicized events, such as fraud-related problems at Health South, Enron, and WorldCom, demonstrate the disastrous impact of fraud. The Sarbanes-Oxley Act of 2002 (SOX), designed to stress the importance of early detection of fraud, requires companies to be proactive in preventing fraud by establishing effective compliance and ethics programs, strengthening their internal controls, and implementing the right tools and technologies.

The broad requirements of SOX include whistleblower provisions, under which companies must establish a confidential, anonymous reporting mechanism for employees. Organizations should incorporate standards and procedures to prevent and detect criminal conduct and train employees about the consequences of fraud. An effective fraud-prevention program has three major components: education, investigation, and preventive techniques. According to Steven A. Lauer, a director of integrity research for Interactive Corporation, the training should include the need for accuracy in books and records and the role of internal controls and all employees in assuring this accuracy (62).

Organizations' compliance and ethics programs should be promoted and enforced consistently throughout the organization through appropriate incentives. Disciplinary measures should be taken by management for those engaging in criminal conduct and failing to take reasonable steps to prevent or detect criminal conduct. Employees should be trained to report fraudulent activities they might observe to the appropriate authorities within the organization. Management, in turn, is responsible for assessing the risk of fraud and implementing appropriate anti-fraud programs and controls to reduce risk and comply with the requirements of the SOX regulations.

SOX contains several requirements for public companies that address important issues related to fraud, including auditor independence, corporate responsibility, enhanced financial disclosures, conflicts of interest, corporate crime, and fraud accountability (Moffett and Grant 3). SOX requires the audit committee of a public company to set up procedures to receive anonymous feedback about the company's accounting methods, internal controls, or audit activities (Adams et al. 58). Of the programs that can advance a company's fraud prevention, a hotline and an ethics program are the two most popular and effective. Through a hotline, employees can report questionable activities. To address ethics, the company usually writes a Code of Conduct and uses corporate ethics programs to train the employees to make correct choices when ethical issues arise. The obtained feedback gives the company information that helps to complete process analyses and identify its areas of greatest risk to ensure that the proper controls are in place to reduce or mitigate those risks and define the desired state. The companies can define the desired state by comparing the organization's current situation and its level of risk with benchmark data (Adams et al. 58).

The most cost-effective way to deal with financial losses caused by fraud is through prevention. David Coderre states in "Computer-Assisted Fraud Detection" that "a systematic approach to fraud investigation involving the identification of unusual activity with the aid of computer-assisted audit techniques (CAATs), including the use of digital analysis, can help to ensure that corrupt activity within an organization is detected" (25). Data analysis software can assist in identifying fraud by highlighting transactions that contain the characteristics often associated with fraudulent activity. Coderre further explains that data analysis programs feature many commands that review records for fraud symptoms, such as the existence of duplicate transactions, missing transactions, and other anomalies (25).

Companies should constantly update their technology to be more effective in detecting fraud. Adams et al, suggest that companies implement new technologies, such as data-mining, to make material differences in fraud prevention efforts (59). According to Adams et al., major credit-card issuers use data-mining techniques to scan purchases for potential fraudulent activities. Data-mining software can be used to sift through the entire database and sort the information along various parameters to locate patterns that may require further investigation (Lindsay et al. 2). The simplest, most logical use of computers in fraud detection in Nita Crowder's opinion is the performance of analytical reviews (17). In these reviews, an expected relationship, which can be based on industry standards and historical relationships, is compared to the actual relationship. Analytical review processes are especially useful in detecting fraud in the purchasing, payroll, and revenue areas where assets are misappropriated, corruption activities happen, and fraudulent statements are made.

Purchasing scams may be the most common type of fraud. Examples of purchasing scams include submitting a fraudulent invoice, avoiding authorization controls, or purchasing from a related party (Crowder 17). To detect fraud, purchasing records can be scanned for peculiarities with the help of computer-assisted auditing techniques. Frauds in the payroll area are most commonly accomplished by setting up a ghost employee, failing to delete an employee who has been terminated, or submitting excessive overtime. Crowder proposes three types of analytical tests or searches that can be performed to help detect these kinds of irregularities: duplicate and validity tests, exception testing, and recalculations (19). These tests help identify unusual items that may be related to fraudulent activities. The main concern in the revenue area is that sales and receipts are properly calculated, recorded, and deposited. Crowder contends that analytical procedures, including horizontal analyses by product type, are an important and effective fraud detection technique (19). By analyzing revenue over a minimum of three years, the auditor can detect unexpected trends in revenues.

Computer-assisted fraud detection is not limited to analytical review procedures. Crowder discusses other practices and technologies, which can be expensive and require a great deal of expertise. Among these technologies are Benford's Law, expert systems, and neural networks. Benford's Law determines which digits appear more frequently in a set of random numbers and helps identify suspect accounts for further analysis and investigation (Crowder 20). Since the expected frequency for each number in the set is known, each time the number appears in excess of the expected frequency is deemed suspicious. These techniques cannot be used when an organization's transactions have logically repeated values like in selling dues or membership, which follow a certain pattern (Crowder).

An expert system is a computer program that mimics human expertise in limited domains of knowledge by using *if-then* rules (Anjaneyulu 46). They recognize logical patterns that are similar to those recognized by humans, and then reason with them to produce expert-like performance. The purpose of such a program is to increase the user's performance of tasks requiring skill or judgment. In contrast to Benford's Law, these systems are rule-driven and therefore are based primarily on reasoning rather than on calculations. Crowder explains that expert systems mimic the thought process of a person who has become an expert in a certain area through study as well as personal experience (20). Neural networks have been used as an expert system. According to Crowder, a neural network is a type of artificial intelligence that uses case-based reasoning and pattern recognition to simulate the way the human brain processes and stores or learns information (20). Neural networks "can learn the characteristics of potential fraudulent schemes by comparing new data to stored data and detecting hidden patterns within large volumes of data" (Crowder 20). They are useful in performing tasks in a shorter period of time than it takes a human to complete.

There is no doubt that fraud will continue to exist. While no company, even with the strongest internal controls, is immune to fraud, strengthening internal control policies, processes, and procedures definitely makes companies a less attractive target to both internal and external criminals seeking to exploit internal control weaknesses. Companies can develop response strategies designed to minimize the impact of frauds that occur, are disclosed, and come to the attention of the company, authorities, and other interested parties. Through technological advancements in data sharing and data analytics, companies can anticipate, detect, and prosecute fraud more quickly and forcefully. To protect the business from fraud, management should be wary of false accounting and assess IT vulnerability. Those companies that approach fraud management as a mandate to protect their reputations and build customer trust will also improve operational efficiencies and realize significant payback to their bottom line through reduction of financial losses.

Works Cited

Adams, Gary W., et al. "Fraud Prevention." *The CPA Journal* Jan. 2006: 56-9. *ABI/INFORM Complete*. Web. 8 Dec. 2011.

Anjaneyulu K.S.R. "Expert Systems: An Introduction." *Resonance* 1998: 46-49. Web. 25 Dec. 2011.

Coderre, David G. "Computer-Assisted Fraud Detection." *The Internal Auditor* 2000: 25-7. *ABI/INFORM Complete*. Web. 20 Dec. 2011.

Crowder, Nita. "Fraud Detection Techniques." The Internal Auditor 1997: 17-20. *ABI/INFORM Complete*. Web. 7 Apr. 2012.

Lindsay, David H., et al. "Detecting Fraud in the Data Using Automatic Intervention Detection." *Fraud magazine. Archive issue May/June*. 2005. Print. 20 Dec. 2011.

Moffett, Ryan C., and Gerry H. Grant. "Internal Controls and Fraud Prevention." *Internal Auditing* 2011: 3-12. *ABI/INFORM Complete*. Web. 7 Nov. 2011.

Steven A. Lauer. "Compliance Programs and Fraud Prevention." *The Metropolitan Corporate Counsel* 2006: 61-62. Web. 23 Feb. 2012.

Sarah Rettew

Brita's FilterForGood Campaign

Take the pledge now and save. Just hearing or seeing those couple of words would make any person want to learn more. Why, though? Through subtle techniques and intelligent placements of words and pictures, Brita has created a program entitled FilterForGood to draw in people to help and be a part of an amazing idea of sustainability. Through buying a Brita filter or reusable bottle, anyone can pledge to save one bottle a day, for one year, to reduce water bottle waste and help make the world more ecologically friendly.

Brita has created an impressive campaign for people to join to help them make a difference. The ways that Brita draws people into joining their campaign definitely contains strong use of rhetorical appeal as well as many other little techniques that may not be completely apparent to the average person reading the advertisements. These strategies, however, cause Brita to be a profitable company that improves the world, making it more of a sustainable place to live. There is really no reason why anybody would not want the world to be healthier because even in the periodical *Mechanical Engineers*, the engineers agree that "'all sustainable design practices are ultimately cost-saving, hence always considered, [and] always recommended'" (Brown). Sustainability is simply filled with positive outcomes and Brita has taken major advantage of their opportunity to make it happen.

When surfing the Internet and coming across the FilterForGood campaign by Brita, the first thing that is noticed on the website are the nine blue water bottles lined up with the number 351,964,390 written across them. Immediately, any observer would want to know more about this, which is why Brita added a little blurb stating that "more than an estimated 340,000,000 bottles have been saved" ("Brita FilterForGood"). With every person who pledges and commits to the cause, this number grows every day. Browsing through the Brita pages, facts such as this are scattered throughout every page, informing observers about important data.

Brita clearly appeals to logos because of its irrefutable facts. Brita hits on main facts on the waste of water bottles, which indirectly benefits their cause to have people buy Brita filters and reusable bottles in order to prevent waste in the world. For example, "69% of bottled water containers end up in the trash and not in a recycling container" ("Brita FilterForGood"). This fact, alone, causes people to have a new perspective about either recycling more often or buying a Brita product to prevent this altogether. Either way, Brita is making people aware that sustainability is important to make this world ecologically friendly.

Another way that Brita draws in potential customers while being sustainable is its appeal to ethos. Obviously, Brita is extremely well known for its trustworthy products. It is simply a credible company that produces products used by an extremely high number of families every single day. Also, the language used is appropriate for any type of audience seeking information on the website. It is simple and to-the-point so that any reader fully understands Brita's attempt to be a sustainable company. As well as appropriate language, Brita also understands that the economy is going through some rough times right now, so it empathizes with its customers. Brita does this by "keeping Mother Earth and your wallet green" by saving customers hundreds of dollars on bottled water ("Brita FilterForGood"). This is important because "'everyone loves [going] green until they have to pay for it'" (Rennie). Fortunately, customers who take part in buying Brita's campaign initially have to pay for a product, but in the long run, they are saving money by not having to buy water bottles again. All in all, these examples demonstrate Brita's reliability and respect for its customers' values and support. The company is profiting off of the purchases made by the customers, but it also knows that its goal of sustainability would not be achievable if it were not for the dedicated consumers.

Brita cleverly has a visual aspect of its advertising that makes its website and commercials appealing to the eye. For example, the main page for FilterForGood has remarkable graphic design, with an image of a droplet of water transformed into the healthy looking world. The bright blues and greens are eye-catching and attractive. Even the page looks like it is under water, with green leaves surrounding the sides of the website. Visually, everything looks healthy and clean—something that most people would not recognize or catch onto, but it subconsciously draws the viewers in, thinking what they are seeing is appealing. Even the commercial in 2008 of all of those connected water bottles representing how enough water bottles were wasted that they could wrap around the whole world over 190 times was eye-opening to many people ("Brita FilterForGood"). If words are not enough to inform people of the harsh reality of plastic bottle wasting, physically seeing hundreds and hundreds of empty bottles lined up definitely strikes people because sometimes numbers do not mean much unless they are seen as empty, wasted plastic bottles polluting the world.

On that note, a striking photo caught my eye when searching for the FilterForGood campaign. It shows two people drinking oil because in 2010,

"16 million gallons of 'OIL' was consumed to make plastic bottles for water" (Rennie). The startling picture places a realization into viewers' minds that oil is being indirectly consumed and wasted because people do not recycle plastic water bottles. Brita uses this image for its campaign not to directly influence people to buy its products, but to make people aware of how unhealthy they are making the world by not becoming more eco-friendly.

Brita's website and commercials never *directly* appeal to the audience's emotions, like some campaigns do. Instead, through a combination of Brita's reasoning and techniques to inform potential customers of all of the positives of buying a Brita product, it indirectly makes them feel something. A need, a desire—anything to make people *want* to buy the product to help make the world eco-friendly and save a few bucks here and there. No, Brita does not have sappy pictures that make viewers gloomy, or humorous photos to make them joyful; it merely has well-described information and visuals that tug at something in each and every one of us that makes us want to give back and keep the world healthy and sustainable. Subtleties that Brita uses certainly promote it as a "green" company and draw people in to be a part of the future success of the business and the world.

In conclusion, Brita influences readers and viewers to purchase its products and help become sustainable by making the world ecologically friendly. Through subtle techniques of intelligent visualizations, logic, and credibility behind Brita's actions, the company can successfully reach its goal of appealing to every viewer's emotions, resulting in them *wanting* to buy Brita products to save money, prevent waste, and help sustain the world.

Works Cited

Brita FilterForGood. Brita: The Clorox Company, 2012. Web. 18 Jan. 2012.

Brown, Alan S. "Sustainability." *Mechanical Engineering* 2011: 36-42. Web. 23 Jan. 2012.

Rennie, Ben. "A Few Facts About Plastic Bottles and the Resistance." *Uncluttered White Spaces*. 2012. Web. 22 Jan. 2012.

Sonia Shah

Creutzfeldt-Jakob Disease

Creutzfeldt-Jakob disease (CJD) is a rare, fatal neurodegenerative disease caused by infectious proteins called prions, and is accordingly classified as a human prion disease. Human prion diseases are a group of disorders characterized by the conversion of the constitutively expressed cellular protein, prion protein (PrPc), into an abnormally folded isoform called scrapie prion protein (PrPSc)[1]. Over time, PrPSc can accumulate and aggregate to the levels that result in brain tissue damage, neuronal death, and development of CJD[7].

Prion diseases are also known as transmissible spongiform encephalopathies because they are characterized by spongiform degeneration or vacuolation of neurons, neuronal loss, intense reactive astrocytic proliferation, and accumulation of PrPSc[7]. The numerous oval and rounded vacuoles in the neuropil give the brain tissue a "spongy" appearance under the microscope. The worldwide prevalence of CJD is one case per million, while the annual incidence is one case per two million, with a slight female predominance[7].

The incubation period of CJD ranges from three years to 22 years, with subacute onset and progressive deterioration[7]. Prion diseases show the highest extent of phenotypic heterogeneity among neurodegenerative disorders[1]. Initially, patients exhibit symptoms including lack of muscular coordination; impaired memory, judgment, and thinking; and blurred vision. The patients' mental impairment progresses rapidly, and they begin to develop myoclonus, pyramidal, and extrapyramidal symptoms. Eventually, the patients enter a comatose state after which pneumonia and other respiratory infections subsequently lead to death[7].

Treatment for all forms of CJD is largely symptomatic, since there is no cure that has been identified to date[7]. However, a number of different pharmacological agents are currently being researched, including quinacrine, which prevents the conversion of PrPc to PrPSc *in vitro*, but there is no evidence of increased survival or significant neurologic benefits in humans[6]. Pentosan polysulfate is a compound that has been shown to increase the incubation period in mice, but there has been no improvement of clinical features in patients with prion disease, although the possibility of increased survival is suggested[8]. Flupirtine is an analgesic that been shown to have neuroprotective properties to improve cognitive function but showed no survival improvement in patients with CJD[7].

Prion diseases in humans occur in three general forms: acquired, genetic (gCJD), and sporadic (sCJD). All three forms of prion disease present a remarkable degree of phenotypic heterogeneity, which is likely to be closely related to the diversity of prion strains[2].

Acquired

The acquired form accounts for 1% of all cases, and includes cases accidentally transmitted from affected humans as in iatrogenic CJD, by ritual cannibalism as in kuru, or from bovine spongiform encephalopathy (BSE)-infected animals as in variant CJD (vCJD)[5,7]. More than 400 patients contracted iatrogenic CJD through the use of neurosurgical instruments, stereotactic EEG electrodes, human pituitary hormone, dura mater grafts, corneal transplant, and blood transfusion[5]. Kuru was first discovered in 1959 in Papua New Guinea among the aboriginal Fore-people, who practiced cannibalistic rituals of eating the brain of the deceased[5]. vCJD first appeared in 1996 in the UK and is thought to be transmitted from cattle to humans when humans consume food from animals that have been infected with BSE-encephalopathy[5]. The most striking feature of vCJD is the young age of its victims, ranging from 14 to 52 years, with an average duration of 7 to 14 months[7].

The critical event that leads to the pathogenesis of the acquired form of CJD involves the interaction between the exogenous PrPSc and the endogenous PrPc of the human, which results in the autocatalytic conversion of endogenous PrPC into endogenous PrPSc and the further propagation of PrPSc[2]. The physiochemical characteristics of the exogenous PrPSc, the site of the initial conversion, and the tissues and organs involved in the pathogenesis of the disease are a few factors that may contribute to variability of the acquired cases[2].

Genetic

The genetic form accounts for 10-15% of all human prion diseases[7]. There are three major genetic forms of the disease with variable but overlapping phenotypic features: Gerstmann-Straussler-Scheinker disease (GSS), fatal familial insomnia (FFI), and genetic CJD (gCJD)[1]. GSS affects the cerebellum, typically has an earlier onset, and progresses over a longer period of time than sCJD. Patients with FFI have severe insomnia in addition to the usual features of CJD[7].

The genetic form of the disease results from different mutations in the coding region of the PRNP gene, which encodes PrPc[7]. The human PRNP gene is located on chromosome 20 and has a simple genomic structure of two exons and a single intron, with the entire protein-coding region located in exon 2[7]. gCJD has been linked to two types of inherited PRNP mutations: (1) missense mutation or (2) frameshift mutation. Affected individuals also often have a family history consistent with an autosomal dominant inheritance of the disease with variable penetrance and expressivity[1]. A few mutations, including E200K and D178N, have been reported worldwide with geographical or ethnic clusters of cases in Israel, Slovakia, Chile, Italy, and Spain[1].

The presence of one of these mutations is thought to alter the properties of PrPc, promoting its conversion to the PrPSc state[2]. Recent studies have demonstrated the additional influence of PRNP polymorphisms on disease susceptibility and phenotypic expression in all forms of human prion diseases. The most important human PRNP polymorphism is the codon 129 polymorphism, which can encode either methionine or valine[1]. A number of studies have demonstrated that methionine homozygotes are more susceptible to CJD whereas heterozygotes are less susceptible[7]. Increasing evidence shows that the physicochemical properties of PrPSc and the codon 129 genotype act as the main determinants of the disease phenotype, while the specific PRNP mutation plays a secondary role in influencing susceptibility to the disease[1].

Sporadic

sCJD accounts for approximately 85% of cases of human prion diseases[7]. The sporadic form of the disease predominantly affects individuals between the ages of 55 and 75, lasts from several weeks up to two years, and disease onset is characterized by a wide range of clinical and pathological phenotypes[7]. The nature of the etiological events which lead to the sCJD is less clear than the other forms[2]. It is hypothesized that sCJD may be caused either by somatic mutations or by spontaneous PrPc misfolding leading to the accumulation of PrPSc[5]. PrPSc purified from hamster brain consisted of 42% alpha-helix and only 3% beta-sheet structure, whereas PrPSc purified from scrapie-infected hamster brain is composed of 30% alpha-helix and 43% beta-sheet[3].

A hypothesized mechanism for the propagation of prion diseases is the self-perpetuating conversion of PrPc to the misfolded disease-causing PrPSc. Several explanations have been proposed for the process by which PrPc misfolds to form PrPSc. One explanation is that there is an error in post-translational processing of PrPc, and a second possible explanation suggests the presence of PrPSc-like oligomers, which acquire the capability to convert PrPc to PrPSc[2].

In 1999, Parchi et al. proposed a classification system of sCJD, which defined six major molecular subtypes based on a comprehensive analysis of 300 subjects[4]. There are two PrPSc conformers named type 1 (21kDa) and type 2 (19kDa). A large series of cases were divided into six groups according to the six possible combinations of their PrPSc subtype (either type 1 or type 2) with each of the three possible codon 129 genotypes (MM, MV, or MV)[4]. This led to a new classification system of sporadic prion diseases based on molecular rather than clinical or histopathological features. The classification provided a molecular explanation for the phenotypic variability and allowed for easier identification of the PrPSc strains in sCJD[4].

In an effort to understand the etiology of sCJD, future experiments should aim to further define the molecular basis of prion strains, including conformational differences, and their distinct cellular targeting. Furthermore, a study should be completed to establish why the two different alleles, methionine and valine, at codon 129 can cause such different behaviors in terms of protein misfolding and strain susceptibility[5]. Additional studies need to be conducted to compare the transmission properties of sCJD and gCJD in order to determine whether any of the specific pathogenic mutations implicated in gCJD generate a prion strain that differs from the six previously defined strains isolated from sCJD[1].

There may also be environmental factors that play a role in triggering the onset of sCJD. Genome-wide association studies and gene-environment interaction studies may reveal other determinants in the pathogenesis of the disease and further our understanding of risk factors that may be associated with different sCJD strains[1].

Works Cited

[1] Capellari, Sabina, Rosaria Strammiello, Daniela Saverioni, Hans Kretzschmar, and Piero Parchi. "Genetic Creutzfeldt-Jakob Disease and Fatal Familial Insomnia: Insights into Phenotypic Variability and Disease Pathogenesis." *Acta Neuropathologica* 2011: 21-37. Web.

[2] Gambetti, Pierluigi, Ignazio Cali, Silvio Notari, Qingzhong Kong, Wen-Quan Zou, and Witold K. Surewicz. "Molecular Biology and Pathology of Prion Strains in Sporadic Human Prion Diseases." *Acta Neuropathologica* 2011: 79-90. Web.

[3] Pan, KM., M Baldwin, J Nguyen, M Gasset, A Serban, D Groth, I Mehlhorn, Z Huang, R J Fletterick, and F E Cohen. "Conversion of Alpha-helices into Beta-sheets Features in the Formation of the Scrapie Prion Proteins." *Proceedings of the National Academy of Sciences of the United States of America* 1993: 10962-6. Print.

[4] Parchi, Piero, Armin Giese, Sabina Capellari, Paul Brown, Walter Schulz-Schaeffer, Otto Windl, Inga Zerr, Herbert Budka, Nicolas Kopp, Pedro Piccardo, Sigrid Poser, Amyn Rojiani, Nathalie Streichemberger, Jean Julien, Claude Vital, Bernardino Ghetti, Pierluigi Gambetti, and Hans Kretzschmar. "Classification of Sporadic Creutzfeldt-Jakob Disease Based on Molecular and Phenotypic Analysis of 300 Subjects." *Annals of Neurology* 1999: 224-33. Web.

[5] Parchi, Piero, Rosaria Strammiello, Armin Giese, and Hans Kretzschmar. "Phenotypic Variability of Sporadic Human Prion Disease and its Molecular Basis: Past, Present, and Future." *Acta Neuropathologica* 2011: 91-112. Web.

[6] Relkin, Norman R., and Cary S. Gunther. "Quinacrine Fails to Stop Prion Disease." *Neurology Alert* 2009. Web.

[7] Spero, Martina, and Ines Lazibat. "Creutzfeldt-Jakob Disease: Case Report and Review of the Literature." *Acta clinica Croatica* 2010: 181-7. Web.

[8] Tsuboi, Yoshio, Katsumi Doh-ura, and Tatsuo Yamada. "Continuous Intraventricular Infusion of Pentosan Polysulfate: Clinical Trial Against Prion Diseases." *Neuropathology* 2009: 632-6. Web.

Week of
Writing

Introduction

Drexel University's seventh annual Week of Writing (WoW) was held in May of 2012. WoW is a weeklong celebration of writing sponsored by the Department of English and Philosophy and the College of Arts and Sciences. This past year's events included such panel discussions as "Writing for Social Change," "Social Media and the Representation of the Self," and "The Intoxicating Allure of Drinks Writing." During WoW, the Drexel Writing Center offered writing workshops linked to the panel topics each day. And, once again, at the reading marathon, faculty and students read their own original creative writing back-to-back, a new reader every few minutes, as the audience came and went throughout the days.

Each year, the lead-up to the marathon is the WoW Writing Contest, used to determine which students will be invited to read at the event. The faculty judging panels determined the best fiction, poetry, creative nonfiction, humor, and opinion/editorial writing submitted by Drexel students in 2012. Those winning students not only read at the WoW marathon and earned prizes, but also now have their writing published in the fifth volume of *The 33rd.*

Creative writing is among the most challenging fields. Even experienced authors who have been writing for years often struggle to find just the right word. As author Gene Fowler famously said, "Writing is easy. All you do is stare at a blank sheet of paper until drops of blood form on your forehead." The writers whose work appears in this section have stared at that blank sheet of paper, or that computer screen. Whether or not blood formed on their foreheads, they have struggled for the right words to touch their readers and bring their vision to life. The Week of Writing will continue to celebrate and reward their efforts.

Zach Blackwood

Tectonics

Steeped in dust—blue air.
The sun phasing through
dry aerial mists.
Atomic particles,
landing arid, on her forearms.

I'm filling these lungs with thick
petrichor—and
poor Tongue flips himself in protest.
Damp muscle refuses to
be beleaguered by must and spores.

A magazine said the tectonics
were irreversibly altered.
That a 1.26 microsecond
scar marred the Earth's
timeline, and would again
every time our sun set.

The slow-moving ebullience
of magma, hot orange
viscosity peeking through cracks
in the blackness, like a charred
sweet potato, crushed.

A tear in the crust and the people
in holes shouldn't act as such cynosure,
but destruction is infinitely more potent
than the conception of novel things,
if only because you can only
demolish a structure one time.

I remember my pedestrian awe,
upon spying your deft
removal of the brittle
shell, when you peeled
that egg in 2 brisk motions.

Laurel Hostak

Summersick

When I think about the summers I spent
chasing a white van
(like a white rabbit)
with the pictures on the side, you know the ones,
I always get a little sick.
Sick from the memory of artificial flavors
stinging my tongue so sweet
and sticking to my face and fingers, leaving stains
of cherry, lemon, blue raspberry, and grape.
Sick with the bellyaches I put up with—
worth it for a taste.
And homesick, too.
For the house on Hollywood (Avenue, not Boulevard).
For the streets and playgrounds
of the old neighborhood
between the highway and the train tracks
where trains no longer run.
Homesick for the body I once inhabited,
that could run long distances
and roll down hills
and jump all the way to the third monkey bar
(Beat that, boys).
For those magnificent bursts of energy
and the heavy slumbers that came after.
I sometimes feel like a hermit crab,
scuttling from body to body
home to home
summer to summer.
The twinkling tune of the ice cream van
is the only connective thread.
What else is there
than the bellyaches
and the sick sick sweetness
and the stains on my hands
to prove that that was me
flying down those streets—

dollar in hand waving
shrieking with the anticipation
of catching that rabbit
and devouring those saccharine treasures?
All other evidence vanished long ago.

Ryan Nasino

A Conceit on My Inability to Write an Extended Metaphor

I think I made a wrong turn
somewhere back there.
And by back there,
I mean about 20 minutes ago.

None of these storefronts
look familiar.
Neither the gelato stand,
nor the one selling glassware,
give me the faintest clue
as to which direction is best.

I know my destination
and what it looks like.
Buildings, acting as walls
on three sides, and the basilica
sitting at the top,
next to Mark's clock tower.

I ask the people on the street
"Piazza San Marco?"
But, without knowing Italian,
I can't follow their directions.

If only I could find a street name,
one that I recognized,
and could follow.
Only, there are no streets.
I'm trapped in a floating city.

I wonder if gondolas
work the same as taxis.
But I don't see a fare counter,
plus, I wouldn't know how to ask
anyway.

I guess I'll just wander
and hope I stumble upon
the right set of words
to guide me
where I need to go.

Kelly Davis

Iron Cross

"Constable! Constable Hawthorne!"

I was roused from a tumultuous sleep by a pounding upon my door, a frenzied voice crying out my name. The night air was still and pleasantly balmy, scented by newly blooming buds. Yet tearing through this serenity, such bedlam! Casting aside my bedcovers, I rose from the bed to retrieve the lantern from the nearby table. In the blackness of nighttime, I shuffled blindly over the well-worn floorboards towards the hall. Here, the candle mounted upon the wall kindled light anew to my lantern and sleep-weary eyes.

I proceeded to the front door, which was still under assault from a driving fist, and pushed it ajar to reveal an ashen-faced boy. He was fitted in the simple scarlet attire of the royal servants, and trembled before me. As chief constable, I was accustomed to unexpected arrivals of such attendants bearing summons to the palace; but I fathomed a more ominous quality to this beckoning. "What is it? What disturbance can there be at such a late hour?" For a moment, he was unable to utter a word, gulping in air with wide eyes. "Speak, boy!" I demanded.

"Prince Edward is dead!"

***

My deputy Jonathan Hitchcocke awaited my carriage as it rolled to a halt outside the palace gates, horses snorting with exertion. I dismounted, and he fell into step beside me as we tramped rapidly through the ingress. "Where is Her Royal Highness?"

"She is in the North Tower in the boy's bedchamber," said he. "We have attempted to have her compose herself and deliver instructions to the staff directly, but she has proven inconsolable. It was a stroke of fortune I was already present for other matters, and summoned you myself." Indeed, he was fully and properly clothed, in comparison to the nightclothes which I had retained in my alacrity to depart, which must have reflected poorly upon my person.

"Have you any idea as to the hour of his passing?" We were ascending the great winding stairs of the tower. I could discern from above us strident sobs, such as only a mother could produce in the depths of profound sorrow.

"Not but an hour ago. A noise was heard from his chambers by a sentinel stationed close at hand. Upon entering he saw nothing amiss, the prince soundly asleep, but upon closer examination he found him without breath or pulse." At last we drew level with the hall that housed young Edward; by this point, the lamentations had diminished. Several armed guards flanked the door to the boy's room; upon sighting us, they immediately dispersed. Together, we entered. "Your Royal Highness, the Chief Constable has arrived," announced my deputy.

The Queen Mother Elizabeth, now silent, lay nearly prostrate across her son's bed, clutching his small body. Her mantle was pushed back from her brow, hair falling tangled across the boy's face. At the sound of the deputy's voice, she gave a start.

"Thank you, Deputy Constable," she responded in a weak voice. Lowering Edward back onto the pillow, she rose, ordering her garment with a look of discomfiture. "I am greatly indebted to you for your swift coming, Chief Constable."

"It is the least I can do, Your Royal Highness." I approached the prince's bedside. In this position, with eyes closed and golden curls framing his youthful features, one would indeed believe that he was merely in the midst of a deep slumber. I placed a palm upon his cheek; it was smooth and cold, more rigid than that of a living being.

Hitchcocke came to my side, and murmured clandestinely in my ear. Disbelieving, I turned to him, finding his face wholly solemn. I accompanied my deputy to a removed corner of the chamber beside the agape window, where I whispered to him. "Are you quite certain?"

"It cannot be an earthly cause, and the sentries assured no commonplace man could have breached the chamber to accomplish the deed. There is no other rationalization."

"Very well." I drew my dressing gown more securely about my person. "Send for judge Seymour at once to assemble a jury and date of trial." Hitchcocke nodded.

As I took my leave, I discerned that this was assured to be a most savage tribunal. There would be no sense of impartiality amongst citizens adjudicating the alleged executioner of their prince aged only twelve years. Compounding the madness to come, if my deputy proved truthful, would be the notion that the accused was not, indeed, human.

***

It would be a full week to consolidate a hearing, Judge Seymour being engaged in a distant town and taking considerable time to contact. By the day of his reappearance, there was not a soul who was ignorant of young Edward's expiry, despite the best attempts of the royals to conceal it. Having so recently and abruptly lost their king to a nameless infirmity, a disquiet verging on mania had overrun the populace.

At last, I stood alongside the podium of the judge inside the grand courthouse, viewing the agitated crowd seated before me. After some minutes, Seymour rapped his gavel upon the tabletop. "Order!" Stillness fell over the courtroom. "Bring her in," the judge pronounced.

The massive oaken doors opened, and two sentries entered. Between them, a flaccid figure hung from their arms, unadorned feet dragging across the floor without any physical effort of supporting the body above. It was a young woman, reedy and long of limb. She would be fetching were it not for the desolate state in which she appeared now, rubicund hair caked with filth, pale complexion darkened by dirt. A strip of cloth, tattered as her soiled green frock, masked her eyes. Her escorts deposited her aggressively onto a stool at the head of the room, where she hunched, shaking.

"Prisoner," I addressed her vociferously. "On this sixteenth day of the month of April in the year of our Lord 1491, you stand accused of the abduction and fabrication of the demise of Prince Edward the Fifth, through the supernatural means of a fey of the dark and most unholy Unseelie court." The assembly issued sounds of shock. "The prince, being of excellent health, would not have died of any physical ailment, and the security of the room eliminates the possibility of an intruder. Unless, that is, they would have had the means to ascend the exterior of the tower through a fey's power of flight."

"I...I have done no wrong." Her voice was barely audible, throat crushed by fear.

"The record stands that at the very hour of the prince's passing, you were witnessed absconding from the grounds about the royal palace with a ponderous mass upon your back, entering the bordering forest, and reemerging unladen when confronted by our guards." I leaned closer. "It is common knowledge that the Unseelie relish in spreading discord through the seizure of children, replacing the absent bodies with wooden replicas to simulate death. Do you deny awareness of this fact?"

"This I know," the prisoner mumbled.

"Have you any word of defense?"

"An errand...merely an errand..." Tears flooded her broken voice, and her shoulders quivered. "That is what conveyed me near the palace...gathering goods for myself and for my—"

"Cease this hesitance!" Hitchcocke interjected, striking a palm upon the table before the girl, who recoiled violently. "Speak plainly if you hold any hope of seeing yourself acquitted."

"I..." Here, all words terminated as she dissolved into a fit of weeping. I tolerantly waited for her to gather her wits; Hitchcocke, in his typical fashion, was less understanding.

"This sniveling gets us nowhere," he huffed. My deputy turned to me. "Shall we initiate the tests?"

"Have patience, deputy. We cannot rush into physical trials until we have further spoken with the prisoner, lest we cause an unnecessary scene."

"The devil with speaking! Words will not settle this louse's deeds! The time has come for action!" My deputy and I gazed heatedly into each other's eyes. After a pause, I nodded slowly, turning to address the crowd.

"As the accusations demand, the prisoner shall be subjected to a series of examinations to determine whether she is truly of the fey kind." Hitchcocke moved to a desk beside the podium, which held two objects. "The first test: primrose and sagebrush, both most repellant to the fey folk." Retrieving a small bunch of these freshly cut flowers and branches, Hitchcocke grasped the girl's arm, pushing back the sleeve and brushing the plants over the exposed skin.

The prisoner's voice instantly returned to her, bursting forth in a cry as red welts swelled rapidly in the wake of the bouquet. Snatching back the limb, she scrubbed at it with her unscathed hand. Hushed utterances rippled through the jury members, who nodded knowingly to each other. I watched emotionlessly as the girl cradled her scarlet arm.

Now, I raised my voice. "Next, the bells, the tone of which is most excruciating to the fey ear." In response, from the steeple above, the lone bell began to toll, softly at first, then increasing to its full volume. A second squeal returned my attention to the girl. Her blindfold had slipped from her face, and her eyes were clenched shut in agony, hands gripping her ears tightly. The crowd's exclamations rose again, more fervently than before. Gradually, the peals ceased.

"Finally," I declared, "the most definitive trial; the touch of iron." The girl's eyes flew open, red and engorged behind their ebony hue, and entirely terrified. Deputy Hitchcocke again took hold of her arm, pinning it flat against the table, palm upwards. From the desk, he lifted a small cross crafted of iron, and pressed it upon her hand.

The sound which the prisoner had made before all paled in comparison to the bloodcurdling shriek which now emitted from the deepest reaches of her body. Wherever the cold metal made contact with her body, it burned into the surface as through it were ablaze. She jerked back and forth wildly, but Hitchcocke remained steadfast, holding the cross to her like a vice. By this point, the courtroom was in an absolute uproar. "Demon!" "Slaughterer!" "Ungodly creature!"

All at once, the pain, horror and screaming subjugated the girl. Her lids slipped shut, and she slumped back against the chair, insensible. The sentries returned the covering to her eyes, then proceeded to drag her from the room. As she passed, people clawed at her, seeking to personally dispatch her that very moment. The judge futilely hammered his gavel, the chance of regaining order gone. At my side, my deputy wore a countenance of utmost satisfaction.

"Now you see what becomes of such hasty action," I remarked sternly. "How do you suggest we come to a level-headed conclusion when every member of the court is in chaos?"

"There is nothing else to be done. Her culpability is settled." Hitchcocke's eyes glittered with a fierce pride.

"And you believe you have proof enough from three rudimentary trials to send a young woman, who had nary a moment to provide a counterargument, to her death? This is not the way of a just man."

My deputy's ears flamed. "What would you have us do instead?" he snapped. "Her suffering is the only evidence required."

I shook my head. "Five years you have served under me, and never have I seen anything but instantaneous judgments and snatching at conclusions.

Leave this matter to me. You have yet to use your mind to resolve a trial as a decent human should."

"Do not presume to tell me what I shall and shall not do!" barked Hitchcocke, temper erupting in an instant. "Never have I had the ability to take a case into my own hands, only standing and watching your infernally mundane methods! You may be above me in station and years, but I am a man of the law and shall be treated as such!"

I stared at my deputy, who breathed heavily, fists clenched, viewing me with palpable animosity. Around us, the jury and observers raved. In the dungeons below, a girl sat bound, having been confirmed in a half-hour guilty of slaying Prince Edward the Fifth.

***

The next day, the court reconvened to provide the final sentence of the prisoner. She sat blinded once more, as invectives were hissed at her from all directions. Copious raps of the gavel were required to bring the room to order. Once silence fell, I stood.

"People of the court," I began, "yesterday you witnessed the trial of one held responsible for the death of the young prince. Her suspected method: using the power of the Unseelie fey to snatch him away, and leaving a model in his stead. This crime was to have held no motivation beyond a desire to cause mayhem."

"However," I continued, "before the jury reveals its verdict, I have final questions to ask." I turned to the desk at which my deputy sat. "They are for Deputy Constable Hitchcocke."

From inside the leather pouch about my waist, I drew a minute glass vial. "Can you identify this substance, Deputy Constable?"

"I know not what you could mean." Hitchcocke's expression was one of irritated perplexity as he regarded the bottle. Delicately uncorking it, I lifted it for the people of the court to view.

"The stinging nettle, in the name of self-protection, produces a potent oil which causes considerable distress to those unfortunate enough to take it upon their skin." I moved my hand over my deputy's hand where it lay upon the table. "This oil is easily extracted by a practiced apothecary, and can be used to anoint other surfaces." I tipped the vial, allowing a large droplet to gather at the mouth. "For instance, a bouquet of primrose and sagebrush." The globule shook, then fell from the bottle onto Hitchcocke's hand.

Instantaneously, a fierce welt red sprung up upon the deputy's flesh. He bellowed, leaping to his feet and clutching at his inflamed appendage. The members of the court gasped. I solemnly stood as Hitchcocke whirled towards me in a fury. "What the devil do you mean by this, Hawthorne?"

"The pain is great, is it not?" I replied with a level voice. "Perhaps as great as the pain one can inflict on a young woman locked away in the muteness and obscurity of a prison, denied a ray of light or a solitary sound, mistreated and malnourished." Approaching the quaking, withered girl, I unfastened the cloth cloaking her eyes. The instant she was confronted with the luminescence of the courtroom, she moaned, clasping her head in her hands. "Even without the toll of a church bell, see how she suffers."

"What is this nonsensical drivel? We look to punish a murderer, not to confront a man of the law!" Deputy Hitchcocke thundered, ruddy-faced.

"Indeed we do. But the two may be hand in hand." I shifted my attention to the crowd. "In the grip of panic, it is a simple matter for one to manipulate facts to his will. A young man, desperate to rise to a level of authority which he could not have previously attained, might view the untimely death of a sovereign as an opportunity to upset this balance of power. How best to accomplish this?" I paused. "Eradicate the next in line to the throne from inside the palace itself. Then find a scapegoat, and use trickery to shift all blame onto that victim and away from himself."

Hitchcocke shook with rage. "If this is so," he spoke through gritted teeth, "how would this person falsify the charring of flesh with cold iron?"

"With the use of a most familiar substance," I replied, tapping the table next to where the cross sat yet. "Something that can burn upon the skin without fire or heat: lye."

A terrible stillness pulsated through the courtroom. Suddenly, with a roar, my deputy launched himself at me. The court fell again into frenzy as he was seized by numerous sentinels, who bound his thrashing hands. "Monster! How can you seek to ruin me? This is madness! Release me! I will wring his neck!" Shouting all the while, he was taken kicking out of the courtroom.

Precariously, the girl climbed to her feet. Looking at me, her lips parted to form soundless words.

"Thank you."

***

As the sun sank in a smoldering orb on the horizon, I unlocked the door to my house. Inside, I stood immobile a moment in the entry hall, a dull ache thrumming in my head. Then, to myself, I gave a secretive smile.

It was foolish of me not to have foreseen the complications which could have arisen in my scheme. Only a burst of cunning and manipulation of the culpability which Hitchcocke had accumulated against himself were able to assist me in redirecting the focus of the trial from a blameless victim. True, a hint of regret lingered upon me for transforming my deputy into a pawn, but in our brief period together I had never held much fondness for the brash, hotheaded man. Such a sacrifice was inevitable to rectify this error.

It was, in the end, a simple matter of deplorable timing. I had known that she departed to procure firewood and other supplies, but had not fathomed that her intended route led her past the palace. Naturally, the odds were absent from her favor, and suspicion and hysteria cast her immediately as an assassin.

It took all my experience as a man of the law to craft a perfectly mundane rationale behind the effectiveness of the tortures she had faced.

Just as trying was remaining placid when faced with the tormented screams of my cherished, innocent sister.

Ultimately, though, all had passed accordingly.

Doffing my waistcoat, the tip of my index finger gave a residual bite of aching from where it had carelessly brushed the iron cross.

The deed was done.

The Unseelie court would be pleased by my triumph.

Ian Micir

Where the Deer and the Antelope Play

It seems odd that life should ever end of natural causes,
being that it takes so damn much to do it otherwise.

At fourteen years old, my first job was at Somerton Springs Golf Center in Feasterville, Pennsylvania. The facility consisted of a pro shop, an 18-hole executive golf course, and a driving range. My job was on the goose-infested range, riding back and forth in one of those rusted, motorized, ball-gathering prisons that are every amateur golfer's favorite target: with each pass, they gear up and try to intentionally top a driver off the mat to produce a low, stinging laser, as though trying to slay the mechanical beast.[1]

Most golfers probably don't know this—or maybe they do and just don't care—but that worker hates that. *I* hated that. See, they don't build the ball-gathering contraption as a single, all-in-one machine. Those don't actually exist. What that poor bastard out there is driving is a regular golf cart with a makeshift cage constructed around it by the lowest bidder who can provide his own scrap metal. He's lucky if it's bolted together; if not, maybe a series of Master locks with lost combinations. Sometimes it's just duct tape and hope between a man and the Almighty, or in this case, a 200-mph Titleist.

My "company car" was impressively dilapidated. A pathetic, abused savage. The rust had spread like an untreated rash, requiring a certain level of faith to believe that the thin metal enclosure was once painted; the color was a blind man's guess. On each side of the dashboard, where the "windshield" cage attempted to run along the hood of the cart, there was an opening as the curve of the vehicle led away from the right angle formed by the metal. The holes could easily be covered by the sole of a shoe, and my legs were just long enough at the time that I could reach to secure the gap. The problem, however, was that there were two of them—and a gas pedal. So in alternating intervals, I would enjoy the security of a 250-yard retreat away from the firing squad of wealthy white hackers, followed by an increasingly terrifying approach run into the teeth of high society. Time and again, I'd have to choose which hole to cover: left or right. At times, I'd consider driving spread eagle, covering both points of entry with my feet while reaching down to push the gas pedal with

---

1This is how amateur golfers stay amateur

my hand—but no, that was impossible. The crowd of yuppies whom I'd grown to despise would laugh at me. And my whole life, every broke teenager's life in Feasterville, was one long struggle not to be laughed at.

They didn't like me very much either, the patrons. When the collection baskets were filled, I would pull the cart in, transfer the balls into a large, gray garbage can and run them through the ball washer next to the tee boxes. Every now and then, someone would approach me with a big smile and strike up a conversation. They seemed genuinely friendly at first, but the small talk inevitably concluded with the request for a few extra balls. They'd tell me they just ended on a bad one and couldn't leave on a shot like that. Sometimes I'd oblige and shell out a handful, but that ended once I realized it just attracted more of them.[2] So I'd receive the courtesy of an eye roll and some sarcastic remark about the lacking importance of my job as they walked away. The general dislike between myself and most of the regulars was at a constant, resulting in mutual ignorance until one day when I was filling the washer and noticed a man a few feet away holding his driver.

"Sorry sir," I said, turning on the machine, "I'm not allowed to give you—"

"No, no. I don't need any balls," he interrupted. He looked nervous.

"Something else I can help you with then?"

"Yeah. I think I, uh, I think I hit one of 'em out there."

"Okay." I stared at him, confused. "Did it go straight?"

"No, not a ball. I mean, I—I think I hit one of them." He nodded toward the range. "A goose. I think I caught one in the neck."

"Oh."

"Yeah."

I walked over to the next stall so the cart wasn't in the way and made my hand into a visor, blocking the late afternoon sun and peering out over the field at a group of geese, one of which appeared to be either dead or very good at yoga. "Alright, hold on," I said.

---

[2] There's a striking comparison to be made here about the remarkable similarity in the relationships between homeless people and loose change, pigeons and crackers, and upper middleclass white men and golf balls, but we'll save that for another day.

Obviously, this sort of thing didn't happen very often. I jogged over to the pro shop where my boss, Bill Franklin, was fitting a customer for a new set of irons. My other boss, Joe Moretti, wasn't around or I would have gone to him. Bill was the one who probably qualified on paper to do the job, but lacked the interpersonal skills and common sense to manage an ice cream stand let alone a golf center. At six bucks an hour, there's just no need to make a kid wear khakis and a collared shirt to clean the goose shit off of yellow golf balls. I called him over and explained the situation.

"Alright," he said. The bell chimed above the door and another customer entered. "Ah, damn. Hang on." He went in the back office and returned with a shovel and a shoebox. "Here, you gotta handle that," he said, "There's a dumpster behind the offices across the little bridge. You know where I'm talking about?"

"Yeah," I said, confusedly.

"You got this, right?"

"Yeah. Yeah, sure," I said, still dazed. He gave me an Attaboy and a pat on the shoulder. Then he went to deal with the customer. I went outside with my—things.

I was fourteen years old, it was my first job, and I'd had it for all of three months. I didn't know any better. My understanding of a job was more likely to fall under the statutes of indentured servitude: boss tells employee what to do; employee does it; at the end of the agreed-upon time limit, employee is released.

The walk back to the cart felt—strange. That's the best I can describe it. I looked at the shovel like a foreign object that came with instructions but they were only in French. Looking at the size of the box, I wondered if my boss had ever actually seen a goose up close.

When I got to the cart, the man was still standing there holding his driver. He was staring at me. I said hello and he continued to stare. In retrospect, I now understand this stare to be one of disbelief that a fourteen-year-old was actually the one responsible for the disposal of animal carcasses.

People continued hitting as I pulled away. Most of them probably hadn't seen what had happened, and even if they had, it was understandable that they'd continue to hit. In my experience, they were all certifiable jerks anyway, and the death of a goose isn't exactly a big deal. That is unless maybe you're driving a golf cart out to scoop it into a fucking Footjoy box or something. Even then, it's just a goose, right?

Just beyond the 150-yard marker, I pulled a U-turn and stopped, covering up both holes with my feet, just in case. People kept hitting as the grief-stricken, golfing assassin made his way down the row to ask people to momentarily hold their fire.

It was rare that I had a moment to myself to just sit motionless out in the middle of the open field without any feeling of guilt over not staying busy. No motor running. No wheels turning. No clang of golf balls being flung into metal baskets. Just the soft sound of leaves blowing in distant trees and the occasional pitter patter of a ball landing, bouncing, rolling to a stop. Suddenly they didn't seem so threatening. The moment was almost perfect.

Through the X's of the metal grate, I stared out at the other geese, wondering why they were still standing there. *Hadn't any of them seen what just happened to Fred?* I shook my head and promised myself I would laugh if another one got hit just then. That might sound sick, but Darwinism-in-motion is pretty funny in that you-had-to-be-there kind of way.

The golfers had stopped and were staring out at me as I emerged from my fortified transport and fetched the shovel from the rear bed. The lid to the cardboard casket had blown open and I looked it over, studying it one last time, trying to figure out how to fit an adult goose inside it while avoiding any sort of impromptu dismemberment. After a short while, I found myself wondering how long it would be before someone grew impatient, teed one up, and hit *me* in the neck with a golf ball. *Do we have bigger boxes?* I grabbed the shovel and approached the goose.

It moved.

I didn't.

A lot happened in the next five seconds.

Up until it moved, I had assumed Bill had given me the shovel to transport the goose from the field to the box. But in those five seconds, my thoughts shifted.

At a young enough age, and in an honest moment, most kids would say they're used to being wrong about most things. They think adults know everything and that Dad is Superman. Thus, in a moment of distress, a young mind often prefers to simply lean on what it's been told; and that's just what I did. I was given a shovel and a shoebox and a "handle that."

So five seconds later, the words "handle that," had shifted from a request to dispose of a dead animal carcass to an order to kill a living creature with an archaic gardening tool, never intended for combat. I stood over the goose, making squeamish faces as it twitched and gurgled. There was a dark purple blood coming from its mouth in bubbles, which caught me off guard. The other geese had waddled away, apparently keeping a 15-yard rule of thumb regarding the minimum amount of space that should remain between oneself and a stranger suspiciously loitering about with a shovel. I looked up at the gallery of now very concerned golfers, waiting to see just what hell I was doing with that shovel. I knew I couldn't back out. It was my job, and I had already come into the public spotlight to execute it. I'd passed the point of no return.

What should not be overshadowed here by my decision to use a swift, downward stabbing motion resulting in decapitation via shovel in the spotlight of a setting Autumn sun, is the fact that I felt an overwhelming amount of sorrow for the animal and thought this the quickest way to end its suffering. It was a humane decision, which I made for all the right reasons, and I stand by that to this day.

It is a common misperception, however, that all it takes to decapitate a goose is the proverbial swift, downward stabbing motion via shovel in the spotlight of a setting Autumn sun. It lived. I tried to quickly remedy the situation with another attempt, but was again unsuccessful. The goose raged on. I didn't understand. It had been half dead and motionless upon my arrival, yet seemed to only gain strength with each besting of the dull-edged farming tool turned guillotine. A third attempt sent it violently flailing about, gurgling out some horrid sound which I can only assume was the goose equivalent of: *for hate's sake, I spit my last breath at thee!* The operation had collapsed to complete chaos—a failed murderous debacle. The bird could not be defeated. Tears of scattered emotion now streaming down my face, lost in the perfect storm of guilt, humiliation, and unfiltered panic, I took the shovel by the handle and using the blunt face of the incompetent weapon, wielded it like a large iron flyswatter, attempting to bludgeon the indestructible monster into submission, forcing a stalemate of unconsciousness.

Several swats later, I looked up with tired arms to a sea of golfers, some with their hands held over their mouths, others cupping their palms over the eyes of their children, and one man running at a dead sprint in my direction. It was Joe, my other boss. He had come back from his dinner break to find his range attendant slaying an animal in front of 30+ customers. I thought I was fired.

"Sorry. Sorry. It got hit in the neck with a ball."

"It's okay. You're okay," he said, out of breath and staring at the goose.

The foul, mangled beast lay there at my feet, alive but severely malfunctioning—frozen somewhere between life and death—dead but not yet deceased. There was as much life in him as can be found in the legs of centipede after being mashed between a sneaker and a bathroom tile; he was trapped in Orwell's lost land of bullet-riddled elephants, dying in agony but in a world detached from this one where not even the blunt end of a shovel could damage him further.

Joe laid the shovel down and took me back to the pro shop, and then he went back out to get the goose. He found a bigger box first.

When he got back, he kept apologizing, which, at fourteen, confused me.

"It was the right thing to do, right?"

"Yeah, kiddo, it was the right thing to do. Just the wrong person to do it, that's all. You okay?"

At the time, I didn't know what he meant by that. Of course *I* was okay. I wasn't the one getting clobbered with the damn shovel. I told him I was fine and he let me go home early after that.

In retrospect, I'm not sure if I was lying or telling the truth. At the time, it certainly felt like the truth: there wasn't a scratch on me and the whole thing felt like it was over in an instant. It wasn't something I'd wanted to do, and I certainly hadn't enjoyed doing it, but it was over—no more significant than eating vegetables. I'd killed a goose, but I really didn't feel much of anything. It didn't matter.

It didn't matter, yet a decade later, it's a story nearing 3,000 words. It didn't matter, yet every time I see a goose, I see the broken one. It didn't matter, yet I still remember the look on the man's face, the 'Size 12' on the side of the shoebox, the blood coming in purple bubbles—the weight of the shovel. Funny how hard it is to forget the things that don't matter.

I kept the job and in the two years following, I'd occasionally catch a stare from a golfer that had a distinct way about it and I'd know that he'd been there that day, staring out into the descending sun to see a silhouette of a young range attendant brutally clubbing a defenseless animal into oblivion. I like to imagine what must have gone through those golfers' heads—seeing what they saw, wondering what the hell happened to the youth in this country. It's what makes it impossible for me to tell this story without laughing. Death's nothing to joke about, but consider the alternative. After all, I'm not the one who can't hit a driver. But even if I was—just a goose, right?

Taylor Bush

The Impression That I Get

We had one rule for that day and one rule only, never spoken or written down, but fully understood by all five of us: no crying. That day was ours, the last of a million summer adventures, and when the morning would arrive one of our own would be taken away from us, but never under any circumstances, no matter what was said or how you felt inside, could a tear be shed. We were better than that.

I still go driving sometimes, late at night when The Universe exhumes a buried memory from the crypts of my mind, and I can feel that day perfectly, hear it in every note on the radio, see every part of it through my windshield like a cloud of smoke fogging up my vision, blocking out the rest of the world for a few infinite seconds before the defrosters kick in and it fades away along the breeze...

There we were, five friends marching along a route we had walked a million times before, through the muddy grass in the spring and across the noisy gravel on tiptoe those summer nights when we didn't want to be caught by the cops.

Tyler leads the charge, rubbing a wad of Skoal Long Cut Apple Blend Tobacco across his gums at all times. He makes me dump out my Aquafina so he can shoot his sticky wads into the empty water bottle when he's finished. Tyler's my best friend and yet there's always something irking me about him. He possesses the inverse component to every single one of my behavioral traits. While I was the taciturn injun dedicated to peaceful negotiations he was the brash gunslinger laying waste to dusty towns, shootin' first, pillaging later, swilling the finest of moonshine and bedding every harlot from here to the Wild Wild West. Growing up, he was always The Pusher, forcing me out of my carefully constructed comfort zone while I assumed the role of The Puller, holding him back from making one boneheaded mistake after another. He was the Huck Finn to my Tom Sawyer, the Dean Moriarty to my Sal Paradise.

Following behind us are Cody, Donna, and Kate. Cody's our team mascot. He only needs two things to survive: attention and any song with a bass-synth backbeat to grind against. Donna's the self-appointed mother of our group, the level-headed one who always knows how to get out of any situation, the one who's gonna be happily married before any of us have even graduated college. Kate, on the other hand, is a tough egg to crack. She's always playing a different role for us. Some days she's a nun, others she's a Lolita or a damsel-in-distress or a lieutenant or, hell, even a fairy godmother. My feelings for her ebb and flow, usually in tandem with the level of grace that she adopts for her latest character. But mostly we just straddle a strange demilitarized zone between friends and lovers.

We limbo beneath the gap in the iron-wrought gate and step into the horror movie vista where the question blossoming in each of our minds is *Who's gonna die first?* Cody's shaking like a sprung doorstop, knowing the fat kid's always the first to go and regretting the three tubs of queso dip he imbibed less than an hour ago at California Tortilla. We now walk along a dirt path that snakes through Linfield Distillery, an abandoned distilment factory that has become a rite-of-passage to visit for high-schoolers and college kids in and around the area of Pottstown, Pennsylvania. Our hearts are hammering inside our chests as our paranoia generates a constant symphony of imaginary police sirens within our heads. Could this really be the night the cops check the factory for stragglers? Every shake in the brush and silhouette in the shadows seems to hint at their imminent arrival.

Kate interlaces her fingers with mine while Donna and Cody latch onto each other. Tyler's the only brave one, walking with his head held high—the position he will one day assume on a battlefield with a rifle laid upon his shoulders. He leads us across the trenches, down a yawning ditch, around a vine-eaten shed, over broken shards of glass and through clumps of thorny weeds, all the while rambling on like a wound-up chatterbox as he smacks on his tobacco.

"We're not allowed to whack off at boot camp," he says. "They say it's for self-discipline or something. Before we ship off they're gonna give us these pills to suppress our hormones. Or is it our testosterone? One of the two. Anyway, they keep us from getting horny so it'll be easier not to touch ourselves for three months. No masturbating for a whole summer. Man, I'd take waterboarding over that any day. Imagine when I come back and rub one off though—it's gonna be like a volcanic eruption. And do you know how much I'm gonna get laid when I come home as a fresh marine? When I wear my fatigues around town, *whew*, all the girls are gonna be all over me!" I roll my eyes.

Tyler leads us behind a mammoth tower and pushes in a metal door. The dying sunlight filtering in through the shattered windows illuminates a shaft stretching up into the stratosphere. A dead bird covered in a sticky slime of blood and feathers lies on the dirty ground. We step over it carefully and charge up the winding metal staircase. Each sound we make echoes off the walls and consumes the shaft, all noises amplified by several decibel levels, every footfall an explosion, every spoken word a scream. Tyler continues to prattle on.

"So Taylor, you still writing that book?"

"Yeahsorta."

"What's that mean?"

"I don't know," I mumble. "I haven't written in a while. Kinda been blocked."

"What's tripping you up?"

I pull up my shirt and wipe the mask of sweat off my face. "My inspiration tank's running a little low. Along with my confidence. I'm not quite sure if I have the chops to reach the finish line."

"I once had an instructor with dragon breath yell in my face that I'd never have the chops to become a marine. But I've passed all the preliminary tests. And I'm gonna go off and carry a rifle and meet every challenge they throw my way because fuck the odds, man, this is what my heart's telling me to do. Ya catch what I'm throwing?"

"I guess so."

We've now arrived at the roof of the tower, the top of the world. Tyler steps out across the gravel and we all follow him. I can see his mood change across his face with every step he takes. He reaches the edge of the tower and stares out into the evening air. The navy blue sky is frosted with pasty clouds and tainted by the magic corona of that evening's perfect sunset. The bloody disk slowly dips towards the horizon.

I watch Tyler as he gazes out into the sunset, the vast world beneath him ripe with countless places to go and things to become. And I think about how he wants to give all that up to become a martyr. It's supposed to go high school, college, then The Real World. But here stands the antithesis to that algorithm. He never was the smartest at Pottsgrove High School (he couldn't even be bothered to put community college on his radar), but this certainly doesn't feel like the right solution to avoiding the land of higher education. I wonder what would happen if I push him off the side of the building right now. He'd fall ten stories and die, but would that be worse than taking shrapnel to the face or being blown to smithereens in a bomb blast?

Then it hits me that in a matter of hours I will have to say goodbye to him for the summer, possibly for good, and I have nothing prepared. How do you say goodbye to your best friend when words and feelings never quite link up the way you want them to?

Tyler spins around, his eyes now mute, somber, devoid of their usual energy. "I wish I could have this sunset forever," he mutters, "because things are never gonna be like this again." The music of the night is beginning to shift for him. "Not like tonight, ever."

The song changes. We're now crammed into my Jeep driving away from Linfield with the radio cranked up full blast. No one speaks because things are different tonight. It's the end of an era and that means all taboos are thrown out the window. Tonight it's all right to wear our shades even though it's dark out. Tonight it's legal to drive thirty-five miles over the speed limit. And tonight it's perfectly acceptable to blast the radio for the entire universe to hear. But we must still uphold that cardinal rule and spill no tears.

We're in the midst of arguing where to go next—the night is still young after all—when The Song comes blasting out of my radio and we all instantly hush, the opening brass strains serving as the only sounds capable of such a difficult feat. The song is The Mighty Mighty Bosstones' "The Impression That I Get," a musical panacea if ever there was one. There's no other song that gets my blood pumping at its mere mention, no other song with more memories of my life stitched into its notes. It gets me high whenever I feel low. It's the nexus of my life, connecting every plane of my twenty-year existence and marking every major emotional epoch, from middle school Sadie Hawkins speakers to graduation party stereos, from that first day I plugged in my Digimon soundtrack to those long summer nights getting drunk and dancing alone to Dicky Barrett's cigarette-and-beer-drenched brio with nothing but a shirt on. *Da da da da da dun dun dun!* Blam! It hits me right in the neck with its sonic dart and I'm incapacitated instantly. My friends and I are religious zealots subscribed to The Mighty Mighty Bosstones, but "The Impression That I Get" is our messiah. For three minutes and fifteen seconds the song surges through our bones, defibrillating our hearts and hijacking our off-key vocal chords. None of us have a care in the whole wide world.

When the song finishes Tyler proclaims, "To The Port-A-Potty!"

I can already sense what he's thinking next. Last Fourth of July after launching off fireworks in a parking lot, Cody, Tyler and I drove to a nearby soccer field and ended up attempting to topple a full-sized port-a-potty onto its side. Many attempts were made, and many muscles bruised, but in the end we never succeeded in knocking it over. But I can see that Tyler's got vengeance on his mind tonight.

We bounce over to the soccer field and park as far away from the road and the scope of a cop's headlights as we can. The girls stand back at the car while the boys resume where we left off last summer, bodyslamming ourselves into the seemingly invincible porta-potty. A year has passed, but despite the weight and strength the three of us have gained, the porta-potty endures our blows like an indestructible capsule. Tyler and I even try pushing against it while Cody charges like a boulder into its back, but it holds its own.

Sweating, and feeling like a Mack truck just collided with our shoulders, we call for the girls. They refuse. Tyler goes to talk to them. I'm not sure what he says, but it must be something convincing because a minute later they're at the porta-potty. We hatch a plan: the girls, along with a drained Cody, will try their hand at pushing against the porta-potty while Tyler and I will lead a charge from the top of the hill, hopefully summoning enough momentum to topple over the portaloo bastion.

Tyler and I stand at the Jeep waiting for the girls to count to three.

"One!"

I turn to Tyler. "You scared?"

He knows I'm not referring to tipping over a porta-potty. After a second, he nods. "Tomorrow's like dying."

"Not necessarily."

"Two!"

He hawks a wad of tobacco into the grass. "I mean that I don't exist after tomorrow. You always make plans for what you're going to do for next week or in a couple days or next month, but now I have nothing to look forward to."

"No," I tell him. "You have something *huge* to look forward to. But you got a whole night before that comes."

"Three!"

We share a look of painful understanding. Then we're off and running, stripped of our cares, two boys, a stampede of elephants, screaming our lungs out, beating our chests dramatically. Faster, faster. Not even the explosion of red-blue police lights invading the darkness could slow our advance now. We reach the porta-potty, leap into the air, channel all of our weight into our shoulders and strike its back. THUD! We ricochet into the grass as the beast begins to lurch. It's going...going...GONE! We hear a gurgling splash as the porta-potty faceplants onto the ground. And the crowd goes *wild!* We're hooping and hollering and high-fiving, Tyler flying around like an airplane, all of us too drunk on the night to care if the cops show up at this point.

Tyler, Cody and I converge in a three-way chest bump as the girls procure a bottle of Smirnoff from the back of the Jeep. No shot glasses? No problem. Tyler flips over his tobacco-filled water bottle and draws a line of vodka across the side. Next thing I know he's taking it up his nose and we're all losing our minds. Cody, always the choir nerd wanting to sit at the head of the cool kids' table, follows suit. The girls opt for a more conventional approach and start taking shots straight from the bottle. Tyler attempts to coerce me into snorting some vodka, but I keep my blanket of teetotalism wrapped firmly around myself.

"Come on, ya puss!" he barks. "It's my last night. Do it for me! It gets you drunk so much faster."

My pulse is running. Tyler draws another line. I can hear the far-off din of the studio audience cheering. I nosedive. Sniff, sniff, sniff. POW! Back up for air. My right nostril feels like a firework just exploded inside of it. I certainly don't feel any drunker. My eyes are watering and I'm spinning. The peanut gallery behind me chuckles like hyenas.

We leave Linfield and head back to Tyler's house where his parents are fast asleep and his refrigerator is well stocked. Tyler takes me up to his room to give me something. He grabs a black G-shock watch off his bureau and chucks it at me. I catch it at the last minute and check the time. 23:11?

"Isn't this your watch?"

"Nah." He holds up a shiny silver watch. "Got a new one. I want you to have that one and wear it every day while I'm gone."

"It's on military time. How do you change it?"

"Don't," he says. "I synced them up. This way when I leave, you might not know where I am in the world, but you'll always know what time I'm on."

I thank him and we return to our friends. I still don't know how to say goodbye.

Like a song, the rest of the night comes to me in a progression of sensations and images. Tyler revs up the heating system of his pool, but none of us brought bathing suits. But nothing can deter us from our fun tonight. I strip down to my boxers and cannonball into the night. We throw on music, play "The Impression That I Get" at least a thousand times. '90s ska-core and bad pop music provide the soundtrack to our revelry for the rest of the night.

I still see it all. Floating in the pool, each of us toasting the summer with a beer can. Green bra straps. Sunburnt skin in the moonlight. Kate. Dripping wet. Her mermaid eyes sparkling up at me. The warmth of those hot tub jets. Kate, dancing in my lap, running her fingers through my wet beard. Kate, pressing her hands against my dripping chest and leaning in for a kiss. I can still taste the way she blew her minty breath into my lungs. Ah, bliss. My head throbs. My bones quiver. And I just want to be her Elvis. As the colors melt together, the two of us become baptized beneath The Music and The Night and The Summer and The Universe.

We turn and see Tyler and Donna back by the pool house. Their lips are locked and her *I want you* hands are running across his back. She'll be his last conquest before he leaves. I'm not sure if I'm proud. They disappear. Cody's practically incapacitated, knocking back his ninth shot beneath the deck table. Kate and I continue dancing in our underwear until the night collapses.

The next morning arrives like a static-filled radio transmission. Through the white noise, the apostles and I gather in the kitchen to have The Last Breakfast together. Donna's the first to leave, opting for a private moment with Tyler to pay her final respects. Then it's Cody's turn. Then Kate's. Then it's just Tyler and me at the foot of his driveway, at the end of five years' worth of porta-potty tippings and distillery adventures, with my equivocal goodbye still gestating inside my mental incubator.

"You know, it's not too late to tell me this is all just one big joke," I say hopelessly.

"No, this is it," he says with a laugh. He clamps his hand down on my shoulder. "Everything changes after this. You better write me every week. And never take off that watch. And try to have fun without me this summer. I know it'll be hard."

That's when the dam breaks. I want to tell him that I think he's wrong. That he's no martyr, but a selfish megalomaniac. He thinks he's sacrificing his life for the lives of millions, but what about all the other lives that'll be destroyed if he dies? What about us? His mom? His sister? His friends? Once he leaves, it's only a matter of time before all the memories fade along with him. If he never comes back then this place will forever feel deficient, a ghost town barbed with regrets, and our summers will be lost forever.

The words come out a little differently than I had them written in my head: "I'm proud of you, Tyler."

He hugs me. I can feel the anxiety radiating off his skin.

"You always get to do the things that I only sit at home and write about," I tell him.

"And you always put into words the things I don't know how to say."

"Don't die." It's the only thing I can think of to say next. "And don't lip off to any of your instructors. I won't be around anymore to make sure you behave yourself."

We pull out of the hug and look at each other.

"Listen," he says, "if I'm gonna fight to make it home in one piece then that book better be ready for me to read by the time I get back."

I try to draw up an image of how he'll look once he returns. Jacked up. An eye missing. Perhaps a robotic arm. PTSD boiling in his eyes. "As long as you come back exactly the same as you are now," I tell him.

"Do you still need to find your ending?"

"Nah, I think you just gave it to me." I salute him with the hand his watch is now strapped to. "Come back with lots of stories for me, alright?"

"I'll do my best. And *pray* that those pills don't make my weiner fall off."

We share one last laugh together, the finale to the thousands that came before it. Then I get into my Jeep, sit in silence for a moment and let the past couple hours sink in. *He's gone.* I turn on "The Impression That I Get" because I'm going to need it to find my way home. But at his neighborhood's stop sign I turn left and head in the opposite direction of my house. It's a disgustingly beautiful day outside and I curse Life louder and louder with every mile I clear. On the return journey I drive by Tyler's house even though I know he's gone. I turn right at the stop sign this time. Suddenly my stomach starts to tense up and no matter how hard I try to fight it, everything that I couldn't express the last day spills out of me.

Then I bawl like a baby the entire drive home.

Colleen McLaughlin

Thanksgiving Relapse

It's morning. I know it's morning, but I don't want to open my eyes. When I do, I'll know for sure that I'm not waking up in my dorm room. I won't be lying in an extra-long twin bed raised impractically high in order to accommodate the mini fridge and storage bins that otherwise won't fit in the tiny two-person standard room. When I open my eyes, I'll be back home. In the same bedroom that, until three months ago, I've slept in for roughly the past eighteen years of my existence. It's my first morning back home since I left for college. It also happens to be Thanksgiving morning. And I would give anything to stay asleep for the rest of my life, as long as it meant skipping today.

Thanksgiving used to be a wonderful holiday. My entire family, on both of my parents' sides, would come to our house. I have a fairly large family; my mom has two siblings and my dad has three. Of these aunts and uncles, all of them are married and almost all of them have children of their own. That makes me one of twelve cousins. My house was always packed on Thanksgiving, and was full of food, games, and traditions.

And it still is. This year will be exactly the same as it has been every other year. On the surface, nothing has changed. But I have. Eighteen years. Eighteen Thanksgivings. Out of those, I've spent eighteen of them with bipolar disorder, five of them with an eating disorder, four of them with social anxiety disorder, two of them with self-harm, and god knows how many with borderline personality disorder. I've spent the majority of these Thanksgivings covering up my problems, lying to my family and myself that I was okay.

But in the span of one year I managed to turn my life around. Last December, after countless serious considerations of pouring drain cleaner down my throat, I figured it couldn't get much worse than this. So I spent an hour sobbing on the bathroom floor with my Mom, and the next day I was whisked into eight months of psychiatrists, therapists, nutritionists, recovery programs, and whoever else made up my ever-increasing treatment team. I emerged a new person. Armed with coping techniques, mental survival skills, medication, and the slightest hint of confidence, I went off to college with big plans, finally excited about my future.

My first three months away at school were fantastic. It was as if everything you read in those cheesy college brochures was actually right. Instead of floating through the halls with a blank stare on my face, I looked forward to going to class each day. Instead of coasting on relationships I built up in my pre-teens, I made new friends who actually enjoyed my company. My laughter was genuine, I was able to talk to people, I was doing well in life. I couldn't believe it was real. It wasn't.

I spent three months on a mental high—a vacation away from all my disorders. I thought I had gotten rid of them, that they were gone forever and I was finally free. I can't believe how foolish I was.

Being mentally sick isn't like being physically sick. Some parts are similar, sure. Whether you "come down" with an illness or not is never in your control. Sometimes it's genetic, sometimes it's developed, or learned. Don't worry, it's not contagious. I once heard that people with eating disorders are born with a gun, and life pulls the trigger. I will always have one. Even if I'm a recovering anorexic, I'm still an anorexic. It'll never go away, always lingering in the back of my mind. After recovery, the disease can stay dormant for months, or even years. But some days, like this Thanksgiving, it can slither forward to remind me it's still there and that it's not going anywhere. It's just my luck that I hit the jackpot when it comes to mental disorders. I was awarded a number of them, all wrapped up neatly into the single care package of my brain. Mini relapses happen all the time, there are good days and bad days, just like with anything. But that doesn't make it suck any less. And today was going to be one of the hardest to get through.

Returning home was like returning to my old self. I wasn't just going back to a place, I was going back to a mindset. Everything around me was horribly familiar—the paisley comforter on my bed, the birch wood cabinets in the kitchen, the lightly stained floral rug in the living room—all reminded me of how things used to be.

These thoughts run through my mind as I lie in bed, still refusing to open my eyes.

I hear her small feet running down the hall before she bursts through the door.

"Colleen! Colleen! Wake up!"

There's no hope of eternal sleep now. Even if I pretend to still be asleep, she won't stop until I'm out of bed. SLAM! I feel her small body crash down onto me. I open my eyes. My view is obstructed by the excited round face of my eight-year-old cousin, Danielle.

"Good morning, Snooch," I lie as I try to sit up.

Despite being a bit too chubby for a typical girl her age, she's nothing compared to the heavy anvil of dread that weighs me down already. Her exhilaration fails to spread into me, but I refuse to do anything that will make her smile disappear.

I follow Danielle into the kitchen. Her family has slept over at my house the night before Thanksgiving since long before she was even born. Dad and Aunt Kathy are making breakfast. Abigail, Danielle's twin sister, sits at the table, already devouring a stack of blueberry pancakes. She looks up as I enter and opens her pancake-stuffed mouth to say something incomprehensible. Dad turns around, frying pan in hand, and offers a "Good morning, Beena!" as he flips over a Mickey Mouse shaped pancake. Aunt Kathy asks me what I want in mine.

When I was younger, before food became the enemy, I used to love making pancakes with my Dad. He'd let me add whatever I wanted into them: chocolate chips, strawberries, bananas, cinnamon, marshmallows, peanut butter. Nothing was off limits. That was a long time ago. I stopped cooking when the ingredients of everything I made started to include shame. But we always eat pancakes Thanksgiving morning, and I'm supposed to be better now. I plaster on my award-winning smile.

"Plain please."

I walk out of the kitchen and into the bathroom, hoping one of the twins snatches my plate while I'm in the shower.

The scalding hot water allows me to breathe calmly. It burns my skin, and I feel as if I'm melting. I convince myself that if I stand here long enough, I'll wash right down the drain along with the shampoo. But before that happens, my older sister Kaitlin is banging on the door, telling me I need to get out so she can take a shower.

Back in my room, I stand in front of the closet, unable to move. It's not uncommon for a teenage girl to have difficulty picking out an outfit. Slightly more uncommon is for a teenage girl to have a full-out breakdown over it. But not for me. I'm used to it by now; the panic that builds inside of me as I yank out each item of clothing, the inevitable hysteria caused by the frantic changing of blouses and leggings and sweaters and jeans. I'm sure it all seems hilarious from an outsider's point of view. This neurotic girl getting so worked up over a few stupid sweater-dresses. But it's different when you're the one with the self-esteem equivalent to a pudgy acne-prone thirteen-year-old who's always picked last for dodge ball. It's different when you're the one with an older sister whose supermodel figure looks gorgeous in absolutely everything she puts on. It's different when you're the one who gained thirty pounds in treatment since last Thanksgiving. I feel disgusting in every article of clothing I try to put on.

It's not about wishing I were skinnier. It's about wishing I wasn't a failure. Wishing I could come back home and have a genuine smile on my face, not the fake one I've put on for so long. It's about wishing my moods weren't still affected so drastically by something as dumb and pointless and inanimate as a scale.

I finally decide on something to wear, and pull myself together just in time to hear the doorbell ring. The rest of my family arrives during the next few hours. With every person that enters the door, the clock ticks a little bit slower. I'm drowning in a sea of holiday cheer, and nobody notices.

Every member of my family asks me the exact same questions. My responses are rehearsed.

"School? Oh it's going great. Yeah, I really love it."

It's not a lie. But it feels so hypocritical to be saying it with a smile that only I can tell is made of wax. I try to be active in the conversations, to stay interested in what each person says to me. But I've forgotten how much work it is to pretend I care about anything they say when all I want to do is crawl under a rock and never think about the world again. I guess once you find actual happiness, it's all the more difficult to fake it when it's gone.

I'm starting to feel pathetic. The same old "starving-children-in-Africa-and-everyone-else-on-the-planet-who's-less-fortunate-than-you" attack circles around my head. Some people don't get to see their families during the holidays, or don't have families at all. And I'm taking everything for granted because of something as lame as depression? But I can't help it. I'm weak. I'm no match against the power of self-doubt and hopelessness.

I successfully avoid the hors d'oeuvres all afternoon. Since leaving treatment, I've eaten proper meals at proper times. I get the designated amount of calories from each of the food groups. I know more about nutrition than the average health student. Realistically, one skipped meal isn't going to make a difference. But I want to feel empty—I *need* to feel empty.

A mind inhabited by an eating disorder becomes very twisted. I know food is life. I know I will die without it. But at the same time, I honestly believe it will destroy me. Of course the logic is flawed, but it's not always easy to operate on logic. During treatment, I had to relearn my ways of thinking. Sort of like re-teaching someone who learned their colors wrong. Green was blue and red was yellow. I know it's wrong, but it's been engraved inside of me for so long, it's difficult to see things any other way. On days like today, it's easier and more comforting to rely on my old methods.

Dinnertime. There are three tables in the dining room, all pushed together to make one long one with multiple tablecloths. Everyone squishes into their seats and begins to ladle food onto the fancy plates that make their annual debut once again. I fill mine, wondering how on earth I'm going to put this into my body. I don't see turkey or mashed potatoes or crescent rolls. All I see is calories. Calories being scooped out of the carrot bowl, calories being poured out of the gravy dish. The numbers fly through the air, adding up and up and up.

It's okay, Colleen. It's okay. You can do this. Don't worry. It's going to be all right. It's not a big deal. It's okay. You're all right. You can do this. I take a deep breath.

"Colleen, can you pass me the cranberry sauce?"

Danielle sits across from me, happy to be sitting at the big kid's table. I plop some of the strange maroon jello-like food onto her plate, hoping she doesn't actually think it's jello, in which case she's in for a surprise. I watch Danielle serve herself at least one of everything at the table. She happily spoons onto her plate things that make me cower in fear, and thinks nothing of it.

I want her to stay this happy forever. I don't want her to grow up and feel bad about herself. I want her do things because they're fun, and eat things because they're delicious. I don't want her to compete with Abigail like I do with my sister, or worry about trying to be perfect all the time. She's not going to stay a kid forever, that's impossible. Thanksgiving won't always be as fun for her as it is today. But right now she's content enough to eat an extra helping of potatoes. And as insignificant as that may be, it means something.

I'm not saying everything's fine, because it's not. There are going to be bad days. Certain things will always be more difficult for me than other people. But I'm in a different place than I was last year, or the year before that. And next year will be different too.

I pick up my fork and begin to eat.

Shelby Vittek

Living in a Bittersweet Paradise

We were floating above a school of angelfish, watching them gingerly peck away at the complex fluorescent coral below, when a sudden commotion in the water caused them to disperse in every direction. I popped my head up, spat out my snorkel, and turned to see a woman treading water alone and flailing her arms in the air. "Somebody help me!" She yelled, "Anybody, help me!"

My younger sister, Lindsay, and I hurriedly paddled the short distance over to the distressed snorkeler, but as we got closer, it became evident that she wasn't in any life-threatening danger. The clear, turquoise waters were not infested with any man-eating sharks. The woman was not a diver whose tank had just run out of air. And she didn't appear to be drowning.

There was, however, a small amount of blood trickling down her left ring finger. "It bit me!" She exclaimed. "The thing came out of nowhere and tried to eat my wedding ring!"

I glanced over at Lindsay and could see her eyes rolling up towards the sky behind the fog of her goggles. "Well, everybody knows the most important rule to follow while snorkeling is to not wear any jewelry," she said with little remorse in her voice. "Barracudas love sparkly things."

The woman continued to whine about her bloody finger, eventually leaving us to swim ashore and continue the dramatic performance for her husband. I shook my head and laughed before adjusting my snorkel and heading back over to the reef. "Ha, stupid tourists." No matter where you went, it was impossible to avoid them.

I can't remember a time that there was ever a shortage of outsiders on the island. Grand Cayman was a popular tropical getaway destination, with a tourist population that often surpassed the amount of residents living there. They polluted the best beaches, lying scrunched up towel-to-towel. When they took beginners lessons in scuba diving, it wasn't in the sea, but rather in a resort's chlorine pool. And instead of eating fresh-caught fish or authentic jerk chicken at a local restaurant, the cruise shippers often flocked to the Hard Rock Café for a burger with fries.

The constant infestation of vacationers hadn't always aggravated me. There was a time when fish nibbled at my fingers as I snorkeled too, when I was as much of a stranger to the island as they were. My family moved to Grand Cayman over the summer of my eighth birthday, after my father was offered a job on the tiny island. Eager for a change, my mother persuaded him to jump on the opportunity, saying that it was "a sign of good things to come." There was, after all, a very convincing tropical fruit basket that accompanied the offer.

So we sold our house by the murky Chesapeake Bay and upgraded to the crystal clear Caribbean waters. Shortly after our one-way plane tickets had been purchased, we landed in paradise, joining the large population of outsiders. And while we weren't typical vacationing tourists, we were far from being locals.

Just like every new visitor did, we reveled in the unfamiliar beauty of the island. My sister and I held green sea turtles above their tanks at the turtle farm, where they were raised before being released back into the sea. Their arms flapped wildly against our hands as they desperately tried to break free of our grasp. We sent our cousins postcards from Hell, a busy sightseeing attraction that was nothing more than a plot of charred limestone the size of a small soccer field.

On weekends we used our American appearances to carefully sneak into lavish resorts with private beaches and swim-up pool bars. One Saturday, when we were rushing toward the side entrance of a resort, my mother told us to slow down and wait for her. I stood underneath the shade of a tall palm tree in a blazing orange full-piece bathing suit that clashed terribly with my fiery red hair. "Just grab one of the courtesy towels in the hallway on our way in," she whispered into our ears with a wide grin on her face, "and they'll never know we don't belong." Once safely inside, Lindsay and I charmed the bartenders at the swim-up bars with our innocent smiles. Exposing my gapped front teeth, I asked, "Can we both have strawberry daiquiris?"

"And make sure it's virgin," she added, even though she hadn't even the slightest idea what that meant. The bartender chuckled as he turned around to add juices and ice to the blender.

But day-to-day island living wasn't always as luxurious as our weekend outings to upscale resorts. As summer came to a close, we rushed to find a school that would enroll us. There wasn't a public school system for temporary residents living there under a work permit. Any native had access to whichever school they wanted, but my parents had no choice but to pay an outrageous amount for our education. Conveniently, the catholic school across the street from our condo was desperate for money and quickly found two spaces for new students.

Many placement tests and plaid uniform fittings later, I sat in a classroom full of dark-skinned locals. Awkwardly tall with pale skin, freckles, and red hair, I stood terribly out of place. Instead of participating in activities like science fairs and singing songs about the first 42 presidents of the United States, I spent the school day playing Oregon Trail with my classmates and smashing coconuts over protruding rocks of limestone on the playground.

"What's an Oregon?" one of my classmates asked. Another replied, "Something in America." I rolled my eyes and grunted, "It's a state, part of the United States," and was met with a sea of blank stares.

I was once asked to write a simple report about the history of the Carib tribes. My mother took me to the public library, a historic shack that may have easily been one of the oldest buildings on the island. We wandered up and down the narrow aisles before finding the right reference books to pull from the shelves. I carried them over to a table, where I sat down and turned to the index of the first one, tracing my finger down the page until I found "Caribs." I flipped to the corresponding section, first reading about Christopher Columbus and his discovery of the island, followed by a description of the native tribes that practiced cannibalism. I had never heard of the word before. "What are cannibals, Mom?"

Her eyes widened with horror. "What are they trying to teach you?" Before reaching over and grabbing the book from me, she spoke softly, "That means that they used to eat the flesh of other humans." The very next day I asked my teacher for a new topic.

It didn't take long for us to notice that we were living in a country whose economy relied heavily on its tourism industry. The tiny island was designed only to impress its wealthy guests, with little concern for the quality of life for its residents. Access to even the smallest, most basic necessities was limited.

At the time, I was sprouting faster than grass does in the summer, quickly growing out of every outfit I owned. Not wanting me to have a wardrobe that consisted of only pastel colored souvenir shirts and cheap beach flip-flops, my mother took me to look for clothes at the local "Cay-Mart." It first appeared to be similar to the supercenters I was used to shopping at in the States, with fully stocked shelves behind the enticing window displays. But as we entered, I saw that the aisles were filled at random with beach balls, hammers, and bulk boxes of processed cookies. "Excuse me," she grabbed the attention of the man sitting behind the one and only register, "Where is your clothing section?"

He laughed at her ignorance. "Lady, if you're looking for something more than what you see in those tourist gift shops in town, you're gonna have to leave the island to find it."

Shopping for clothes wasn't the only hurdle we faced. If a type of food couldn't be caught in the sea or found on the island, it had to travel far to get there. And once it did, its level of freshness was questionable. Most trips to the grocery store were paired with humiliation when my mother sniffed out every package of meat as I pushed the cart behind her. "You're so embarrassing," I whined to her as other shoppers glared at us with disapproving looks on their faces. Nose deep in the middle of a pound of ground beef, she looked up at me and my sister and replied, "Unless you want food poisoning with your dinner tonight, you better get used to it."

At some point, though I don't know if it was a few months or closer to a year after the move, my parents' marriage began to fall apart. My father began spending more and more time at his office, working on multiple projects with approaching deadlines. Late one night, I was woken up by an argument brewing in the bedroom next to mine. I did my best to ignore my father's demeaning tone, but a loud crashing sound that followed made it difficult to do so. That night I cried myself to sleep, in sync with my mother's sobs on the other side of the wall.

As tension built higher inside our tiny rental condo, our family outings became a thing of the past. My father rarely left his office and my mother spent every night in a bed sleeping alongside one of her daughters. It was heartbreaking to watch my parents drift apart. Even being surrounded by the most beautiful beaches in the world couldn't save their relationship.

Not knowing how to handle the situation, Lindsay and I did what we knew best, and returned to the familiar tourist-ridden beachside resorts on our bikes. As we approached the lobby of the Hyatt, I took on the cautious role my mother usually played. "Remember, we have to pretend like we've never swam in this pool before." Lindsay nodded. "And if anybody asks us where our parents are, we tell them they walked out to the beach to go for a swim."

We sat in the powdery soft sand among all the foreign vacationers. Parents generously lathered sunscreen on their children before helping them build the perfect sand castles. Families swam in the shallow water, playfully splashing water at one another. Couples relaxed on the beach, holding a drink in one hand, and their partner's hand in the other. As I watched these tourists I saw how joyful being in paradise made them. I envied their happiness, and wanted nothing more than for my idea of paradise to be as carefree as theirs.

My mother had been wrong about the good things to come. Just two years after moving to Grand Cayman, we packed up the contents of our lives into suitcases, and bought one-way tickets back to the States. In the end, the island remained a land built for tourists, polished and glossy on the surface, with nothing of substance hidden underneath. We may have inhabited it briefly, but we always remained outsiders—caught between two worlds, never belonging fully to either.

Elizabeth Galib

Dear Future Husband Applicant:

Thank you for your interest in applying for the position as my future husband. I want to express my gratitude for your interest in looking out for our marriage, our future, and our credit card bills, which could possibly be a result of my extravagant lifestyle. As you know, you are one of many competing for only one position, which promises a loving, caring, and demanding future with me. Forever. Your application will only be considered once you have indicated your knowledge of the following terms and conditions, by signing and dating below.

In addition to this form, the second step of the application process requires an essay or video (attached separately) distinguishing yourself with your unique and positive character traits. The following questions are prompts: How do you stand out? (Answer: you are over 6 feet, with a muscular build. If not, please stop reading here and retrace your steps to the exit). What are your skills and talents? (Ans: you are a fitness, health, and sports buff. Athletes such as yourself display a chiseled body with washboard abs, carved by Michaelangelo himself. You understand and appreciate music, and are willing to sacrifice your favorite artists in exchange for mine: Disney soundtracks, Selena Gomez, Nsync, and Nikki Minaj). What makes you different? (Ans: you will learn to read and understand the complexity of my mind. You may think you have the extraordinary gift of insight into the female brain, but they failed to tell you in med school that in addition to the female race, there is me.)

Required materials to be submitted with the essay or video include: a minimum of two un-airbrushed topless photos, a recorded orchestral composition or song displaying operatic or classical training, SAT scores, high school diploma, college degree and GPA, MCATS, LSATS, et cetera.

Please read the terms and conditions below describing the position for which you are applying:

1. Considering my highly irritable state of being, due to my attentiveness to details and miniscule sounds that are not easily heard by the average human eardrum, it is advised that for the duration of our marriage (forever), you will refrain from superfluous and extraneous noises such as: heavy breathing, snoring, chewing, crunching, unwrapping plastic wrappers, bubble gum

popping, loud teeth brushing and flossing, off-key singing or humming, sipping or slurping, unwanted bodily sounds, et cetera. This list is subject to expansion at my convenience.

2. I have enforced a "no touch" policy on my hair and face. I invest a large portion of my morning in aesthetically enhancing my long, brown locks, acne-free ivory skin, dusty rose lip pout, thick and long fluttering eyelashes, and perfectly arched eyebrows, that to have this work of art disgraced by the oily hands of the male species would simply ruin the masterpiece and is strictly unacceptable.

3. There are five days out of every month that I am permitted to temporarily forgo our marriage, and focus on myself and my wellbeing. Throughout these five days, I am to have unrestricted access to Midol, hot water bottles, tissues, carbohydrates, romance novels and movies. Your judgments are not included on this list. Arguments or negative discussions during this five-day period will result in tampons being placed elsewhere, to achieve my desired silence. It will be uncomfortable. Therefore, a positive attitude with empathy and love is required. Sympathy gifts are encouraged, and include but are not limited to: heels, jewelry, bags, hats, make-up, carbohydrates, et cetera.

4. I am an excellent, hard working cook, baker, and cleaner—when I want to be. However, such hard work merits leisurely activities. My off days are Sunday, Monday, Tuesday, Wednesday, Thursday, Friday and Saturday. Should a dire situation arise, you may find me at any of the following stores: Pretty Nails, Ulta, Guess, Fredericks of Hollywood, Victoria's Secret, Anne Taylor, Armani, Love Culture, Dior, Forever 21, Gucci, Brooks Brothers, JCrew, Prada, Coach, Fendi, Sephora, M.A.C., Versace, Polo Ralph Lauren, Chanel, Marc Jacobs, and other brand name stores. Any questions pertaining to credit card bills will be ignored, as you can view the expenses at the end of the month. Due to my extensively full schedule, it is crucial that you be at least on par with, or better than, my level of skill in the areas of housework stated above, should I ever become overwhelmed in the many challenging tasks presented to me.

5. I am very strict with my fitness and nutritional regime. This is top priority in my life, and is not to be questioned, judged, or downgraded. Yes, my trainer is over 6 feet, has a chiseled body and washboard abs. Yes, I flirt. Please commit my fitness regime to memory:

    a. Sundays: off

    b. Mondays: 20-30 minutes cardio, 45-60 minutes weight
       lifting

c. Tuesdays: 20-30 minutes cardio and boxing rounds

d. Wednesdays: 20-30 minutes cardio, 45-60 minutes weight lifting

e. Thursdays: 20-30 minutes cardio and boxing rounds

f. Fridays: 20-30 minutes cardio, 45-60 minutes weight lifting

g. Saturdays: 20-30 minutes cardio and boxing rounds

*I must ingest a high protein meal (in the form of whey isolate) and fast–acting carbohydrates (preferably fruit) right after my workout is completed. The meal is to be anxiously awaiting my return home from the gym. It is cooked by you.

6. Additionally, please commit my favorite foods to memory: Chinese food, specifically sesame or General Tso's chicken, lo mein noodles, brown rice, dumplings, spring rolls, and avocado or vegetable sushi. Thai food, specifically steak in teriyaki sauce, chicken and vegetables in curry sauce. Pizza, made with whole-wheat crust, low fat cheese, a garden of vegetables, pineapples, and ham. Pasta, made with Asian shiritaki noodles and a light creamy sauce, preferably one by Classico found at your local supermarket (please note that this type of pasta repels red sauces). Grilled chicken salads, dressing on the side. Always. Peanut butter, with added cinnamon, maple syrup, and vanilla flavoring. Fage Greek Yogurt, the brand that has traveled thousands of miles in turbulent air flow and unpredictable weather to fulfill the only two purposes of its existence: to bring the manna from the Greek gods into my stomach; and to make my otherwise dull, all-American lifestyle a little more European, in exchange for a thinner wallet. Well, your wallet. I am not a chocolate fan: any sort of chocolate received on holidays shall be taken with extreme offense, and returned immediately.

7. In the likely event that I will be carrying my own mini-me, whom I have taken the liberty of pre-naming "Samantha," I require your undivided attention at all times throughout the 9 months to ensure the following: I can still walk comfortably in heels, wear my size 0 jeans, and indulge in a double fudge brownie at 4 am, while madly cursing Poseidon for tearing apart the beautiful romance of Jack and Rose on the night of April 14, 1912. When the neighbors complain of loud emotional outbursts, simply hand them an information brochure of Timbuktu; I hear it is quite peaceful and free of hormonally imbalanced pregnant women. Actually, on second thought, it is your responsibility to only allow me to indulge in healthy foods, prevent weight gain, and ensure a healthy mini-me.

8. My collection of heels, jewelry, hats, and bags must not be touched or tampered with, as they bear great personal significance and serve as a medium for art and expression. Should you decide to splurge your hard-earned money from your medical practice to expand my collection for the advancement of my self-expression, you are highly encouraged to do so. Your services are always welcomed and greatly appreciated.

8.5. On third thought, cocoa powder is healthy; therefore, a double fudge brownie is healthy.

9. The ability to carry deep, philosophical and psychological discussions is crucial to maintaining healthy communication. Topics include, but are not limited to: the deepest secrets of life, elements that comprise one's identity, physiology's significance in dictating gender roles in society, developmental changes in behavioral patterns, failure's significance, a guilt-tripper's mindset, reverse psychology's useful (or abusive) power, the location of King Triton's Kingdom under the sea, the ingredients to concoct a potion to transform into a mermaid, useful bargaining tactics and techniques to practice on a mini-cooper salesman, pros and cons of acrylic nails versus gel nails, Solia tourmaline ceramic flat iron versus the Chi ceramic flat iron, and probability of Maybelline 24 Hour Super Stay Lip Color paling in comparison to Max Factor Lipfinity Lip Matte. And lastly, which heel to wear on my next night out. Just to name a few.

10. I do not apologize in advance for any potential outbreaks, arguments, and/or fights. Should these happen, I declare ownership of the bedroom, kitchen, and bathroom, while I await your apology. According to Ronald T. Kellogg's Second Edition Advanced Cognitive Psychology book, there is a 99.75% chance that the average woman will sincerely accept a man's apology, and forgive all grudges. However, since I am not the average woman, this percentage has been reduced to 3.74%. But, I encourage you to remain positive and hopeful, because 3.74% is still greater than 0%.

10.5. Peanuts are healthy; therefore, snickers bars are healthy. Just saying.

11. I have the right to know your exact location and company at all times. In the unlikely event that I find unauthorized relations or interactions with unknown females, I will investigate the matter with interrogation, and examination of all technologically socially connecting devices, including but not limited to: cell phone, Facebook, emails, etc. And do not use the excuse of having a female boss. You are a self–employed doctor. Also, please buy our mini dog a new shock collar, as her current one will be around your neck, for your own protection, out of my deepest love. You'll thank me later.

12. If I gain weight, it's your fault. Please have easily accessible money set aside for when I splurge on the latest fad diet.

By submitting this application, I, _____, have read and agree to the terms and conditions above on _____/_____/_____. If chosen, I will abide by them for the duration of the marriage. Forever.

Printed_____

Signature_____

Kerri Sullivan

A Reflection On My Paranoid and Highly Secured High School

Someone fell down the stairs today and there was blood everywhere. This should probably be a major concern for the administration (especially considering the recent outbreak of MRSA), but they instead occupied themselves with the all-important matter of student IDs. See, the catastrophe is that the boy who fell down the stairs wasn't wearing his ID. So for the first ten minutes, no one was sure who he was. Was he a teacher, terrorist, student, janitor, registered sex offender, bus driver, suicide bomber, a member of the marching band, or a drug dealer?

One student tried to save the administration time by revealing the boy's identity. "I'm telling you, it's Casey Perez—I was standing right in front of him... we were talking moments earlier...I *know* it's him!"

"That's a very nice story, Leslie, but we need you to go back to class," the principal told her.

"I'm just trying to help! You're not doing anything," she said, "He's passed out unconscious and bleeding to death and you're checking his bag for a gun?"

"We're not checking for a gun," one of the other administrators said. "We're looking to see if he has his student ID. If we can't find one, *then* we'll look for the gun. But if we happen to stumble upon a gun, then we'll take care of that matter immediately."

Leslie rolled her eyes and jumped over the pool of blood. She rushed off to her next class, leaving smudged, bloody Uggprints as she left.

While the suspected terrorist/possible student/alleged Casey Perez lay unconscious, someone finally found his ID—that all-knowing piece of plastic that informed them that the body belonged to Mark Terrace. He was not a terrorist, didn't deal drugs, nor was he a sex offender (registered or otherwise). He was, however, a member of the school marching band, and this concerned the administrators very much. "There's a jazz band concert tonight! They need their solo trumpet player!" And so, Mark was rushed off to the nearest hospital while someone broke the news to the band teacher. His parents were also notified.

***

Aimee Henderson, a junior, left her fourth-period geometry class to visit the school nurse. She felt like she was moments away from throwing up, and wanted to sit down for a little while. Or maybe get an aspirin. When she reached the door, she saw a sign that read, "NO PASS, NO ID, NO MEDICAL HELP." She tried to open the door, but it was locked. She knocked. Several moments passed, and she looked awkwardly at the colorful array of pamphlets warning students about the dangers of sharing things—from pencils (you never know if they chew on the erasers!) to clean gym clothes (this is how people get MRSA!) Then, a small slot opened up and the school nurse peered at her through it. "Do you have a pass?" she asked. Aimee held it up. "Do you have an ID?"

"I switched purses last night and left it in my other one," she admitted with ashamed, downcast eyes. "But, I'm really, really sick," she said. "I'm going to throw up."

Upon her failure to display proper student ID, Aimee sealed her fate. The nurse said, "I'm sorry, but due to the common occurrence of random people coming in off the street and needing band aids, we don't allow anyone in without a student ID."

"I can show you my schedule, my homework, anything! I go to school here!" Aimee begged, but the little slot soon slammed shut and left her once again awkwardly standing in the hall. She looked at a brochure that said "1,001 Things That Are Killing You Right Now, and What You Can Do to Stop (Some of) It" and threw up right there, in the middle of the hallway. She banged on the door, yelled, "I told you so!" and wandered back to geometry.

***

Leslie sat in English, tapping her pencil on her desk impatiently. She glanced periodically at the door to see if Casey would enter, but he didn't. "Hey Leslie? Can I borrow that pencil?" Mark Terrace asked her. "I'm marking my sheet music for tonight's concert."

Just as Leslie was about to hand him the writing utensil, another student stopped her. "No! Don't share pencils! What's wrong with you? Don't you know that if you share pencils, there's a 30% chance that someone will chew on the eraser and spread a cold?"

"You're thinking of sharing chapstick," Leslie said. "Or a juice box."

"No! Pencils!"

Before the debate could get heated, a school administrator walked through the door. "Is Leslie Cathcart here?" She raised her hand. "I just wanted to tell you that Mark is going to be just fine. He is sedated and about to get his stitches. With some luck, he'll be able to play in tonight's concert!"

"What are you talking about?" she asked. "Mark Terrace is right there." She pointed to the boy sitting across the aisle from her, using her pencil to write a concerto. Mark looked up upon hearing his name.

The administrator looked at him. "Who are you?"

"Mark Terrace."

"Show me your student ID."

"I lost it somewhere," he admitted slowly.

The administrator panicked. He pulled out his walkie-talkie and said, "Code red! We have a case of identity theft in room 203!"

Mark's concerto was confiscated and he was told to stand against the wall. Four school officials and one of the more muscular gym teachers soon rushed in. They took turns interrogating Mark Terrace on his real identity. None of the students bothered to speak up for him. They too were unsure if it was Mark, considering he didn't have his ID.

It was then that the band teacher rushed in. "What are you doing to my star trumpet player?" Everyone was confused. He continued, "I was bringing a floral display to Mark in the hospital, but when I got there I realized it wasn't Mark! When he woke up from surgery, he said his name was Casey Perez, and that he found Mark's ID on the stairs when he tripped."

Everyone was dumbfounded. "Well," said the nurse, "where is *his* student ID?"

"He was wearing it," the band teacher said.

"Oh," said the principal. "That's the last place we would think to look if we wanted to find a student's ID."

Eric Friedensohn

Down with Stairs!

Do you hate stairs? If so, you likely suffer from Climacophobia, the fear of climbing or falling down stairs. But you are not alone. Seventy-nine percent of people above the age of one are climacophobic. Rightfully so, I might add—stairs are the most dangerous form of skyward transit. The average person walks across forty-one and a half stairs each day. I have made it my life's goal to reduce that average significantly and make the world a safer place for everyone.

Four out of five people agree that walking up stairs is the worst part of their day. I know what you're thinking. It's not because people are lazy. In fact, that is very rarely the case. The vast majority of good people are subconsciously freaking out when they are walking up or down stairs, even if it's just a couple of baby steps. Stairs are everywhere! For these people, daily life often feels like an MC Escher drawing. You just never know when you're going to turn a corner and find a flight of stairs staring you right in the eye. Why do you think people run up stairs two at a time? It's because they just want to safely make it to flat ground as soon as possible.

We have all seen someone stumble on the staircase once or twice, and sure it might make us chuckle inside. But it's not so funny when it happens to you, or even worse, your loved ones. It may seem like after crossing the same flights of stairs each day you would be all right. But just when you least expect it, there's that one centimeter you didn't account for and before you know it you are on the hard earth, bleeding from all orifices. This year with the release of the new iPhone, the number of stair-related injuries has doubled. This is no joke, people. Last year, stairs were present in the crime scenes of nine out of ten unsolved murders. Maybe the police are willing to look the other way, but not me!

Whoever invented handrails was obviously in the same boat. There's nothing that comforts me as much as clinging to a sturdy bar to help me balance. But sometimes hand rails work against us. Just last month there were two deaths and one injury due to splinters from the same wooden handrail. A couple of days ago, I discovered an entire YouTube channel devoted to stair prank videos. These evil people trick others with faulty handrails! When people lean on the rail, it falls out of the sockets and the poor, innocent walker tumbles to the ground. I can't believe that there are people in our world that find this to be funny.

Some people use stairs as an exercise tool, jumping up and down them and such. This is clearly inappropriate, but the real problem in stair exercise is the Stairmaster. The sleek appearance hypnotizes the eyes until you get sucked into a whirlwind of never-ending stairs! Somehow people seem to gloss over the horrifying aspects of these machines, and they end up in gyms across the country. No matter how many steps you climb, you will never master the stairs.

It's plain to see why all stairs should be exterminated and forever banned across the world from new architecture plans. I firmly believe that ramps, escalators, elevators, chair lifts, gondolas, and funiculars should be installed in place of every last stair set. If you believe in the cause, join the Climacophobes Union in the first ever strike against stairs on April 1st in the Underground City Hall Plaza.

Ian Micir

An Incident Involving a Grizzly Bear

On my way to work this morning I stopped at Dunkin' Donuts to pick up a breakfast sandwich. The gym where I work opens early enough that I'm usually the first person there when the D.D. opens. But to my surprise, I wasn't first today. There was a bearded man in his early forties and a grizzly bear in a blue polo in line in front of me and the following scene took place.

(I enter the store wiping sleep-boogies out of my eye and get in line behind the grizzly bear. He nods to me.)

BEAR: Hey, how ya doin'?
ME: Not too bad, yourself?
BEAR: Can't complain.
ME: Chilly out there again, eh?
BEAR *(casually shrugs)*: Eh, supposed to hit 50 a little later this week.
ME: Wish that was today. Just gotta bundle up I guess.
BEAR: Not me. I'm a grizzly bear.
ME: I see that.

(The man in front of the grizzly bear is handed his order and exits the store. The cashier returns to the counter. She appears to be the only one working. She is a short Indian woman with a gentle voice.)

INDIAN WOMAN: Welcome to Dunkin Donuts, sir, can I take your order?

(The grizzly bear places an order for a sausage, egg whites, and cheese sandwich and a Tropicana orange juice with no pulp. The cashier deftly types his order into the computer. One can tell she's on her way up. A real go-getter.)

INDIAN WOMAN: That'll be $4.95, sir.

(The grizzly bear hands her a ten and she hands him back a five and a nickel and goes back to make his order. He stands there for a moment, staring down at the change in his massive, furry paw.)

BEAR: God damn it.
ME: Wrong change?
BEAR: No. It's these damn tip jars.

ME: Tip jars?

(*The grizzly bear makes a nod to the bowl on the counter that reads: Gratuities accepted for exceptional service. He looks down at his change again.*)

BEAR: So what the hell am I supposed to do with this?

ME: How do you mean?

BEAR: A nickel and five bucks. There's no way to win this one. I give her the nickel and she's gonna be like, Oh wow thank you so much, sir. How can I ever repay you for your unprecedented generosity?

ME: So keep it.

BEAR: Yeah that'll go over well. Oh thanks a lot fuzz-ball. We finally integrate you into society and you goddamn bears can't even tip a nickel? She would have to be Indian, too. It's damn near a hate crime now.

ME: Hmph. I see your dilemma.

(*A few seconds pass. The bear thinks. Then he shakes his head. He thinks again. Then he looks up at me as if I had said something.*)

BEAR: I'm not giving her five dollars for making me a three-dollar sandwich.

ME: No one could expect you to.

BEAR: If she'd done something exceptional, that'd be one thing, but I've seen nothing prodigious here.

ME: Agreed. An average performance at best.

(*He puts the five in his pocket. The Indian lady returns with his sandwich. The grizzly bear peeks in the bag, then turns and looks around the store for a few seconds.*)

BEAR (*mumbling to himself*): Ketchup, ketchup, ketchuuuuup...

INDIAN WOMAN: Oh, I've got them right here, sir.

(*She reaches under the counter and pulls out a handful of ketchups and holds them out to the grizzly bear. He stares at her for a second. She continues to hold the ketchups.*)

BEAR: I suppose you think this qualifies as exceptional.

INDIAN WOMAN: Sir?

BEAR (*shoving his hand in his pocket*): Here. You win, okay? Just take the five dollars. I don't even want your goddamn ketchup!

(*The grizzly bear slaps the five dollars down and the nickel goes bouncing around the counter. He frantically tackles it with his other paw, picks it up, and holds it up to the cashier. She is understandably puzzled.*)

BEAR: I'm keeping this.

(*The grizzly bear exits the store, defeated. The Indian woman blinks a few times, picks up the five dollars, and looks at me.*)

INDIAN WOMAN: What a generous bear.

ME: Agreed.

The End.

Ian Micir

Beyond All Recognition

A bum makes his way down a train platform asking every already-shaking head if they can spare some change. Bum is a harsh word, but these are harsh times. Ten years ago he might have been a homeless person; now he's a bum—the economy affects everyone. When he finally reaches me, I'm sitting hunched on a bench with my elbows on my knees pretending to type something important on my phone. My clever ruse fails.

Heyscuzemesir, dyavalilsomnucdspare?

I don't blame him. If I had to say anything that many times a day, I wouldn't give a shit about pronunciation either. I shake my head without looking up and he shuffles on to the next person. On an eighth-grade class trip to D.C., I handed out four consecutive twenties to shaking Styrofoam cups full of dirt and dried coffee. Now I don't even look up. The world has a funny way of finding what's best in a man, pulling it out of him, holding it in front of his face, and burning it, all slowly and quietly enough that he doesn't realize what's happened until he looks up a decade later and all that's left is smoldering embers and ash—or maybe he doesn't look up.

The bum asks some poor woman if she could spare a token for the bus. He's a veteran (of the craft, not the war). She says, *No, I'm sorry, I don't have any.* I shake my head. Six words too many, rookie. Anybody who knows anything knows never to elaborate on *no.* If the lack of a token is the justification for the answer, *no,* it implies that if one had a token, the answer would change. So he asks her for the two-dollar equivalent. She has it, knows it, and can't think quickly enough to duck the haymaker and get off the ropes. The poor woman never had a chance. Welcome to street rhetoric.

Two dollars richer, he skips a few people and starts over farther down the platform. The woman knows now that the money wasn't for the bus, but it doesn't seem to bother her. She's probably been swindled into three timeshares that she doesn't use, but they don't bother her either. The warm and fuzzy feeling is worth two dollars.

My train arrives and I climb aboard. For most of the ride, I dwell on the images of all the people shaking their heads before the bum had spoken, of forty people with iPhones—all unable to spare a quarter, of my own refusal to even look up and my classification of the kind woman as a sucker. It's a sad reality that we're now surprised by the rare person who reaches into her pocket to help a stranger. Most of urban humanity has fallen by the wayside.

I can't explain its origin, but as I sit on the train watching the headlights on the highway flicker and fade, a thought creeps into my head: a scene where I attack the bum the moment he asks me for some spare change.

He's weak and malnourished from life on the streets and I follow two workouts a day with smoothies made of frozen fruit, skim milk, and whey protein—it's not a competitive bout. As he mumbles his first pathetic words, I stand quickly, plant my shoulder into his ribcage and drive him to the ground. Upon impact, I feel more than one of his ribs break and the back of his head hits the concrete. A circle of blood pools and expands behind it. It's darker than it is on TV. I straddle his torso, pinning him to the ground as my left hand grabs what it can of his filthy, thin T-shirt and my right delivers blow after blow to his mouth. The neck of his shirt tears like paper and he chokes on the weakly rooted teeth that come loose and the pieces of the ones that shatter from lack of enamel. All the tension leaves his body and his eyes roll back in his head.

Two men of about forty who'd come running from the bum's direction tackle me, breaking up the fight, if it can be called that. The bum continues to bleed, unconscious on the ground. A few people attend to him and another calls 9-1-1. Not far away, the two men ask me what the bum had done. I tell them that that wasn't the point. They give a confused look and I ask them to show me the contents of their pockets. If only out of curiosity, they oblige: one of them has a black pen, and they each have a cell phone and some loose change. I smile, but not out of happiness, and ask them why they would come running to the bum's aid when not even two minutes earlier they wouldn't go so far as to reach their hand into their pocket for a nickel—

I snap out of it as the windows shake from a passing Acela train. I'd never hurt someone who didn't deserve it, but the idea stands: many of the people who would go out of their way to help someone in physical danger are the same people who walk past empty cups and cardboard signs without a single thought of helping. It's not self-righteous to say it, because I've become one of them. There's no real explanation or justification for it, either: to say that there are too many people to help shouldn't have anything to do with a person's willingness to help one person at a time and to think that everyone living on the street is there because of a drug problem is an unfair generalization.

The truth of the matter is that most of us who live in major cities just don't give a shit. Maybe we do in the beginning, but with enough time, we just grow numb to it—summer soldiers and sunshine patriots scurrying from place to place on the fucked up battlefield of capitalism, passing by the wounded with noise-canceling headphones and a thousand-yard stare, always thinking the medic is right behind us to patch them up. Dog-eat-dog doesn't even do it justice. We're closer to cannibalism. FUBAR.

Faculty
Writing

Introduction

Writers render their perceptions from far off places and times; rarely do they live close to us, and rarer still do we know them or have the opportunity to know them, if only because they have died. They're almost always strangers with disembodied voices to whom we have no easy access. This can be a source of frustration to anyone who has wanted to ask a writer to elaborate on a particular point or share their experiences with the nuts and bolts, from conception to execution, of a written subject.

In the following section, examples of the work by Drexel faculty have been included in *The 33rd* as representations of fine professional, creative, and scholarly writing. The authors are alive and kicking and on campus; some may be your teachers now or in the future. You can see from the pieces that the approaches and subjects range from original works of poetry and personal essay to scholarly articles on topics like forgery and the role of science in mental health care. You can assume that each subject presented particular challenges that the authors had to grapple with in the same way that all writers must, including, of course, those in a composition class.

Scott Barclay

Has the Tide Turned on Marriage Equality? From the Controversial to the Mundane, From the Unusual to the Routine

In the politics of marriage equality, there are six important indicators that the tide has turned for lesbian and gay rights around this issue.

From Unusual to Routine Politics: At one point in time in the last 20 years in 17 separate states (CA, CT, DE, HI, IA, IL, MA, MD, ME, NH, NJ, NY, NV, OR, RI, VT, and WA), either a state's legislature successfully passed a bill though both legislatives houses in support of same sex marriage or civil unions *or* a state's highest court judicially ordered the establishment of same sex marriage and/or civil unions. Based on 2010 Census figures, 117 million residents—38% of the US population—currently live in one of these 17 states. Although simple math indicates that 33 states remain, 17 states constitutes over one-third of all US states. The important point being that full or nearly full recognition by a state government for lesbian and gay couples in long-term, committed relationships is no longer aberrant or unusual. In fact, there is increasingly a sense of inevitability associated positively with the future prospects of the issue. The very presence of gubernatorial vetoes on this issue, such as in California in 2005 and 2007 or in New Jersey in 2012, and the new possibility of overriding such vetoes, evidences a politics-as-normal aspect that has become attached to the issue.

The Shift in the Default Category: As researchers and social movement activists have recently noted, the introduction of civil unions, rather than simple rejection of any relationship recognition, has increasingly emerged as the default position for those opposed to marriage equality. In states that raise the issue for consideration, opposition within legislatures and courts has largely adopted civil unions as their own base position. This is consistent with the framing of published editorials and op-eds in a wide variety of newspapers throughout the 2000s, as noted in research by myself and Daniel Chomsky. Notwithstanding that civil unions now occupy this category, in six states over the last 15 years (CA, CT, NH, NJ, VT, and WA), either a state's legislature has successfully passed a bill though both legislatives houses in support of moving the state from civil unions to marriage equality or the state's highest court has judicially ordered such a move.

From Controversial to Mundane: Based on the truly muted media coverage nationally of the legislative and gubernatorial actions in Illinois, Delaware and Rhode Island in 2011, the promulgation of civil unions by a state barely draws sustained national media attention at this point in time. More sustained media attention appears reserved for those few states that introduce marriage equality at this time. Gerald Rosenberg (in *The Hollow Hope*, 2nd Ed) has argued that civil unions are less controversial in general, but the recent media coverage of state legislatures that initially introduced civil unions appears in marked contrast to coverage of similar actions in earlier years in Vermont, Connecticut, or New Jersey.

The Decline in Legislative Opposition: Voting behavior within those state legislatures that have revisited this issue on several occasions over the last eight years demonstrates a marked decline in opposition to marriage equality. Part of this decline is accounted for by changing legislators, which acknowledges the shifting electoral success enjoyed by supporters of marriage equality. But, part of the change in level of opposition reflects a change-in-heart of existing legislators who are slowly coming to support the issue. This may occur for the electoral reasons noted above or it may be reflecting the change in larger cultural norms around the issue, as noted below. Similarly, in some states, including as evidenced in New York in 2011, much (but not all) of the legislative opposition now eschews the stereotypical anti-gay tropes in favor of rejection without explicit explanation of their vote. This action appears to be motivated by their apparent understanding that their use of these former stereotypes risks potential future electoral damage. Interestingly, electoral "backlash" now appears of greatest fear to those who vote against marriage equality or civil unions, rather than their supportive colleagues.

The Decline in Popular Opposition: Gallup is reporting, based on their public opinion polls, that as of May 2011 the majority of adult, US residents are supportive of marriage equality. Polls conducted since that date support this basic finding and the national trend appears well-established at this point. This trend can be expected to be reflected in future voting trends, including the possibility of successfully fending off hostile popular initiatives and state referendum.

The Age and Experience of the Groups: There is now over 20 years of social movement activity—from 1991 to 2012—to account for in the current wave of marriage equality cases and legislative activity. At this point in time, the major interest groups are now constituted by seasoned political and legal actors who reflect the value of their extensive experience on this issue. Their experience shows in the strength of the movement in terms of its ability to simultaneously maintain local, regional, and national activities, as evidenced recently by the contemporaneous nature of the timing of legislative activities in Washington, New Jersey, and Maryland.

In the complexity of day-to-day activities related to a social movement, the general public can occasionally lose the larger thread of action in ways that over-emphasize either losses, such as the effects of the California initiative in November 2008, or wins, such as very recent legislative actions in Washington, New Jersey, and Maryland. Yet, if we look at these six indicators over time, we can note a marked shift in the general political environment for the recognition of relationships of lesbian and gay couples. It is by no means a completed struggle, but it does reflect positively on the idea that the tide has turned for lesbian and gay rights around this issue.

Genevieve Betts

Pest vignettes

1. A beetle is crawling up my leg—
it is the driveway
oiled in a moon blue sheen,
turned teal, then oyster green.

2. The glittering trail on the sidewalk
leads to the snail—
        half-stepped on,
the shell is cracked like an egg,
        the yoke
a steely gray,
but its antennae is still erect.

3. On Bishop Drive, you and I
would find molted cicada shells
clutching the bark of mulberry trees.

They held so still, as if waiting
on the slow honey-drip of sap.

Almost perfect replicas—
        every striation of the body
        outlined in brittle wax paper—
if not for the open seam
split thick down the back.

It pained our childhood fingers and thumbs
to so gently pluck each one off
without crushing it to crumbs,
        to place it with the others
        in the large glass jar.

Genevieve Betts

Eggshells

The anatomy of a baby
is all Humpty Dumpty
pre-fall—

soft skull
covered in soft spots,
        even soft eye sockets.

Parenting is wincing at imagined injury,
hypotheses of could,
like what really happened
to my friend Ryan in preschool—
        shattered glass
against garage floor,
crystal shards lurching toward
one of his soft white orbs.

Some hand and mold
composed its replacement
from the same substance,
the glass eye,
light blue iris,
a piece of the enemy inside.

In school, he popped it
in and out with ease, teased us
with a chase around chairs and tables—

always in his little hand
the older eye, unblinking.

Paula Marantz Cohen

The Meanings of Forgery

My subject is forgery—its function and meaning in the context of artistic representation.

Literally defined, forgery is the shaping of metal through the application of high temperature, a process whose development marked a major stride in the progress of civilization. But in a second, more common meaning—and the one that concerns me here—forgery is a process of copying a valuable artifact so as to deceive a viewer into thinking that it is original or real. This sort of forgery, though a crime, is associated with a more advanced point in the progress of civilization.

Forgery of this second kind prompts us to ask practical questions: how was the thing done?; how long did it remain undetected?; how was it exposed? It also raises conceptual questions: what does a forgery, which manages to fool us for a time, say about our ability to perceive and judge accurately?; what, to extrapolate, does it mean to be accurate in perception and judgment?

In prompting such questions, forgery has a kinship with magic. Both trick us through sleight of hand and call into doubt what is real. Both capture our attention and fascination. One way to get a work looked at closely is to suspect it of being a forgery.

Beginning in the late 1960s, a group of art experts calling themselves the Rembrandt Research Project began reviewing hundreds of works worldwide attributed to the seventeenth-century Dutch painter. In the course of their study they concluded that at least half of these works were forgeries, copies, or misattributions. This revelation was startling to those familiar with the art in question. It was as if it had suddenly disappeared off the walls of museums and private collections and been magically replaced by different works. The substitution, moreover, was not one-way. As research progressed, some art that was initially presumed to be fraudulent was reinstated—as if the magic wand had been waved again, putting these works back where they had been.

In magic, of course, the effect is connected to hiding the mechanism of transformation, while forgery, to have an effect, requires revealing that mechanism. If we don't learn through scientific analysis, connoisseurship, or the confession of the forger that the thing is fake, we continue to be fooled but not know that we are, which thereby precludes the effect.

Part of the mystique of forgery is that it only pertains to certain kinds of artifacts. The philosopher Nelson Goodman has explained that representations can be delineated into two kinds: *allographic* (works that are based on a notation that exists outside the representation itself) and *autographic* (works that have no antecedent notation and exist as singularities)—and that only autographic works can be forged. Thus, one *can* forge a painting or sculpture, a signature, an original manuscript, or, for that matter, an identity (though once the human genome has been thoroughly mapped, this may change). One can *not* forge a novel, a piece of music, a play, or a movie (there are exceptions of a sort here—as when the original manuscript of a written or musical work is said to be lost but a later forged transcription is attributed to the master based on stylistic affinities). The preferred crime for allographic forms is plagiarism, in some sense the reverse of forgery: instead of passing off one's own work as the work of another, the plagiarist passes off the work of another as one's own. One can see why forgery is the more glamorous crime. The plagiarist is both self-aggrandizing and talentless, while the forger is self-effacing (at least for the purposes of the crime) and must possess a modicum of talent (or at least skill) in order to succeed.

Forgery can be further demarcated in its association with certain kinds of artifacts within the autographic realm. One speaks of forging rarities rather than more mundane objects, for which the preferred term is counterfeiting. The difference is that the counterfeiter makes fraudulent merchandise in mechanical, mass-produced form (jeans, handbags, currency), while the forger makes discreet, careful imitations and is most often associated with fine art. (Note that a forged check is really a forged signature, which is to say, a highly idiosyncratic, personalized representation).

The forger also tends to take advantage of our nostalgia for work associated with a remote, artisanal past: art that exerts the singular "aura" which Walter Benajmin described as a function of capitalist values. One thinks of "gentleman forgers" with their scrupulous methods and special tools, working alone in private studios. The forger, in other words, looks a lot like the artist—a point I will return to.

One could argue that artists need forgers quite as much as forgers need artists. This is because a work of art is a non-utilitarian object: it has no "use value," as Marx would say; only "exchange value." Forgery performs a service in this context by helping to solidify what is by definition subjective and uncertain; it gives free-floating exchange value an anchor by announcing that the art is worthy of being forged. It performs this service, of course, only after it has been exposed.

In the following pages, I want to consider in more detail the paradoxes attached to forgery, to explore the ways in which this criminal activity can be understood in the context of our culture, and how its meaning might change in a culture different from our own.

Let us begin with a thought experiment:

A billionaire has recently decided to donate his art collection to a museum, but his attachment to one painting in the collection is so great that he wishes to have a copy made to keep in his home. He offers to pay $10 million to the artist who can render the best copy. Many artists enter the competition, and the billionaire chooses to purchase the painting by X, which he judges to be the best copy. At this point, another painter, Y, announces that he has perpetrated a hoax: his rejected copy is actually the original painting, while the one donated to the museum is a copy that was sold to the billionaire at an earlier date (details of this transaction need not concern us here). The billionaire has thus purchased a copy of a copy, and rejected the original.

How should we respond to this revelation?

Probably, our first inclination in hearing this story is to blame the billionaire for his poor judgment. We are likely to assume that he was swayed by the famous name affixed to his painting and played for a sucker by an unscrupulous art dealer or bogus expert. So long as we have no interest in the billionaire's estate, we are liable to be amused by his ordeal. We may even think that, given his presumed ignorance and gullibility (and the fact that he can afford to lose the money), he deserved to be duped.

The assumptions here derive from what we have been taught about the importance of training in discerning good art from bad. The practice of judging artistic quality dates back at least to Vasari, whose *Lives of the Artists* included a number of anecdotes regarding the nature and provenance of certain well-known works (including a discussion of a Michelangelo sculpture, now lost, that the artist tried to pass off as a work of antiquity). Still, up through the end of the eighteenth century, cultural historians wrote only anecdotally on the subject of forgery and were not engaged in evaluating such acts in a professional, systematic way. This changed in the nineteenth century when the practice of connoisseurship—the professionalized act of judging the quality and authenticity of rare artifacts—came into being as an offshoot of the new field of art history.

Ironically, the first person to use the term in a professional context was himself a forger, one Louis Marcy, who is said to have flooded the antiquities market with falsified objects in late nineteenth century and early twentieth century London. After moving to Paris, he appears to have given up forgery and taken to exposing it, even publishing a journal entitled *Le Connaisseur* to help in the process. Marcy's career path has become a familiar one in the modern era where con men retrofit themselves as gatekeepers or are recruited to catch other con men. The contemporary forger, John Myatt, followed a similar career path—and now does a brisk business selling his copies of famous paintings on the Internet.

If Marcy was among the first to use the term connoisseur, Bernard Berenson was the first to give the vocation cultural prominence and respectability. The son of poor Russian-Jewish immigrants in Boston, Berenson earned a scholarship to Harvard in the 1880s, where he began his study of art history. (He wrote several well-regarded treatises on Italian Renaissance art.) As part of his early research in the field, he traveled through Europe, developing a network of contacts and potential patrons. Eventually, he became the expert consultant of wealthy American collectors like Isabella Stewart Gardner in their purchase of European art, mostly Old Master paintings. Berenson's role, which continued into the 1920s (when his expertise was tarnished by a scandal involving the British art dealer Joseph Duveen), was to determine whether a work was worth buying: identifying who painted it, how important the artist was in the tradition, and what its quality was within the oeuvre of that artist.

By the middle of the twentieth century, connoisseurship had become an entrenched part of the art establishment and began to assume a wider influence as museums broadened their mission, seeking to appeal more directly to the general public. Thomas Hoving, the flamboyant director of the Metropolitan Museum of Art from 1967 to 1977, was an exemplar of the new connoisseurship. While Berenson's clients were American nouveau riche industrialists, Hoving's were the American populace who, though they could not afford to buy great art, could nonetheless pay to visit it. Connoisseurship became an important part of Hoving's marketing endeavor—and the concept of forgery became the dramatic means he hit on to make connoisseurship interesting to the public.

Early in his career at the Met, Hoving delivered a public seminar on the subject of forgery, comparing authentic works in the museum's collection with forged or misattributed ones: "Contrast the vigor of the good one, on the left, with the sickliness of the other," he instructed his audience. "Of course you can tell that the one on the left has a life and a light and a feeling to it, while the painting on the right is wooden, hesitant." Hoving's language implied that, with a modicum of training (by him), telling the difference between an authentic work and a fake one could be easy. Those who didn't "see" would appear, in this context, to be philistines or dunces.

However different their goals, Berenson and Hoving assumed that distinguishing the authentic from the fake was possible if one brought the right tools and qualities of discernment to bear. It is the legacy of this idea that underpins our sense, in reading the billionaire's story above, that he is a fool for having been duped, *twice*, with regard to his painting.

Still, it is possible to view the story differently. For even as Hoving put forward the notion that distinguishing the authentic from the fake was not only possible but easy (if one knew how to look), such ideas were coming under siege from a spate of scholarship in the 1960s that addressed the problematic aspects of forgery. This scholarship was inspired at least in part by the famous case of Han Van Meegeren, whose Vermeer forgeries had deceived experts before and during World War II, with the result that a large number of collectors and museums had purchased them at high prices. Van Meegeren's most notorious client was the Nazi second-in-command, Hermann Goering, an association which resulted in the forger's trial as a collaborator after the war.

The fact that Van Meegeren was able to pass off his forgeries to experts as authentic puts the billionaire's case in a different light. We have up until now assumed his mistakes were the product of his ignorance. But using the Van Meegeren case as a model, it is possible to see these mistakes as the result not of ignorance but of knowledge.

Let us postulate, for example, that the billionaire is not lacking in discernment at all but is a connoisseur in his own right, with years of presumed experience and scholarship behind him. (Thomas Hoving, it should be noted, was himself responsible for acquiring some of the Rembrandts that are now subject to dispute.) If we imagine the billionaire as an expert rather than a novice collector, this suggests that his valuation of the paintings he purchased was based on what he knew about the artists in question. This was indeed the case in the mistaken view of the Van Meegeren forgeries. Abraham Bredius, one of the foremost Vermeer experts of the period, was led, through a series of circuitous associations, to see many of the elements that now strike us as flagrantly *unsupportive* of a Vermeer attribution as supportive of one. The very differences became sources of confirmation, as he expounded on Van Meegeren's most ambitious forgery, *The Supper at Emmaus*: "The subject matter is nearly unique in his oeuvre, and it expresses a depth of sentiment such as one sees in none of his other works." Convinced that the deviation was a mark of authenticity rather than the reverse, he concluded: "When this masterpiece was shown to me I had difficulty controlling my emotion. . . Composition, expression, and color all unite to form a whole of the highest art, the highest beauty!"

An obvious difference between the billionaire's case and that of Van Meegeren is that the forged Vermeers were not copies of original works but calculated deviations from Vermeer's characteristic style. Van Meegeren knew the scholarship on his subject. He knew that because Vermeer had married into a Catholic family, scholars had postulated that he may have painted "Catholic" paintings during an unexplained, seven-year lacuna in his career. He also incorporated into his forgeries references to a Dutch *volk* identity which had appeal during this period of nationalist foment (and which had particular appeal to Goering).

Since no paintings of the sort Van Meegeren created in Vermeer's name actually existed in the Vermeer oeuvre, one could call the Van Meegeren paintings original forgeries or forged originals. Remove the Vermeer attribution and they look less like Vermeer's known work and more like Van Meegeren's, who exhibited similar paintings in his own name earlier in his career.

To adjust my fictional scenario to approximate the situation of the Van Meegeren forgeries, I would have to make the three paintings in the story a series of forgeries in the presumed name, if not the style, of another painter. The so-called original would simply be the first in this line of forged attributions. I should note that Van Meegeren's own work gave rise to such a situation. After he was exposed after World War II, he became so famous for his forgeries that they were themselves forged. Some of these were done by his own son, whom Van Meegeren had trained as a painter.

But let us return to my original scenario and reconsider the billionaire's case in yet a third light. Let us suppose that the original work, which one of the artists had copied and replaced, was not a forgery but a misattribution of another artist from the same period as the great artist to whom it was attributed. This original artist was little or unknown. What should occur now in valuing the work with respect to the two copies made of it? What if the original is a lesser work but still an "original" one (though not by the artist to whom it was attributed), and if the copy of it is an improvement on that work, bringing it closer to the quality of the famous artist for which it was mistaken? Indeed, one can even say that the copy of the mediocre original was done by that mistaken master (perhaps early in his career as an apprentice to this lesser artist). How does such a scenario compare with the one above in which the original painting is a forgery rather than a misattribution?

Such paradoxical situations, which do, in fact, occur periodically in the art world, raise the question of comparative assessment, which stands at the root of ideas about the distinction between an authentic work and a copy put forward by Goodman in his 1968 essay. Goodman makes the point that if one is confronted with an original and a forgery that seems to exactly duplicate it, knowing that one is original and the other is forged informs the esthetic experience of looking at the two works together. Even if we can't see the difference between original and copy, knowing there is one makes us think that in time we can learn to see the difference.

This idea—that two apparently identical works encode the possibility of difference—assumes that the connoisseur, like the artist himself, has embarked on a journey to enlightenment. What the artist hopes eventually to achieve in the way of mastery, the viewer, as Goodman sees it, hopes to achieve in the way of "perceptual discrimination." As he explains: "what one can distinguish at any given moment by merely looking depends not only upon native visual acuity but upon practice and training."

Goodman does not address the idea of esthetic value—the possibility that the copy might be better than the original and that training might lead us to appreciate, not the original, but the copy (what one might argue happened for the connoisseur billionaire in the last version of my scenario). This postulate finds refutation in the work of Goodman's contemporary, Alfred Lessing, who in his essay "What's Wrong with a Forgery?" argues that the original, even if undistinguishable from the copy—or even if superficially less good— is nonetheless *better* for the reason that it has "artistic integrity"; it is the authentic product of a particular cultural context which the copy is not. In a later variation on the same idea, Dennis Dutton calls the difference between original and copy the "performance" aspect of the work, which relates to how artists "solve problems, overcome obstacles, make do with available materials." Thus, even if one thinks the copy as good or better, the original, by being the original, "performs" in a way that the copy does not. Taking this idea further, Sherri Irvin draws on T.S. Eliot's argument relating art to a historical tradition which it both fits into and alters:

> what happens when a new work of art is created is
> something that happens simultaneously to all the works
> of art which preceded it. The existing monuments form
> an ideal order among themselves, which is modified by
> the introduction of the new (the really new) work of art
> among them. . . for order to persist after the supervention
> of novelty, the *whole* existing order must be, if ever so
> slightly, altered; and so the relations, proportions, values
> of each work of art toward the whole are readjusted. . .

Thus, to insert a forgery (that has not been exposed as a forgery) falsifies the historical record and throws tradition into disarray.

And yet this conclusion does not entirely hold up. Our tendency is to think that we are dealing with a long time period here—that the work in question is a more contemporary work and that it is copying an Old Master. But, as noted, it could be an Old Master copying an Old Master, an Old Master copying a lesser artist early in his career, or a more contemporary artist copying a more contemporary work—all cases where the time between original and copy is much shorter, changing our sense of the importance of the historical element. Moreover, history (no matter how long or short the period in question) is both always present and to some degree relative in its importance. There is a historical component even in a forgery that connects it to the past and to the present. And integrity, problem-solving, and performance are themselves relative things. A copy can have its own sort of integrity, encode its own problems, and perform in an admittedly unorthodox way. Van Meegeren's case, a subject of fascination to cultural historians, seems to be a striking instance in which the performance of the exposed forgery approaches the status of a conceptual artwork (a point to be discussed further below). In any case, one should remember that Goodman's own theory posits that a difference is always there, even when works look identical, which means that difference, no matter how small or seemingly negligible, may encode elements that are personal and historical with regard to the artist, even if the artist is copying another.

This raises the question of how originality—or if you will, honesty with respect to origins—connects to creativity. Here it is helpful to consider what it means to be original—and how much difference is required for originality to happen.

The philosopher James Elkins has addressed this question by noting that an original work is always to some degree the derivative of some earlier original, and enumerates seven steps in the process of moving from one original to another. His schema serves not only as an abstract index for the relationship between continuity and change in art but also as a practical guide for the movement from student to master. In other words, each of the points he describes can be viewed both with regard to the artifacts themselves and to the developmental stages that artists follow in achieving mastery and becoming original in their own right.

The developmental evolution Elkins describes is from an original (or as he puts it, an "originary" work), to a strict copy, to a reproduction, to an imitation, to a variation, to a version, and, finally, to a new original. This trajectory supports a traditional form of art education in which copying marks an apprenticeship in a student's development that leads eventually to a new personal style. Not all artists, of course, arrive at this desired end point—indeed, one could argue that most don't, which is why we have misattributions: works by artists who have been stalled in their developmental process at a point that makes it easy for them to be confused with more original masters. Still, the overall sense of Elkins' trajectory is toward an independent expressiveness, even if that end point is rarely achieved or if a given artist gets stuck at an early or intermediary step. This was one of the defenses mounted on behalf of Van Meegeren—that his personal style was that of an earlier age (that could be equated with an earlier stage of artistic development), so that, unable to be acknowledged or make a living in a contemporary context, he was obliged to pass his work off as that of the Old Masters who had inspired him. (This self-representation has been called into question, but it has persuasiveness in the context of Elkins' developmental trajectory.)

But the evolution that Elkins describes—moving incrementally from one original to another—is a schematic one and, as such, artificial. Although, traditionally, artists were expected to apprentice to other artists—to work in their workshops, copy their work, and only gradually acquire their own style—this is an outmoded form of training and one that even many Old Masters did not follow. Modern artists clearly deviate to various degrees from such a trajectory (which is behind the familiar complaint that modern artists never learn how to draw), and avant garde artists will explicitly thumb their noses at tradition and claim to spring out of the void. (How much of this is posturing—itself a learned behavior that stands at the end of a developmental trajectory—is open to question, and may well complicate my point in provocative ways.)

Avant garde art seems the opposite of forged art, yet the two share a kinship in eschewing a traditional developmental trajectory. An example that in some sense encompasses both—idiosyncratic originality and exact copying—is Sherri Levine's photographs which use Walker Evans' original negatives to reduplicate his work under her name. Levine's photos are saying something original while technically occupying the intermediate developmental stage that Elkins calls "reproduction." (Indeed, one can argue that Levine's work is original insofar as it alters the nature of the representation from allographic to autographic in Goodman's terminology.) The point, Levine would no doubt argue, is that her copying is a transparent gesture—it doesn't hide the fact that she is using Evans' negatives—and in being so, can be placed at a later point in Elkins' trajectory (and change the work from an allographic to an autographic one). Copying that is not transparent—where the work is being put over on a credulous viewer—seems a different sort of thing entirely.

Elkins acknowledges this distinction in setting up his developmental trajectory, noting that forgery is "a perversion or failure of the normal process of increasing distance between student and master." But the statement also begs the question of what "a perversion or failure of the normal process" means. For one could say that all original art is a deviation (if not, more extravagantly, "a perversion or failure") of the "normal process" of learning about the world—that art is, by its definition, a duplicitous act insofar as it distorts reality even when it seems to render it accurately, which it by no means always intends to do.

This would seem to apply to Van Meegeren, who was able to turn his apparently mercenary decision to forge Vermeers into a kind of performance that involved both a poignant personal story about being misunderstood and frustrated as an artist and a literal spectacle of "proving" that the painting he sold to Goering was a forgery by painting another in the same style. As a result, he entered the annals of art history as "the genial forger"—a figure who laid bare some of the misleading assumptions in the scholarship on Vermeer and some of the flagrant blind spots in the marketing of fine art more generally. This makes his work conceptually valuable, if not esthetically so. (And again, the absence of esthetic value is open to question, given that his paintings were extravagantly praised for their beauty when they were thought to be authentic Vermeers.)

One may say that in forgery a legal crime is being committed and that this falls outside the bounds of what should be considered artistic. But again, the distinction between proper and improper transgression—of "boundaries" for artistic expression—is hard to prescribe. Artists are often the first to condemn bourgeois support of law and propriety when its falls outside of their interests. Is the tendency to condemn forgery a kind of hypocrisy, then—an action which artists castigate because it involves their own livelihood? Perhaps the context in which a forgery is presented may determine how we view the artifact or the process more generally. The finger-wagging in Hoving's lecture on the subject, for example—"Don't hesitate to use derogatory adjectives in describing forgeries. They should not be given any sort of adulation"—might, by its very smugness, incite artistic opposition.

When a forgery is finally revealed—and the longer or more complicated the process before revelation the more intense the effect of the "reveal"—it produces something of the same perceptual jolt that an original work of art creates when it is successful: It captures attention, it makes us look, and it makes us think by raising questions about originality and comparative value. By the same token, it also reasserts the sense of value that it has violated. The paradox of forgery is that it is at once transgressive and reactionary—artistic and highly conventional. The exposed forgery grabs us and excites us, but it also, in Goodman's view, trains us to see in "proper" esthetic fashion.

Elkins' statement that forgery is "a perversion or failure of the normal process of increasing distance between student and master" also strikes me as having broader implications. It suggests that in any process of artistic development, a perverse eruption may occur that can throw things off—not only mislead us as to where we are in the process, but call the process itself into question. For if the copy is taken for the original or even, as in the example of billionaire's story, is able to supersede the original, what does this say about the validity of orderly learning? If, as Elkins notes, the "steps [moving from old original to new original] are historically determined categories and habits of thought," then what does it mean about our relationship to history and about our habits of thought when those categories are duplicitously (rather than transparently, as in the Levine photos using Walker's negatives) traduced?

But the issue has broader implications still. For the artistic enterprise can be understood as a metaphor for the existential enterprise; as with art, so with identity. We need to copy others not only to become ourselves but to validate the idea that others deserve to be copied. And to extrapolate, we hope to be copied ourselves by those who succeed us: to live through them after we are gone. We want to be singular and special but also to be assured that we are part of some ongoing sense of value and meaning. Once we see this existential paradox as underlying the hierarchy of authentic and inauthentic, real and copy, original and forgery, we can also see how it might be turned on its head.

In a study of the Kwoma tribe in Papua New Guinea the anthropologist Ross Bowden notes that the very idea of copying is viewed in a different way than in the West. Kwoma art, used in spiritual ceremonies, is replaced when it grows worn out or shabby. It is evaluated not as good or bad art but as correct or incorrect copying. The disposability of the old art, once it has been replaced by a new copy, is hard for Westerners to understand, and Bowden notes that critics who castigate the purchase and display of this art in western museums are confusing their own notions of value with those of the tribe, which has no problem selling what has become expendable. Not only is the original work less valuable than the copy for the Kwoma, but the further one gets from the original the more relevant and valuable the art becomes.

If we return to the original anecdote about the billionaire collector, we might recast our understanding of the story in light of Bowden's description of the Kwoma. We can imagine him now as a wealthy member of the tribe, who has a wonderful ability to discern distinctions in art and is intent on choosing the most correct and latest copy of the original work, no longer in circulation and no longer of particular value. His home is the temple where the copy will be installed. The museum is the repository for the artifacts that no longer hold value for the tribe but are hung with its predecessors to satisfy the gaze of Western observers with their interest in the obsolete earlier versions of this sacred art.

One may, in considering the sacred nature of Kwoma art, make a connection between it and medieval Western art, where a religious sense of the world predominated and where the identity of the artist was less important than the rendering of the sacred subject-matter. Both limit what is worthy of representation and how this subject-matter can be depicted. Both pay are indifferent to the individual artist and exist outside a market economy.

But the Kwoma art, as much as it may be said to resemble medieval western art, makes for a more dramatic contrast with our current notion of art. Images of, say, the Virgin and Child, though highly valued in the Middle Ages and often involving conventional poses and prescribed coloration, were not literal copies of earlier work. Moreover, looking at medieval art we can see a clear continuum moving us from the flatly stylized figures in altarpieces of the 1100s and 1200s to the more modeled, distinctive ones of the 1300s to the recognizable individuals in signed works of the 1400s. Art in western culture seems predicated on an idea of development and change, and art historians are able to show how the seeds of the present are to be found in the past. No such evolutionary distinctiveness is to be seen in Kwoma art that simply continues the process of copying into the present.

And yet, if we dig deeper we can see that the larger impulse behind both forms of representation is not so different. Indeed, by providing a schematic contrast to our individualized, authentic art, Kwoma art is particularly useful in revealing the underlying relationship of art to civilization. For while western art and Kwoma art might seem to have different superficial purposes—one religious, the other personal and esthetic—they both involve a relationship to time. In the case of western art, this relationship takes the form of an ever-unfolding innovation—an evolving sense of art history that is a phylogenetic version of the western artist's evolution from copying to independent mastery. In the Kwoma's case, the temporal relationship takes the form of a sustained repetition in the service of a larger idea. And these are flip sides of the same coin. Both tie the past to the present and the future. This sense of continuity, abstracted, so to speak, into the realm of representation, is a necessary foundation to culture. It is that basic substrate of orderliness upon which meaning can be erected and elaborated.

This view of art provides a final insight into the issue of forgery. To substitute a copy for an original work in western culture, as, by the same token, to substitute an original (or at least a *more original*) work for a later copy in the Kwoma culture, is to violate the idea of continuity that these cultures have devised with respect to past, present, and future. This continuity is more existential in western art, more spiritual in Kwoma art, but, either way, it exalts the idea of continuing human life and enacts an orderliness through which that continuity can be felt and understood. Forgery—ingenious, dramatic, skillful though it might be—is a violation of the human spirit within the formal system of our culture. It cannot ever raise itself to the level of art, which must, by definition, always seek to exclude it.

Richardson Dilworth

Does Political Reform Exist?

The United States was formed on the basis of political reform and progress; the colonists were motivated to declare revolution in part because of suspicions that the British government had become irrevocably corrupt, and they believed themselves to be, as the historian Bernard Bailyn put it in his classic *Ideological Origins of the American Revolution* (1967), "uniquely placed by history to capitalize on, to complete and fulfill, the promise of man's existence." Ever since, American politicians have made careers out of presenting themselves as the saviors who will rescue the electorate from corruption, and who will usher in a new dawn of virtue, transparency, and efficiency.

In a country so infused with the spirit of reform, does reform actually mean anything? If everyone is a reformer, does reform actually exist? I am not the first person to question the existence of political reform—or at least that its existence might not be as common as might be suggested by political campaigns. Historians and political scientists have long made a cottage industry out of suggesting that the people who we previously thought were reformers were really up to something possibly less virtuous, and those who we thought were corrupt "bosses" were really more like reformers. For instance, in her recent book *Political Monopolies in American Cities* (2008), political scientist Jessica Trounstine contends that "machine and reform were different versions of the same political phenomenon." The main goal of both types of politicians was to maintain their power indefinitely by changing the rules of politics, though in different ways.

Indeed, many politicians and political powerbrokers throughout U.S. history have looked like both machine and reform politicians at the same time. Of the twenty purported "bosses" that Harold Zink profiled in his classic *City Bosses in the United States* (1930), he noted that six of them ("Czar" Martin Lomasney of Boston; "Duke" Edwin Vare of Philadelphia; Roger Sullivan of Chicago; Martin Behrman of New Orleans, and "Senator" William Flinn, and Christopher Magee of Pittsburgh) all "threw their support to progressive measures on frequent occasions." The same might be said of later "bosses," such as Pittsburgh's David Lawrence.

The American electoral system often makes it difficult to distinguish between bosses and reformers. The classic Progressive "reforms" were mostly attempts to change the rules by which politics was played, such as the official ballot, personal registration, primaries, nonpartisan elections, civil service, and commission and council-manager government. Yet in the "winner take all," majority-rule elections by which most American politicians win office, the focus is on the virtues and vices of the individual candidates, and not the formal rules of the election, and thus "reform" comes to refer less to systems of rules, and more to the individual virtues of the candidates. And in a nation whose political culture has its origins in Protestant beliefs of personal perfectibility, "reform" becomes synonymous with "good," so everyone claims to be a reformer.

Furthermore, most politicians, both reform and machine alike, are, practically by definition, experts at manipulating organizations and organizational rules to their own advantage. Thus machine politicians can promote organizational reforms, knowing full well that they will be able to use those reforms to maintain, or possibly even bolster, their control. The classic example is Frank Hague, arguably one of the most autocratic political bosses in US history, who was a champion of the commission form of government, and campaigned for its adoption in Jersey City. In 1917, Hague ran for a commission seat on the "Unbossed" ticket, became mayor, and was reelected every two years until 1947.

That the Progressive era reforms were relatively easy for politicians to manipulate is reflected in the fact that the traditional big city machines only began to fall apart after World War II (as was the case with Hague's machine), primarily as a result of larger unintended changes, such as economic restructuring, the rise of the suburbs, and new immigration patterns. The political reform movement that arose in the postwar era was not so much an independent, proactive movement to clean up city government, as it was the recognition that cities existed in a new economic context that required a new type of politician—as elegantly summarized by the journalist James Reichley, who noted of Philadelphia's reform mayor Richardson Dilworth (who, it's probably worth noting, was my grandfather), that he was to the city's business interests, their "able servant instead of their grafting inefficient slave."

Reichley succinctly makes the point that Dilworth (and his political partner Joseph Clark) did not arise randomly as a reformer, but was instead a product of a unique moment when Philadelphia and other American cities were adjusting to the new world order that was emerging after the convulsions of the previous decades. The same can be said of Philadelphia's reform mayors both before and after the Clark-Dilworth era. For instance, the turn of the twentieth century was a period of change after several years of economic depression, marked by increasing technical sophistication and professionalization in industrial production. Thus the reform mayor elected in 1910, Rudolph Blankenburg, appointed people to run the city departments who were trained as experts and devoted to the emergent discipline of "scientific management." Similarly, the 1980s and early 1990s were a period of adjustment after the economic and social upheaval of the 1970s, especially in Mid-Atlantic cities that suffered unprecedented population losses, teetered on the edge of bankruptcy, and endured a long crime wave. The mayor elected in 1991, Ed Rendell, moved aggressively to reform the financial structure of the city, took a more aggressive stance toward street crime, promoted service-oriented industries, and sought to revamp the city's image so that it became more of a tourist destination.

To say that reform in Philadelphia has mostly been a response to larger economic restructuring is not to deny the importance of individual reformers. Philadelphia would have been much worse off had Blankenburg, Clark, Dilworth, or Rendell not been elected, which was in each case a distinct possibility. At the same time, it is worth noting that these reformers could likely only have gotten elected and pursued reform at specific historical moments, and the specific types of reforms they could pursue were largely preselected by economic circumstances.

It may thus be more accurate to speak not of reforming cities, but rather of *re-adjusting* them to a changing political economy, which then begs the question of what genuine reform might look like. I will conclude by simply suggesting that genuine reform might include a radical re-imagination of the role and status of cities, so that they might be capable not just of adjusting to broader political and economic contexts, but of actively shaping those contexts as well. For instance, what if cities set their own immigration policies? What if city borders could span across state borders? What if city governments were allowed to establish banks and thus engage in monetary policy? Such reformations would make cities practically unrecognizable from what they are today, and they would have myriad unintended and potentially negative (and positive) consequences—but that is in the nature of genuine reform.

Ingrid Daemmrich

From Erasmus to Twitter: Parody as Medium for Local and Global Social Networking

This paper was originally designed to initiate a discussion among humor scholars at last year's International Society for the Study of Humor Conference in Boston. Instead of that local, scholarly audience, this version envisions a Web-based interchange by linking with a Google Docs site that contains a PowerPoint with illustrations and invites readers to contribute their examples and comments to an exploration of social media's influence on a traditional form of literary humor.

In his groundbreaking study, *Community and Civil Society: Fundamental Principles of Sociology* (1887), Ferdinand Tönnies asserts that social networks link individuals into either a rural, intimate, "organic" community that shares practices, values, and beliefs or a wider commercial and urban public world. He names the former *community* and the latter *society*. Today's theorists of social networking speak instead of *nodes* or ties that connect individuals simultaneously to local communities and broad, even global society, an idea echoed by Amy Carrell in her 1997 article, "Humor Communities." Thanks to the lightning speed and outreach of the World Wide Web and devices like today's smart phone, social networking can instantly erase the distinctions between community and society. I propose that in appropriating this versatility, parody, often considered literature's most sophisticated form of humor, opens unlimited potential not just for literary but also for social game-playing, and not just locally but globally.

Before the advent of the Internet and mobile devices, parody had two networking functions. The first was closely associated with its traditional role: to mock previous works, whether literary, artistic, architectural, or musical, as for example, the noses doodled by the Renaissance philosopher Erasmus do. The network was text- and work-centered. A single writer would make fun of a previous work for the entertainment of intelligent readers who, as Neal Norrick observes so aptly, had passed "intelligence tests prefaced by quizzes in literary history" (118). The second was socially oriented by offering an incentive for appreciators of literary "intertextual jokes" to meet in a tavern or other public venue and play a social game of "mutual admiration." They would compete for applause for the most hilarious parody of a work they selected on the spur of a moment. Food, drink, literary conversation, and literary-game-playing were seamlessly interwoven into a night of fun.

Erasmus's parody of an ancient Greek caricature in his satirical colloquium, "In Pursuit of Benefices," is an example of mocking a text known to his classically educated audience. In it, the character Cocles enumerates the hilarious uses of Pamphagus's oversized nose, such as a "lamp extinguisher," a peg, a bellows, a "shade," a "grappling iron," a shield, a wedge, a trumpet, a spade, a scythe, a fork, or a fish-hook (47). The reference becomes an amusing literary hide-and-seek game for those readers who can recall and interrelate Erasmus's humor with epigram 203 by "Anonymous" in the *Greek Anthology* caricaturing Castor's nose as a series of incongruous implements such as "a hoe for him when he digs anything, a trumpet when he snores and a grape-sickle at vintage time, an anchor on board ship, a plough when he is sowing, a fishing-hook for sailors, a flesh-hook for feasters, a pair of tongs for ship-builders, and for farmers a leek-slicer, an axe for carpenters, and a handle for his door" and ending with the absurd statement: "Such a serviceable implement has Castor the luck to possess, wearing a nose adaptable for any work" (11.169). The ending is a wink at the ancient connection of the nose with the phallus and male prowess. That wink recurs in Cyrano's inventive self-caricature of his nose as he addresses the mockers of his oversized nose in Edmond Rostand's *Cyrano de Bergerac*:

> You might have said at least a hundred things / By varying the tone, like this, suppose:
>
> *Dramatic*: "When it bleeds, what a Red Sea!"
>
> *Admiring*: "Sign for a perfumery!"
>
> *Lyric*: "Is this a couch?" . . . "A dwarf pumpkin or a prize turnip?" (1.3)

The popularity of Rostand's play is so apparent that Saleem in Salman Rushdie's contemporary *Midnight's Children* can simply refer to his nose as a "cyranonose" and knowledgeable readers can connect the dots.

But text-based networking also has a robust existence on the Internet. For instance, an amateur classics lover, Michael Gilleland, assembles Erasmus's and the *Greek Anthology*'s caricatures of the nose, along with the "Slawkenbergius Tale" in Laurence Sterne's *Tristram Shandy* in his blog entitled "Noses." English professor Scott Rice has moved his perennially popular "It was a dark and stormy night" parody-writing contest to the Web. Based on the first sentence of Bulwer-Lytton's 1840 novel, *Paul Clifford*, "It was a dark and stormy night; the rain fell in torrents—except at occasional intervals when it was checked by a violent gust of wind . . . etc." the contest invites participants to submit "bad opening sentences to imaginary novels." The move to the Internet has resulted in worldwide contributions, extending from the 2010 winner, Seattle author Molly Ringle:

> For the first month of Ricardo and Felicity's affair, they greeted one another at every stolen rendezvous with a kiss—a lengthy, ravenous kiss, Ricardo lapping and sucking at Felicity's mouth as if she were a giant cage-mounted water bottle and he were the world's thirstiest gerbil.

to the 1992 French winner Laurel Fortuner:

> As the newest Lady Turnpot descended into the kitchen wrapped only in her celery-green dressing gown, her creamy bosom rising and falling like a temperamental soufflé, her tart mouth pursed in distaste, the sous-chef whispered to the scullery boy, "I don't know what to make of her."

Two consequences of Rice's ongoing parody contest: First, it was adopted and made fun of by cartoonists like Charles Schultz. Snoopy repeatedly submits his creative "It was a dark and stormy night" to the contest. But he's constantly disappointed because his contribution just isn't "bad" enough.[8] Second, Scott Rice's website links to an interactive secondary website, called "Sticks and Stones," which announces a variation of the venerable "dark-and-stormy night" contest:

> We the custodians, guardians, and stewards of the Bulwer-Lytton Fiction Contest propose a new game. We propose that you locate, isolate, and otherwise identify samples of bad published writing (that is, writing by those who are paid to write), and that you submit them to this page along with any commentary you wish to provide.[9]

There is no visible monitoring of the site: anyone can post. The outreach for social networking through parody on this site is limited only by its ability to attract readers and writers. Here is a posting from Berkeley California. It begins by quoting the opening sentence of Susan Fromberg Schaeffer's *The Golden Rope*:

> It was the last of the gray hours, when there are no colors left in the world, when his face on the sheets would be gray and set, like stone, when the wrinkled sheets on the bed

look like a frozen slate-gray sea, or like plowed land dead beneath the first killing frost."

and then critiques it:

> The similes don't work and there are too many of them. If I were to try to sneak this into the Bulwer-Lytton contest (Purple Prose) I'd continue thus: "and not like the funerary sculpture that Pietro ... makes, but like that cheap stuff made in Taiwan or someplace and sold through mail order catalogues, except that with the Internet they don't publish them any more, so I was really kind of down and wanted an Egg McMuffin, but they weren't open yet."

Piggy-backing on Rice's site, "Sticks and Stones" opens his game of parodying "purple prose" to anyone throughout the world who would like to join in playing it without the constraints of Rice's rules.

The second function of parody, to stimulate social game-playing for a group of friends, provides an interesting footnote in the history of American literature. The networking began in mid-nineteenth-century Boston with a group of Harvard graduates (all male, of course) who met monthly in the Parker House, to talk about literature over dinner and drinks. The group included such New England luminaries as Emerson, Longfellow, Agassiz, Motley, and Holmes and later, Henry James, William Hunt, Judge Lowell, Bishop Brooks, and James Thomas Fields, the editor-publisher of the prestigious New England literary magazine, *The Atlantic Monthly*. The men called their group the "Saturday Club." Oliver Wendell Holmes gave it the subtitle of a "society of mutual admiration."

That subtitle gave a brash New York writer, Bayard Taylor, the idea to challenge the preeminence of New England intellectual life in a series of articles named "Diversions of the Echo Club" and to have *The Atlantic Monthly* publish them. Their purpose was clearly to mock the Saturday Society. Like its parent, Taylor's Echo Club meets monthly, not in an upscale hotel, but in "Karl Schäfer's lager-beer cellar which Karl calls his Löwengrube or Lion's Den" (Jan. 1872:77). Its pub-like ambience immediately reminds *The Atlantic*'s knowledgeable readers of Auerbach's cellar in Goethe's Faust, where the satanic Mephisto magically produces first wine and then sparks of fire from the tables. In Taylor's series of articles, between four and eight men meet to write, read, and mutually applaud each other's parodies of current poets. Proclaiming: "We can come together, here, and be a private, secret club of Parodists, of Echoists," they all agree that "It will be capital sport." The sport starts with names of well-known poets being thrown into a hat and shaken up together. When, for example, the name Edgar A. Poe is drawn, Zoïlus writes and reads his parody of "The Raven":

What is time, time, time,
    To my rare and runic rhyme,
    To my random, reeling rhyme,
    By the sands along the shore,
Where the tempest whispers, "Pay him!" and I answer,
        "Nevermore!" (77)

Zoïlus continues: "Now, I don't mean to be wicked, and to do nothing with the dead but bone 'em, but when such a cue pops into one's mind, what is one to do?" The others agree that "boning" the dead Poe is "within decent limits," before proceeding to pick apart the poetry of Browning and Swinburne, two other names drawn from "the Ancient's hat." The evening's entertainment ends with a clink of empty glasses and the shout, "To be continued!"

Bayard Taylor's fictitious parody of Boston's eminent Saturday Club inspired the New Jersey turn-of-century humor anthologist Carolyn Wells to continue the parody in the form of the *Re-Echo Club*, published by New York's Morningside Press in 1913. "Little is known of the locale or clientele of this club, but . . . it takes pleasure in trying to better what is done," she announces (1). One of the most amusing sessions is parodying different English poets' imaginary reactions to Duchamps' Cubist painting, *A Nude Descending the Staircase*. The challenge is: "Take this, you fellows, and throw it into poetry."

"Any rules or conditions?" asked Billy Wordsworth.

"Absolutely none. It's the Ruleless School" (13).

So, for example, Ben Jonson responds with a laughable jingle that inspires the next silly poem, as the group plays at poetically mocking contemporary art.

Today, the congenial game of a group of friends parodying a famous work has moved to social networking sites like Twitter and Facebook. Here, for example, is a parody of Wallace Stevens' famous poem "So much depends" as a series of tweets collected by Drew Magary into *A Compendium of Horrible Horrible Twitter Poetry*: "*The catnip's in bloom besides the porch; clusters of tiny white blossoms dotted in purple, each with a front stoop to tempt passing bees.*"

Drew Magary tweets: "The old cliché was that Twitter was where people went to tell the world what they had for breakfast. But . . . it's much more than that. It's a bowl of cream of wheat, each granule glistening like a baby pearl..." The tweets from anonymous amateur writers are quick, quirky, and casual.

Club meetings in taverns, publishers and printers have given way to smart phones whose owners tweet their instant parodies on the run.

Still, as Michele Hannoosh has observed, the game of parody never stops. It just changes directions. So, Sarah Schmelling's book, Ophelia Joined the Group Maidens Who Don't Float uses old-fashioned print to mock precisely the new-fashioned social networking sites. Here is an excerpt of her take on Lewis Carroll's protagonist in *Alice in Wonderland* joining Facebook:

NEWS FEED

Alice joined the Wonderland network.

• Alice is trying to make sense of this brand-new place full of "friends" she doesn't remember ever seeing before.

• Alice also can't sort out how to change her profile photo.

Huck Finn: Excuse me miss, something seems to be awry with your type.

Alice: Oh dear, how puzzling it all is! I'm ever so confused. Perhaps I should have a drink.

Holden Caulfield: Boy, do I remember this time I got all tanked up and went to Central Park looking for the lagoon (103).

Like Bayard Taylor, Carolyn Wells, Scott Rice, or even Drew Magary, Schmelling envisions parody as a social game through which participants (here Lewis Carroll, Mark Twain, and J.D. Salinger) enjoy socializing. The texts that they post are as trivial as the earlier parodies. Far more important is just socializing on Facebook.

So, do Facebook and Twitter with their instant, abbreviated texts erase Ferdinand Tönnies's distinction between the local community and broad society by creating social networks of parodists that are simultaneously local and global? Is there any difference between the text-based game played by Erasmus, Sterne, Rostand, Rushdie, and others and parodies inviting verbal games among friends, such as the Echo and Re-Echo Club, Twitter, or Facebook? Or do the web-based capabilities simply extend the sociable pleasures of parody's traditional literary game-playing to ever new players on worldwide sites?

Works Cited

Attardo, Salvatore. *Linguistic Theories of Humor*. Berlin: Mouton de Gruyter, 1994. Print.

Carrell, Amy. "Humor Communities." *Humor* 10.1 (1997): 11-24. Print.

Erasmus, Desiderius. "On Benefice-Hunters." *Collected Works*. Trans. Craig R. Thompson. Toronto: University of Toronto Press, 1997: 39: 45-49. Print.

Gilleland, Michael. "Noses." *Laudator temporis acti*. http://laudatortemporisacti. blogspot.com/2007/02/noses.html. Web. 14 April 2011.

Greek Anthology. Trans. R. Patton. Cambridge: Harvard University Press, 1918: 11.169 Print

Hannoosh, Michele. "The Reflexive Function of Parody. *Comparative Literature* 41.2 (Spring 1989): 113-127. Print.

Ludwig, Richard and Clifford Nault. *Annals of American Literature*. New York: Oxford, 1986. Print.

Magary, Drew. A Compendium of Horrible Horrible Twitter Poetry. http://deadspin.com /5592733/a-compendium-of-horrible-horrible-twitter-poetry. Web. 14 April 2011.

Norrick, Neal. "Intertextuality in Humor." *Humor: International Journal of Humor Research* 2.2 (1989). 117-139. Print.

Rice, Scott. *The Bulwer-Lytton Fiction Contest*. www.bulwer-lytton.com. Web. 18 April 2011.

Rostand, Edmond, *Cyrano de Bergerac*, translated from the French by Charles F. Rideal Print. London: F. Tennyson Neely, 1896.

Schmelling, Sarah. *Ophelia Joined the Group Maidens Who Don't Float: Classic Literature Signs on to Facebook*. New York: Plume, 2009. Print.

"Sticks and Stones." *The Bulwer-Lytton Fiction Contest*. www.bulwer-lytton.com/sticks.html. Web. 18 April 2011.

Taylor, Bayard. "Diversions of the Echo Club." *Atlantic Monthly* 29 (1872): 79-80, 169, 26 Print.

Tönnies, Ferdinand. *Community and Civil Society*. Cambridge: Cambridge University Press, 2001. Print.

Wells, Carolyn. *The Re-Echo Club*. New York: Franklin Bigelow, 1913. Print.

Valerie Fox

Incorruptible

The sun set. We saw it off. At that moment there was still an outside chance of being corrupted.

This waiter has flair. He has my cousin's nose. He takes the least number of steps. The dog looks on. I have a memory of my father lifting and carrying boxes of bread.

Just at that moment you spoke to the dog. You explained that we could not take him inside the building, so he'd have to loiter outside a bit longer. He was left to think about not belonging.

Why worry? Why count the broken hours? You say something like that to no one in particular, or to someone you love.

You assign the roles. I get to be the bad luck owl. Everything is steady, or tries to be, like we're on a stately barge. Everyone is alive again. Except for me. My paint is flaking away. Apples are falling pretty far from our trees. On nearby Hanover Street a once inviting and cared-for house has been recently demolished. An upright piano stands slightly elevated at the top of the front steps. Someone should remove it, but it looks nice there, surrounded by blue skies and summertime.

Just at that moment I was incorruptible. We were interrupted by the radio. You floated the idea and cloud-like, I rained.

Valerie Fox

One day

one day you're barreling over the cement median, drunk
in the orange Karmann Ghia convertible
next thing you're married, then you're still married
careening and declining, going left and going
right, on foot in circles, attending Mass, on a dare,
climbing into the dire taxi

meeting up by the Don Quixote statue in Fishtown
stature all wrong, loping along
beginning again, being less married
donning a paper hat, making your way
into a room, this makes sense
to you, like being a savior, you save
you don't hoard, you appreciate the angularity
of High Modernism and insomnia

you don't discard your printed napkins—
Ponzio's, The Bluebird—
peppered with rhymes and telephone numbers
another dated and signed, punctured by thumb tacks,
having fallen at least once, abject, to the floor
see shoe print, size 9

young you, never at a loss for trying,
for staying up late, or inventing
evidence, necessary to replace the stolen boxes and bags of it,
noting the smell of the hoof and the horn,
of your own ice age, finding pictures of actual people
having a sense of conviviality and snow-preparedness
just ask anyone, you'll try anything

one day attracted by the moon, hiding from it
the next, or else you just can't find your true compass
not in this sky, never lucky or believing in luck, one good thing is
no one ever told you what to be, just what not to be,
and they left out a lot
for you to be

James Herbert and Richard Redding

When the Shrinks Ignore Science, Sue Them

In 1793, there was an outbreak of yellow fever in Philadelphia. Benjamin Rush, a leading colonial physician and signer of the Declaration of Independence, accepted the conventional wisdom that the condition should be treated with bloodletting. This treatment contributed to the demise of many of his patients. Nevertheless, as the epidemic waned, Rush was more convinced than ever of the efficacy of his methods. When Rush's patients recovered, he attributed their recovery to his intervention. When they died, he chalked it up to the inevitable course of the disease.

Medical practice has come a long way since Rush. Antibiotics and vaccines, to name two obvious examples, have been transformative. Without exception, these advances have been driven by the application of science to healthcare. Science substitutes controlled scientific data and statistical predictions for the practitioner's intuition and clinical lore, which are prone to biases in decision making, as Rush illustrated.

By promulgating practice guidelines, institutions like the United Kingdom's National Institute for Clinical Effectiveness and the United States' Comparative Effective Institute work to codify medical practice based on the best available scientific evidence. But not everyone is sanguine about dethroning practitioners' judgment in favor of science, and spirited defenses of clinician autonomy have emerged in both the professional literature (Hagemoser 2009) and the popular press (Greenfield 2010).

But consider recent cases involving mental health care. A father lost custody of his child because the mental health evaluation of the parent relied upon the scientifically unfounded Rorschach "inkblot" test. A depressed patient experienced severe side effects from antidepressant medications but was never informed about the option of equally effective treatments like cognitive-behavior therapy. And a number of therapists promise that repeatedly tapping (yes, tapping!) on their patients will cure serious disorders and addictions by adjusting the body's invisible "energy field" (Gaudiano and Herbert 2000).

One of our own patients suffered from severe obsessive compulsive disorder. He would spend hours each day showering and washing his hands until they bled. He sought treatment from a psychoanalyst, who insisted that his symptoms reflected unconscious drives that he must "work through." After his symptoms gradually worsened over several years of this analysis, he eventually sought behavior therapy and within weeks was completely cured of his condition. Although many psychological interventions may be ineffective but otherwise benign, research has demonstrated that others can be quite harmful (Lilienfeld 2007). Crisis debriefing is promoted to decrease post-traumatic stress reactions following a trauma, but in fact it actually increases the risk of such problems (McNally et al. 2003). So-called "attachment therapies" have led to the death of several children (Mercer et al. 2003). Facilitated communication, a technique promoted as allowing otherwise severely impaired individuals with autism to communicate fluently via typing on a keyboard while a facilitator supports their hand or arm, has led to parents being falsely accused of sexual abuse (Herbert et al. 2002; Romanczyk et al. 2003). These are only a few potentially harmful interventions. Despite data illustrating their potentially harmful effects, they remain surprisingly popular and continue to be used.

Such practices represent the tip of the iceberg of a persistent problem in mental health care: the chasm between science and practice. To close that gap, several steps must be taken. Of course, we need malpractice reform, but not as it is usually conceived. The pernicious effects of frivolous malpractice suits in encouraging unnecessary diagnostic and intervention procedures are widely discussed. But when mental health practitioners use methods that are totally lacking in scientific support, particularly when the treatment has been demonstrated to be harmful and evidence-based alternatives are available, they should be liable for malpractice.

Yet unlike lawsuits against other medical professionals, lawsuits against psychiatrists and psychologists have been exceptionally rare—and successful suits even rarer. Mental health practitioners have been able to escape liability by relying on prevailing community practices—no matter how misguided—to define the permissible standard(s) of care. A defendant can always round up some likeminded community practitioners who will testify that the procedure in question is widely practiced, even if it is scientifically unfounded.

Although suits against mental health professionals remain uncommon, litigants can and should make use of a Supreme Court case to make their claims viable. In *Daubert v. Merrell Dow Pharmaceuticals* (1993), the Court ruled that expert testimony must be based upon reliable "scientific knowledge" rather than common practice. Thus, when a mental health professional is sued for treating a patient with harmful or unscientific techniques, expert witnesses called upon to describe the prevailing standard of care must base their testimony on science. No longer can defendants argue that they met the standard of care merely because they employed techniques often used by others in the profession.

We acknowledge that clinical practice is complex and often does not lend itself to a simple application of scientifically established treatment protocols. For example, patients do not always fit neatly into diagnostic categories; this requires clinicians to use interventions established for closely related conditions. Patients do not always respond to first-line evidence-based interventions, therefore modifications of an established treatment or even a different approach may be necessary. Evidence-based treatments may not yet be established for some disorders or symptoms, so modifications of established treatment strategies or even a novel or experimental approach may be required. Moreover, in the case of psychotherapy even relatively straightforward cases necessarily involve some degree of tailoring of the treatment to each individual's unique circumstances. Each of these scenarios requires judicious clinical judgment. But such judgment should always be informed by the best available scientific evidence. Clinical judgment does not represent a *carte blanche* to escape scrutiny or legal liability.

A related issue is informed consent. Despite being ethically mandated, mental health practitioners rarely obtain fully informed consent from their patients for their interventions. An interesting issue centers on the question of whether clinicians should be permitted to offer services that are completely devoid of scientific support as long as the patient is fully informed of this fact, is informed of any known risks associated with the treatment, is informed of alternative options, and is paying out-of-pocket rather than through a private or governmental insurer. Without resolving this particular issue, it is clear that clinicians should always obtain fully informed consent, and such consent becomes even more important the further one deviates from scientifically established practices.

It will take time for case law to sort through the nuances of these real-world complexities. In the meantime, clinicians can minimize their risk of malpractice liability by using scientifically supported procedures whenever possible, ensuring that modifications to established treatments are scientifically informed, avoiding interventions that have been shown to be harmful while providing little or no benefit, and obtaining fully informed consent, especially for experimental procedures. In contrast, by seeking relief through the courts, not only can consumers who have been harmed by unscientific mental health practices seek appropriate damages, but they can also exert a positive influence on the field as a whole by encouraging scientifically based practice.

In addition to malpractice suits, other changes are needed to place routine clinical practice on stronger scientific footing. We need an unequivocal commitment to scientific practice by professional organizations, third-party payers, and state licensure boards. Organizations such as the American Psychological Association pay lip service to scientific standards, but they leave gaping loopholes that allow psychologists to practice all kinds of pseudoscientific nonsense. All too often psychiatrists, psychologists, and other mental health clinicians use unproven and even demonstrably harmful assessment and treatment procedures, even when alternative scientifically supported methods are available. A key principle inherent in healthcare reform is that in order to save cost and improve outcomes, medical practice should be driven by the best scientific evidence (The Hastings Center 2009). That principle should also be applied to mental health professionals, particularly because research has found a number of psychological and psychiatric interventions to be effective (sometimes more so than treatments for physical disorders).

Next, we need user-friendly practice guidelines that are based on the best available scientific evidence and are free of undue influence from interest groups. Reflecting the influence of the pharmaceutical industry, the American Psychiatric Association's guidelines for the treatment of depression are heavily skewed toward drug therapies despite many scientific studies showing that certain forms of "talk therapy," such as cognitive behavior therapy, yield longer-lasting effects with fewer complications. (Of course, the best guidelines are not overly rigid but allow the practitioner to tailor them to an individual patient's unique clinical picture.)

Finally, we must improve consumer education. Paradoxically, the growth of the Internet and advertising of pharmaceuticals makes information more available to consumers but also makes it more difficult to filter good science from potentially harmful pseudoscience.

Each of these strategies has an important role to play, but malpractice suits against mental health professionals may become *the* critical motivating force behind change, so that the shrinks, too, are guided by science rather than their modern-day versions of bloodletting.

References

Daubert v. Merrell Dow Pharmaceuticals, Inc. 1993. 509 U.S. 579.

Gaudiano, B., and J.D. Herbert. 2000. "Can we really tap our problems away? A critical analysis of Thought Field Therapy. " Skeptical Inquirer 24(4) (July/August): 29-36

Greenfield, S. 2010. In defense of physician autonomy. *Wall Street Journal* (September 7): A23. Hagemoser, S. 2009. Braking the bandwagon: "Scrutinizing the science and politics of empirically supported therapies." *The Journal of Psychology* 143: 601-14.

Herbert, J.D., I.R. Sharp, and B.A. Gaudiano. 2002. "Separating fact from fiction in the etiology and treatment of autism: A scientific review of the evidence." *Scientific Review of Mental Health Practice* 1(1): 23–43.

Lilienfeld, S.O. 2007. "Psychological treatments that cause harm. "*Perspectives on Psychological Science* 2(1): 53–70.

McNally, R.J., R.A. Bryant, and A. Ehlers. 2003. "Does early psychological intervention promote recovery from posttraumatic stress?" P*sychological Science in the Public Interest* 4(2): 45–79.

Mercer, J., L. Sarner, and L. Rosa. 2003. *Attachment Therapy on Trial.* Westport, Connecticut: Praeger.

Romanczyk, R.G., L. Arnstein, L.V. Soorya, and J. Gillis. 2003. "The myriad of controversial treatments for autism: A critical evaluation of efficacy." In S.O.

Lilienfeld, S.J. Lynn, and J.M. Lohr (Eds.), *Science and Pseudoscience in Clinical Psychology*, 363–98. New York: Guilford.

The Hastings Center. 2009. Cost Control and *Health Care Reform: Act 1.* Garrison, New York.

Henry Israeli

A Canticle With Dashes of Remorse

The mother in the movie *Mother* would kill for her son.
Not so my mother, who, if anything went wrong,
laid blame squarely on me. If a kid hit me,
I probably deserved it. And why was I bothering her anyway?
And how about hitting him back? That never worked out well for me.
One kid who boxed my ears so expertly left no bruises
but a pain in my head so excruciating you'd think
he was professionally trained in torture.
A thousand of me felled into myself, swimmers
choreographed to look like the petals of a closing flower.
I held in my tears.
               I confess that when I was six
I snuck into the house they were building next door
and painted the walls myself.
I mixed pink insulation with several cans of paint
and reached as high as a six year old could
to spread my personal vision across the newly built house.
Still, I was surprised when police officers
came knocking at our door, asking to speak to my mother.
I hid in the garage, waiting to be turned in,
envisioning life behind bars with prison slop on metal trays
and baggy clothes that practically dripped off me.
But no one called for me. Not for questions, or punishment.
Not a word was mentioned but there was plenty of talk
around the neighborhood about who the vandals probably were
and what they had done.
               I never told my mother,
and eventually it seemed too silly
to bring up at all. Would she even remember?
But now, for some reason, I wish I could ask her
if she protected me from the law that day
or if she just thought her little angel was incapable of the destruction
I did so easily and dutifully, with hardly any effort at all.

Miriam N. Kotzin

How to Write a Sustainable Love Poem

First wonder if the love you celebrate
will prove sustainable. Will it endure,
renewed, a lifetime guaranteed amour,
or does it have an expiration date?

Then ask, if love should die, whose heart (or mind)
will be the first to slow then turn away;
then mark the watched-for changes day by day—
who's first indifferent, then disinclined.

If you're the one who's left behind, then write
about enduring grief. Take care to tune your moan
with rhyme and meter. Do control your tone:
use lots of sugar; serve up honeyed spite.

And though your love limps off to die, your verse
will stride along to pass the grinding hearse.

Miriam N. Kotzin

How to Write a Sustainable Poem

Of course you'll want to write in free
verse. Decry the rising tide,
but scandalize the bourgeoisie
with your naughty thoughts implied
and then revealed by simile
and metaphor: Jekyll, Hyde
.

But scandalize the bourgeoisie
with your naughty thoughts implied
by clever phallic imagery
(pines and windmills); you've denied
and then revealed by simile
and metaphor: Jekyll, Hyde.

By clever phallic imagery
(pines and windmills) you've denied
all hope of passing for PC:
what you've dreamt you've pushed aside
and then revealed by simile
and metaphor: Jekyll, Hyde.

All hope of passing for PC?
What you've dreamt you've pushed aside?
Just praise sustainability
and keep your margins wide
and then revealed by simile
and metaphor: Jekyll, Hyde.

Michael Leone

From the Terrace of the Hollywood Hotel

Larry P. Zemlinski
C/O The Hollywood Hotel
2145 Yucca Street
Hollywood, CA 90028

May 8, 2007
Traci Pereki, President
International Documentary Institute
1201 Waverly Boulevard, Suite 550
Los Angeles, CA 90017

Dear Ms. Pereki:

I am not writing to you because the documentary feature "Movie Maniacs: Three Moviegoers in Manhattan," of which I am arguably the star, did not garner any Academy Awards, nor because I was not nominated for Best Actor. (I hope you catch my wryness: I'm fully aware that such a category for documentaries doesn't exist.) However, in your speech, which I obtained an expensive transcription of from Video Monitoring Services, delivered at the 2007 IDI Gala Reception for Academy Awards Documentary Nominees at the Academy of Motion Picture Arts, you made a few remarks about my film that puzzled, and frankly, disturbed me.

You said that the documentary was about "three lost, disenfranchised souls." I suppose you are including me in that number. However, and I find it tedious to assert, I am hardly "lost." I wonder how you can conclude that somebody such as I, who has a unique collection of vintage San Pellegrino bottles, including the very vessel the great Pakistani actor Prakash Bahadur Thapaseen sipped from on the set of his most famous film, "Every Bengal Boy," is lost. Somebody—though I no longer partake in such frivolous activities—who was a former member of the International Federation of Competitive Eating and champion of the 1977 U.S. Matzah Ball Eating Contest held in Crown Heights, Brooklyn.

I think perhaps that the portrayal of me in the film has led you to presuppose this about me. (I won't go into details about the craven irresponsibility of the director, Leeza Saavedra. And no—I am not "obsessed" with her, as the *Post* has reported, and though I was found residing in a canvas tent outside of her apartment building, I most assuredly was not doing anything "perverted," but merely making a point: I refused to allow her to continue to cruelly and unprofessionally ignore me.)

I agree that the other two people featured in the film would fit your description. I in fact live in a very fashionable tenement house in the Bronx. There is quite a charming take-out Chinese bistro on the first floor where on very special occasions I partake of a hearty dim sum before I venture to see a film. I subsist on a modest but plentiful trust bequeathed to me by my late uncle, who was a lifelong member of the Ancient Arabic Order of the Nobles of the Mystic Shrine. This income allows me to indulge my film passion full time, as long as I don't overextend myself. (I have a very strict diet: I buy a bundle of homemade knishes from the local Jewish delicatessen, freeze them accordingly, and eat one for breakfast, another for lunch, while snacking in between on a variety of grains, from pumpkin seeds, hazel nuts, and—a constant weakness of my sweet tooth—saltwater taffy. At night, of course, I eat full-course microwaveable meals.)

I don't think you could say the same for the other people in this picture, one of whom resides in a cardboard teepee beneath the Williamsburg Bridge, and the other in a halfway home in Woodside, Queens. Unlike my co-stars, I have actually *studied* film, at NYU. And no, I did not get expelled for attacking a certain woman who will go unnamed in a certain dormitory that will go unnamed. True, I did not obtain my degree; I opted to leave the department because of insufficiently devoted teachers and talentless students.

And the incident with the woman—I will say this: it's not my fault that she lacked imagination and creativity. Indeed, the entire freshman class was participating in a Movie Masque held at the auditorium in Weinstein Hall. We were all to dress like our favorite film characters. I chose the golem, from Galeen and Wegener's movie of the same name. I stitched together my own cardboard suit, which I daubed completely with a red, oven-baked polymer clay, and I wore a very expensive pair of shin-length hobnail boots. But how was I to know the masque ended at midnight?

Further, I have made regular appearances on Raymond Bremmer's cable network show "Foreign Flicks" (very underrated, in my opinion, and a must-see for real cineastes). I have a trove of personal correspondence with a wealth of international film directors, including the Icelandic animated short director Guðbjörg Jónsdóttir, who penned me a note on the back of an embossed napkin from Café Cultur in Reykjavik before drowning herself in the icy waters of Faxaflói Bay. (It is presently listed on eBay for seven dollars; I might give you a discount if you are interested.)

I agreed in principle to star in Ms. Saavedra's film because I thought my presence, when juxtaposed against those two other hopeless stumblebums, might inject an element of integrity to the film. Do you know that the usher at MoMA actually reserves a special coat hanger for my cape, a privilege he grants only to me? That the barista at the Anthology of Film Archives is kind enough to proffer me free, day-old but very fresh scones? That I was once featured prominently in the background waving a sign "American Film is Dead" during a "Good Morning America" episode featuring that arch destroyer of American cinema, Steven Spielberg? Is any of this important information about me in the film? No.

Again, the problem is how I was presented in the film. Allow me to explain:

Yes, I gave the filmmaker Leeza Saavedra complete access to my life. She approached me in the lobby of the Film Forum, hands tucked into the pockets of her tight jeans, and told me she had been watching me. And yet *I* am portrayed as the stalker?

"I'd like you to be in my film," she said.

This might astonish some people; not me. I have often been the object of curiosity of many gawking, camera-carrying tourists. (I am a very handsome and sturdy—not "stout," as one reviewer referred to me—Sephardic Jew with a baronial forehead and austere jaw line.)

"What is this 'film' about?" I said. She was very attractive, this young woman, but I certainly wasn't going to let her charm distract me.

She told me. "I like people who have obsessions."

"I have a passion," I said. "There is a difference."

"How many films do you see a day?" she said.

I pondered. "Depends on the day, but if it's a good one, at least six. That doesn't count shorts, of course."

She told me more about her project: she wanted to lump me in with two other moviegoers in Manhattan, documenting their lives.

"Who are these people?" I said.

She described them to me. One of them, Phil, was, of all ungodly things, a George Lucas fanatic, who at forty-eight years old, wears Star Wars-decorated pajamas and sleeps under a R2D2-painted coverlet; the other, Sally, the teepee twerp, spends most of her evenings in giant Cineplex theaters, scuttling from one movie to the next on the same ticket until the theaters close.

"But I am unlike these people," I said. "Obviously you haven't read my many articles on film history."

She confessed she hadn't.

"Where are they published?" she said.

I told her they were readily available on Gopher.

"I'm sorry?"

She was obviously unacquainted with this remarkable document retrieval network protocol, vastly more efficient than the current monstrosity known as the "Internet." I explained it to her. "Unfortunately," I said, "thanks to Bill Gates, Gopher is only available on a hundred or so servers in the world. But I will see if I can procure you a copy of one of my pieces."

"I really want to tell *your* story," she said.

"I'll admit I lead a fascinating life," I told her, "spending the day doing what I love. But what makes you think it will be appreciated by the general public of this moronic country?"

"I guess I'm going with my instinct."

I allowed her and her sound and cameramen to inhabit my studio and my entire life for six weeks. They recorded my daily peregrinations, and I granted them intimate access to my emotions and thoughts. For instance, during one trek through Central Park—I was rushing westward to a screening of Bernard Swenson's neo-naturalist film "The Sprinkler Fitter" at the Natural History Archive—a bombastic rainstorm started. People scrambled for shelter, but I, an otherwise agnostic, felt suddenly possessed of the crushing divine beauty of life and I ripped off my fleece-lined Inverness cape and stomped about howling out the haunting lyrics of Verdi's "Rigoletto." I was not, as Ms. Saavedra reported in her film, suffering from a "manic" episode. Yes, I allowed the paramedics to assist me, but it was only because I was suffering from a middle ear infection and had gotten a bit winded. Despite being given access to this and other unique moments, Ms. Saavedra managed to piece together a film that makes me look like nothing more than a dreary dilettante who never bathes!

A few things about the latter. Though there is a segment in the film where I mention that I have not bathed in two weeks because my water was turned off, I would like you and everybody else to know that I shower *every* other day. And while it is true that I suffer from a skin condition, it in no way absolves me of using soap. I did state this at one point in the film, but I had been grossly misinformed by my ex-naturopathologist that *all* soap solutions exacerbate the chafing effects of atopic dermatitis.

I also object to my stepmother's presence in the film. Here is where I feel I have been truly sabotaged. I had no idea Ms. Saavedra would go slithering behind my back interviewing my relatives. I haven't seen my stepmother in at least ten years. She is an "activist," and I use the term loosely, because the only thing she presumes to act upon is my father's wallet. (My real mother died when I was ten. And yes, I was laughing at the funeral—how only the most anomalous aspects of my character have made it into this film!—but only because I was remembering a joke my mother, a free spirit, often used to tell me: Why did the hippie go to the North Pole? To meet cool people.)

"He is a very sick man," my stepmother says, in her Bronx accent. "He is filthy, degraded, and has serious psychological problems. He lives in a complete fantasy. He once showed up at Juliette Binoche's vacation home in the Hamptons. He *loathes* women."

No, Henrietta, you harpy, I loathe *one* woman: you.

And how I wished Ms. Saavedra had the courage to present my side of the story about my strained relations with my father and stepmother, how it was she, against my father's wishes, who demanded I be put into a sanitarium at fifteen years old, she who insisted that I receive the "proper" medications that left me addled and sluggish and bloated and inarticulate and defenseless. She, I am sure of it, who is responsible for whittling away at the otherwise robust health of my father, turning him into, after ten years, a stooped old stick of a man with early Alzheimer's.

But I do not mean to prate.

Many reviewers of the film have remarked upon my intriguing, charming character. Here are a few samples:

From Roger Ebert: "The most interesting character, to be sure, is Larry Zemlinski, an immensely intelligent, if not unhinged, man, who has tried, literally, to spend every moment of his life watching a movie;"

From Joel Siegel: "Gosh. I don't even know where to begin with this guy. He is just so wonderfully wacko."

From A.O. Scott of the *New York Times*: "Zemlinski is hyper and hypnotic, his love of film as intense as his hatred for modern life. Seldom have we seen captured in film such a . . . [i]ndividual."

There are many more snippets I could spit at you, but I don't want to boast. The real purpose of my letter is this:

I have seen your early work, including your thesis for the UCLA Department of Film Studies, called "Dumpster Divers," a cinéma vérité account of a crew of homeless desperados in the suburbs of Oakland. Though I thought your student film was marred by a propensity for over-exposition, you have talent. I also read an interview with you in the *Journal of Film and Video* where you decry your lack of inspiration because you just haven't found a subject worth pursuing.

Here is where I come in:

Obviously, the public and press agree that I am captivating; obviously, Ms. Saavedra, despite our artistic and emotional clashes—by the way, it was she who suggested we go out for sushi, and later to a session of skee-ball—had the instinct to realize I am an intelligent and engaging personality. Thus, I am willing, at my own expense, to allow you to film me. As you will see at the top of this letter, I am, in fact, already in LA. My recent explosion of fame has forced me to flee New York; I am writing this now from the terrace of the Hollywood Hotel on Yucca Street.

I like you, Ms. Pereki. You are *extremely* fine looking, with an excellent figure—sculpted daily at the Karma Karballa Center in Beverly Hills—and I am positive you are the person to do the job. I do not care that you fly off regularly to the Red Mountain Spa in St. George, Utah not with your husband but with the super agent Ronald Dworkin from the William Morris agency. (I must confess incredulity at your taste: isn't the guy responsible for foisting upon the American public that no-talent homosexual, Tom Cruise?)

This is your opportunity to correct all of Ms. Saavedra's wrongs. I have a half-century's accrual of knowledge to present to you. Though living in Los Angeles has cramped by cinematic lifestyle a bit, I still manage at least three films a day at the Indie Film Lounge and the Retro Theater in Silver Lake; I think you, of all people, should appreciate the sacrifices I am making on my part to appeal to your reasonable judgment.

Lastly, I do not appreciate the temporary restraining order you filed on me in Los Angeles district court. I am not harassing you, nor being abusive or alarming; I am merely trying to ingratiate myself to you, if you would only tear your pretty mouth away from that cell phone and speak to me for a moment.

I hope this letter finds you peaceful and beautiful.

I anxiously await your reply.

Truly,

Larry P. Zemlinski

Lynn Levin

How to Eat a Pet: A Gastronomic Adventure in the Andes

I have been known to eat foods that others snub. As a student, I lived off back-of-the-store, reduced-price vegetables and fruits. Day-or-more-old muffins and danish were a treat. My best company dish was a cheap and tasty enchilada casserole that I made with chicken necks and backs. So it was only natural I should one day undertake a real gastronomic adventure. I should try to eat a pet, a nice small one. A guinea pig would do, and the place to accomplish that was Peru where *cuy*, as guinea pig is known, was said to be a staple of the traditional diet.

Of course, I didn't travel to Peru just to challenge the frontiers of dining. It had long been my dream to explore the cloud-crested ruins of Machu Picchu and to glide upon Lake Titicaca in a reed boat. I wanted to brush up on my Spanish. I wanted to experience the Andes. I wanted to try a dish so repellant that I could brag about it for the rest of my life. No matter that the furry beasts were the hapless servants of science, or that my sister and I once kept them as pets, or that every single person I spoke to curled his face in revulsion when I announced my intention to dine on a creature normally at home on a bed of cedar shavings. The more folks made retching motions, the more I rubbed my palms together with anticipation over a dish of something I imagined as a kind of mammalian Cornish game hen. I pledged to myself that I would consume cuy and then return home to triumphantly proclaim to my sister that *I had eaten Fluffy.*

How fondly I remembered my sister Judy's sweet-tempered little calico guinea pig. Fluffy loved to be held and stroked. We had tea parties for her. We made her salads with tough outer lettuce leaves. Fluffy nibbled on carrot tops and rabbit pellets. She didn't exercise much, but neither did anyone in our family. She lounged through a placid life until we felt she needed a mate and introduced Mickey into her cage. A hefty albino, Mickey had beady red eyes, a nasty attitude, and a pair of tusks that drew more than their share of our blood.

The match, I think, was a cruel one. I have often regretted it. Therefore it would have been more fitting to imagine myself biting into the hostile Mickey in retribution. But I imagined him as bitter and tough. There would be no pleasure in his degustation, none of the delight of eating Fluffy.

In Peru, I learned that cuy was prepared in a number of ways. You could make it stuffed and roasted, piquant and quartered, or flattened whole and fried. And while my host family in Cusco, the Mariscals, never served it at *almuerzo*, our main midday meal, cuy is said to be widely consumed in Peru. According to the author of *Unmentionable Cuisine*, veterinarian and food expert Calvin Schwabe, cuy provides over 50% of Peru's animal protein. Many people raise guinea pigs at home, and others buy them killed and cleaned in the meat section of the market. Ask a Peruvian if he or she eats cuy, and you will hear that person wax sentimental about the way his or her mamá prepared it—just the same way an American will rhapsodize about Mom's apple pie or fried chicken. Still, as much as the Peruvians boasted of their favorite cuy fricassee or roast cuy, not once did I see an Andean or a Criollo actually eat cuy.

So why should my mind and guts rebel before a carefully prepared dish of pet? Was I just too ethnocentric? Did I think it barbaric or taboo? If I were starving, I would probably see things differently.

Cuy is by no means the most stomach-turning thing one can consume. In some parts of the Amazon jungle, people eat monkey, an animal whose genome is too close to human for my taste. Apropos of the human genome, food writer Jen Karetnick, who has done considerable research on Peruvian witchcraft, reveals that in some remote areas of Peru certain cooks may stir stew with a human femur or scrape bits of skull into a marinade of fish. Karetnick explains that this is part of a spell-casting ritual, adding that the use of human remains in cooking is strictly illegal in Peru. Good to hear that since fish with skull is another no-brainer for me. But in the Andes what did I eat unawares? There's a mystery.

The issue of cannibalism or quasi-cannibalism aside, food tastes and food taboos are relative. The Chinese eat cat and dog. Moses declared that locusts were kosher. The Japanese challenge death by indulging in the poisonous *fugu* fish. The Philippinos drink and chew the delicacy of *balut*, the nearly mature embryo of a chick cooked in its shell. And what about haggis, the stuffed sheep's stomach so dear to Scottish palates and my own? I did not want to be ethnocentric. I wanted to overcome a food prejudice and eat a pet, a pet that, unfortunately, also happened to be a rat.

Rodent eating, however, is not unheard of even in America. Squirrel is a classic ingredient in Brunswick stew. In some parts of New Jersey, fire companies and churches hold muskrat dinners. On the Internet, you can find recipes for muskrat, or marsh hare, as it is sometimes known. I also found a recipe for rottweiler with sweet potatoes. But I digress. The Peruvians think it is bizarre and hilarious that Americans keep guinea pigs as pets.

For the first two weeks in Peru I demurred when it came to cuy. I dined on *ají gallina*, a spicy chicken stew, and *lomo saltado*, a yummy stir-fried beef dish gilded with french fries. I particularly liked alpaca, a meat which I found a little chewy, but very tasty. Grilled and attractively plated, it looked just like scallops of beef. At most every meal I ate *choclo*, the bland, starchy, mega-kernelled corn that is a staple of the Peruvian diet. It didn't taste as good as it looked, but served with a chunk of salty cheese—a bite of *choclo*, a bite of *queso*—I learned to like it better. I developed a fondness for *mana*, a kind of giant marshmallow-sized sweetened popcorn, a popular snack you could buy from street vendors. Peru, of course, is the birthplace of corn and potatoes, and one is served spuds of all types: yellow, white, purple, dried and reconstituted, and then some.

It was not until I was in the town of Aguas Calientes, a maze of repetitive souvenir shops, restaurants, and hostels that served the budget tourists to Machu Picchu, that I bellied up to the challenge of eating guinea pig. It was now or never, I thought, for after Machu Picchu I would journey on to Lake Titicaca, and I didn't know if I would be able to order cuy there.

This was February, the height of the rainy season. In Aguas Calientes, torrents niagara'd off the awnings of the shops and restaurants. Deluges turned the staircase-like streets into tributaries of the Urubamba, the river that roared and rushed through the town and by the base of Machu Picchu. The town itself is called "Hot Waters" after its thermal springs, which are popular with the younger hikers. While my traveling partners, Michelle and Nancy, dared the spa, I passed, being fastidious, if not about eating strange things, then at least about stewing in a pool of backpacker bacteria. The rain had put a damper on our spirits. We did not look forward to hiking the ruins during a downpour, but magically the skies cleared the morning we were to visit Machu Picchu, and I even saw a flock of green parrots wing by a mountainside.

Never discovered, hence never destroyed by the Spaniards, Machu Picchu stands in silent majesty along the eyebrow of the rainforest. We spent a glorious morning exploring its emerald agricultural terraces and its common, royal, and sacred precincts. It was a sublime and strenuous visit. By the time we returned to Aguas Calientes, we had worked up an appetite. It was time for my next adventure. It was time to try cuy.

Together we searched for a suitable restaurant. We dismissed quite a few: too expensive, too pretentious, not clean, no guinea pig, overly expensive guinea pig. At last we settled on a homey little place called El Candamo, mostly because of its comically mistranslated menu, which was headlined: "Plates to the pleasure give the victim."

Here, the Roasted Alpaca or *Asado de Alpaca* was known as Roasted He/She Gives German Nickel. Trout Roman-style or *Trucha a la Romana* was Trout to the Roman One. *Milanesa de Pollo* or Chicken Milanese-style became Milanesa Gives Chicken. Then there was my favorite: *Milanesa a la Napolitana de Res* or Milanesa to the Neapolitan One Gives Head. Michelle ordered trout. Nancy asked for spaghetti. Though I regretted having to pass up that Milanese and Neapolitan combo, I went for the *Cuy al Horno*. Oven-roasted cuy. It cost thirty-two soles or about ten dollars, and I watched with some trepidation as the cook took the small prepared mammal, laid it on a shallow white tray, and slid it into a wood-burning clay oven. Soon after I finished my Cusqueña beer, the dish was ready. The waitress smiled at me ironically.

Fluffy lay on the plate congealed and scorched, paws up, claws and head on, ringed with papas fritas, a huge log of choclo, and a few slices of cucumber and tomato. The garnishes surrounded her the way flowers garlanded the body at a funeral parlor. Fluffy was helpless. Her hind legs were splayed in indignity. Her orifices winked at me. Lest one take her for a pig, her two pairs of chisel-like incisors classed her at once in the order *Rodentia*. Fluffy had bits of herb over her eyes. Her mouth was frozen into an unmerry rictus, that sarcastic grin born by Death who always has the last laugh. "So, living stiff," she chortled silently, "eat me. I dare you."

The body of the cuy was pierced at various points to let the fat run out. With much difficulty I split it open with the dull table knife. Inside there was a dark green stuffing, made mostly of parsley and flavored with various herbs. It was potent and aromatic, but as I dipped in a second time, I came up with a fork of noodle-like stuff; the animal's intestines were mixed in with the green. So much for the stuffing. I took a deep breath for courage then cut and mostly combed at the meat with my fork. It was a labor-intensive dish. I found I had to separate the thin sheets of meat from the leather and subcutaneous fat. After giving Michelle and Nancy as much as they would accept—about two teaspoons each—I tried the meat. It was pungent, perhaps from the herb stuffing. There was a slipperiness to it. It was stringy and chewy and tasted like pork. And that was enough cuy for me.

Partly out of respect for my companions, partly out of respect for the corpse, I drew some tiny flimsy restaurant napkins over Fluffy's face and body. Thankfully Nancy was generous in sharing her spaghetti, and Michelle gave me some of her guacamole. The Cusqueña beer helped. All that plus a serious loss of appetite made for an adequate lunch.

My friend, Odi Gonzales, who is not only a noted Peruvian poet but also a genuine ethnic Inca with a passion for cuy, later told me that you are supposed to pick up the cuy whole with your hands and suck the meat off the thin bones.

You then draw out and discard any bones that end up in your mouth. Clearly my knifing and forking had not contributed positively to my rodent-eating experience. I thought of the waitress at El Candamo and her sly smile. It must have been routinely funny to see the tourists struggle with the varmint. In her heart I think she knew that I would have been better off with the Milanesa to the Neapolitan One Gives Head.

Those of us who are not vegetarians eat dead things. This is the common fact. If you accept that humans are omnivores, which I do, we as a species kill and cook so that we may eat and live. I have never had much patience for sanctimonious vegetarians who tell me that morally I should be able to kill a cow if I want the right to eat steak. Nevertheless, there is something shocking about the frankness of seeing the cooked body entire. Of seeing the thing with its teeth. Many people, said Dr. Schwabe, have a bias against eating an animal served whole. Some will not eat fish with the head on or roast suckling pig. Well, it was that, of course, but it was also that the darn thing was a rat. As far as the gastronomy of disgust goes, I'd give whole roasted guinea pig at least an eight. So when it came time to report to my sister about eating Fluffy, I had to confess that I had eaten her, but not very much.

On the other hand, I obtained a new degree of self-knowledge. I discovered that when it came to eating strange things, I was not as brave as I thought. Some might even call me chicken.

Yet, if you, too, wish to overcome a food prejudice and eat a pet, you may want to know how to prepare cuy. I came across this recipe for stuffed guinea pig in Peru.

You will need:

>one clean guinea pig
>onion
>ground chili pepper and ground red chili pepper (both very spicy)
>cooking oil
>parsley
>oregano
>mint
>huaycatay (an herb that tastes and smells like a blend of black mint and marigold)
>walnuts
>salt
>butter

The recipe, obviously not one for the beginning cook, instructs you to open the guinea pig ventrally, then to salt and drain it. After salting and draining, remove the organs and intestines, but do not wash the cuy anymore. Parboil the innards separately, then pierce them and dress them with onion, chili pepper, and oil. In another container, prepare a finely chopped mixture of the parsley, mint, oregano, huaycatay, walnuts, and salt. Combine the mixture with the cooked organs and intestines and stuff all that back into the body cavity of the guinea pig. Coat the guinea pig with butter and ground red pepper. Place the critter in a roasting pan and cook it in the oven "until it's done."

Revised American instructions: First, go to a pet store....

Works Cited

Karetnick, Jen. "The Culinary Art of Peruvian Witchcraft." *The Drexel Online Journal* 2004. <http://www.drexel.edu/doj/essays/karetnick_witchcraft.asp>.

Schwabe, Calvin. "Food Prejudices and the Gastronomy of Disgust." University of Pennsylvania. 20 Nov 2002. Lecture.

Joanna Lyskowicz

Try or Not to Try to Learn a Foreign Language?

Learning a foreign language can be daunting task for people who have been speaking only one language their entire life. As children, people 'acquire language' by immersion in the family environment rather than by classroom schooling. No task is too much of a challenge simply because everything is new and attractive; effort is made without being conscious of it; parents are constantly applauding their children who have yet to learn the words "to complain."

Yes, learning a new language in the classroom requires much more effort from the language learner, especially since the process is conscious. This means that language learners must purposely set aside time to study and practice because they are older and more resistant to language acquisition (read: complain a lot). The most important element of the language learning at this point is motivation. The student has to know what the purpose of learning a new language is. Motives can vary from personal enrichment to professional ambitions (for examples, desiring to learn the language of your ancestors, wanting to travel abroad, communicating with friends from foreign countries and learning their culture through language, or aspiring to use language to further their career and become more attractive on the job market).

Why should you learn a foreign language?

You must answer this question before you enroll in a language class. If you are unable to find a motivation in yourself to study the language aside from the fact that it fills a requirement or an elective, you will suffer through the process and the results will be mediocre at best.

Now, once you are enrolled in the class, what should you expect?

Much depends on your previous experience in learning another language in general, or maybe this is the first time you are brave enough to begin your journey of language learning.

With the right attitude your journey will be a blast, but if you get discouraged at the beginning, you may never want to study the language again.

The same way as you prepare and pack your luggage to go to a new place, you should prepare before you join the language class. You will need an open mind, humbleness, a positive attitude and a willingness to try. If you are shy, get rid of your shyness for the sake of success in language learning. You are learning. You have the right to make mistakes, but you need to practice to make them and to, eventually, avoid them.

Let me explain why I said you need to be humble.

As a native speaker of English or another language, it is easy to assume that you are an expert, that you know your mother tongue the best and that you make no mistakes. You may dislike the fact that once you start learning a new language, you may come to a realization that you don't know your own language that well. You speak it, but you cannot explain why some tense has to be used or you are unable to name parts of speech. So when your foreign language teacher comes to the rescue, you need to be all ears, as you can learn your own language along with the new one.

The more you understand your own language, the easier it will be to acquire the foreign one. The more questions you have about your own language, the better your will understand the new language you learn.

Lots of students tend to be passive learners who wrongly believe that a few hours of class time will make them fluent in the foreign language. Unfortunately, this is a big fat lie. Taking classes will impose on you a certain studying routine: new subject taught, activities to practice it, quiz/exam, ability to ask questions of your teacher, but the real deal comes from the exposure to the language outside of the classroom. I'm not only referring to talking to native speakers—which seems to be a mission impossible to students learning the language in the U.S.—but also to reading articles and books, listening to the radio, and watching TV on foreign channels.

If you do everything mentioned above and are still struggling, then maybe you are a language anti-talent, but I haven't met one yet.

Also, if you are a musician with a sharp ear who has never yet considered foreign language study, you should take advantage of the gift God gave you and stop by the foreign language class. It will be a breeze.

And one last (but not least) reason you should consider studying a foreign language is to improve your memory. In the era of cell phones and smart phones with instant access to any information that we desire, we barely make an effort to memorize things. With language learning, you have no option; you have to memorize many things.

The more you train your brain while young, the more efficient it will be at an older age. There is a study showing that memorizing foreign words works to prevent Alzheimer's disease. Prevent and don't worry about the cure later.

Learning any foreign language will be an adventure, but since Spanish is the second most-spoken language in the U.S., it is also the most commonly taught in schools before you reach the university level, and lots of you, at some point in your past education, have studied it.

Now let me give you a short review lesson from your Spanish class. Let's see what you remember.

Estudié, estudiaba o había estudiado español—which of these verbs means "I studied Spanish"?

You learned that Past Tense is a tense that describes actions that happened in the past. Is this explanation good enough? Could you say something more specific about this tense?

If the answer is NO, you are correct. The tense that you call in English Past Tense in Spanish divides into Preterit, Imperfect, and Pluperfect and depending on its function in the sentence can be translated in a few different ways into English: I did, I was doing, I used to do, I had done.

I know, it all seems complicated, but the constant analysis of your own language makes you realize how different foreign language may be from yours and how differently people can perceive and express the same things.

¡Aprende a hablar español! or ¡Aprenda a hablar español!—Which of the two commands is the correct one?

Another thing that you learned were commands. Just the thought may overwhelm you. You struggled with them, but little by little you will get the idea.

Can you tell me why commands in Spanish are so difficult to learn for the English speaker?

You may be hesitant to learn them, thinking that you don't need to know them. Well, it turns out that you already make plenty of commands in your daily communication in English. "Call me later! Wait for me! Don't worry! Stop doing it!" With that in mind, what's the problem with making those same commands in Spanish? Don't get discouraged! Get bossy in Spanish!

I am not going to answer these questions here, but if you are curious, it's a sign that you should visit a language class.

Do you know what you are learning for?

Which one, POR or PARA, would you use to translate the preposition "for" from that question?

Spanish is complicated, but really? Behind each thought there is a specific use; it's not as hard as it seems for you. For you? Por or Para?

As long as you open your mind to new concepts, language learning will enrich your life. Just like there are differences in different cultures, there are differences in the way people express their thoughts. Not everything can be translated literally, not only in grammar and words, but also in proverbs and expressions that represent a cultural background like, for example, this one: *A quien madruga, Dios le ayuda* (lit. God helps to those that wake up early), which has its equivalent in English "The early bird gets the worm."

I hope to see you in the foreign language class!

Anne-Marie Obajtek-Kirkwood

Exquisite Meals, Exquisite Words

French cuisine is famous for its award-winning chefs and their star distinctions, its being part, in November 2010 thanks to UNESCO, of the "world intangible heritage," but it is also encountering some serious issues with globalization and its consequences: fast food, restaurants serving reheated frozen dishes, invading MGOs. It is celebrated in literature, and has anthology pages like Emma Bovary's wedding meal (Flaubert), Gervaise's feast (Zola) or the little *madeleine*[1] (Proust), to mention just these. Closer in time, Noëlle Châtelet has "served" us *Histoires de bouche* (1986), Muriel Barbery, *Une gourmandise*[2] (2000), and Chantal Pelletier *De bouche à bouches* (2011). Pelletier also has, with Nile Editions, created in 2007 the collection "Exquis d'écrivains,"[3] which, at the end of 2011, numbers thirteen small books about good food. They are centered 'round keywords, and according to her, "Each author presents his own travels in the land of food, in different narrative forms (stories, dialogues, short stories, tales, poems...) that make you feel like putting your feet under the table or preparing dinner on the kitchen-stove[4]."[5]

This short study proposes the reading of ten of these books written by the following authors: Anne Bragance, Michèle Gazier, Denis Grozdanovitch, Michel Hubert, Chantal Pelletier, Pierre Pelot, Claude Pujade-Renaud, Alina Reyes, Dominique Sylvain, and Martin Winckler. Their books include texts about childhood memories; that describe the transmission of tastes and culinary knowledge; and that define individual, familial, regional, and exotic gourmet pleasures. They also portray our times, adding economic and social criticism, and visions of our future food.

Whether our ten selected authors originate from the countryside or the city, they enjoy a well-paying employment and good eating is normal for them, except for Chantal Pelletier, whose worker-parents believed that "wasting food was a deadly sin" (33). They all have experienced the former French decades of prosperity since they are on an average between fifty-five and sixty-five years old. They are descendants of good eaters, and families cemented around meals, where food is prepared, eaten, and narrated from generation to generation. If

---

1 A very buttery, round and fat cookie.

2 Translated into English as Gourmet Rhapsody. Europa Editions: 2009.

3 Literally Writers' Exquisite [food].

4 http://chantalpelletier.free.fr/exquis.htm

5 The translation is mine here and for all the various quotations from the books, since they exist only in French.

some do little or no cooking, they have observed the cooks, and participated more or less actively in the preparation of meals. They all are enthusiastic and share their gustative pleasures with readers for whom food is as enjoyable as for them. Including us in their families of good eaters, they pass on their pleasures to us, hand down few recipes though, or rather make a mystery of them to better seduce us, like in "Crêpes," by Hubert Michel, where crêpes from Brittany remain a "pillow secret" (80).

There are as many authors as different culinary influences because of their regions of origin, and their subsequent choices of dwelling. The most faithful to his native turf is the science fiction writer Pierre Pelot, a farmer's son born in a Vosges village where he still lives. Next come two country-dwellers by adoption, Alina Reyes, born in a resort of the Aquitaine and then settled in a barn in the Pyrénées, and Anne Bragance of Andalusian origin, raised in Morocco, later established in the Cévennes countryside, and last in Avignon. Martin Winckler, a native of Algeria, practices medicine in Pithiviers, in the Loiret. Michèle Gazier, of Spanish origin, born in Béziers, lives in Paris, as do Claude Pujade-Renaud, Denis Grozdanovitch, and the very nomadic Chantal Pelletier, partly raised in the Bresse region and in the city of Lyon. The youngest of these authors, Dominique Sylvain, a native of Metz, currently resides in Japan.

This geographical diversity acquires great importance in shaping the writers' taste-identities. Each book's opening narrative gives their metaphorical self-portrait by defining the writer's basic food tastes. Larger than life is the Garden of Eden invented by Alina Reyes (*Cueillettes* "Jardin" 12-16), with a generous cherry-tree in its center and a nurturing mother figure fond of leaves and flowers. This is the garden that Reyes will copy later on in life in the Pyrénées for herself and her family. Even more natural and wild are the nettles in Pelot's *La Croque Buissionière* (Orties 9-12), an unloved, skin-rash giving plant, unmistakably recalling the disorder of Pelot's bearded face and his nettle-soup delight. Anne Bragance, a cook from sunny climes, has us admire a lemon birth and slow ripening, later preserved with great care (*Un Goût de soleil* "Citrons confits" 11-17). The tomato, appreciated since his earliest days by Martin Winckler, gives his Mediterranean origins a place of choice (*A ma bouche*, "Tomate" 11-13) in his collection of texts rather oriented towards Jewish holiday cooking. From Bresse and Lyon, the milk-based béchamel sauce from Chantal Pelletier (*Voyages en gourmandise*, "Sauces" 11-17) magnifies the success of her relationship with her mother as well as culinary transmission by the mother, and very freely opens to other types of cuisine. *Minuscules extases*,[6] by Denis Grozdanovitch develops in the chapter

---

6 *Tiny Excstasies.*

"Maïzena"[7] (11-12) the "divine and likely primordial Oedipal taste sensation" of his childhood dessert. Claude Renaud Pujade, in her short story "Mère"[8] (15-24) in *Sous les mets les mots*, acknowledges flirting with food proscriptions due to her malfunctioning relationship with her vegetarian mother. Michèle Gazier confesses her childhood anorexia (*Abécédaire gourmand*, "Anorexie" 11-13), refusing her mother's "force-feeding" and living a malaise that only a "petit rose" pastry, a tiny pink shortbread, covered with vanilla icing, and with chestnut cream inside, could comfort. In *Mes péchés bretons* ("Sucette" 13-18), Hubert Michel tries to amuse us with his impertinence when in May 1968, as a child-king watching TV, he told his mother that it is forbidden to forbid one more "lollipop." For Dominique Sylvain, the expatriate in Japan, only "Champagne" which plays "cha cha cha" and has the "scent of return" to the country can serve as a standard to her *Régals du Japon et d'ailleurs*[9] ("Champagne" 47).

In these prologues, the qualifying food or beverage of natural, maternal, or industrial origin, is a witness to tastes or smells and likings acquired in a given familial, regional, or cultural context. Once favorite tastes have been identified, the various authors just need to make us travel according to their love for food.

As participant and editor, Chantal Pelletier travels extensively through her love of food, in her own texts, and in the twelve writers' she discovered, collected, and accepted, constituting thus the *Exquis d'écrivains* collection of Nile Editions. To this end, Chantal Pelletier recommended that writers avoid "cooking recipes," and compose literary texts focusing on "delights," "food," and "pleasures." She specified, as an editor, that food in the texts should be described from the eater's point of view, not the preparer's. While most book titles do not specify the geographic origin of the eating experience, such as: *Sous les mots, les mets, A ma bouche, Minuscules extases, Abécédaire gourmand, Un goût de soleil*, some do indicate countryside (*La croque buissonnière et Cueillettes*), or regional origins (*Mes péchés bretons*), and some books state that this culinary experience is accompanied by a change of scenery: *Voyages en gourmandise, et Régals du Japon et d'ailleurs*.

"It all starts in the garden" (12), Alina Reyes writes in *Cueillettes*. She describes her garden surrounding the house where parents and children plan some beautiful gatherings, which will become the natural and magical basis of daily family fare. Roses attract by their smells, they'd nearly eat

---

7 Corn flour.

8 Mother.

9 *Treats from Japan and elsewhere*

them; perennials such as mint and lavender repel household pests and are gathered, just as are wild thyme and sorrel; tomatoes are not harvested but eaten on the spot. Parsley and lettuce come from gleaning at neighbors' since they allow it. The family goes to the nearby forest to collect the eggs of a generous neighbor's wild hens, and berries on which they feast. Later on they think of transforming nature's fruitful presents into purees and jams, or dry mushrooms. Alina Reyes's vision is pantheistic; for her, picking and gathering provide "happiness" (81) "being blessed by the divine" (82), a gift paid back to the hundredth by the gift of self "every day until the last, in consciousness" (42).

Pierre Pelot, a Vosges countryman, talented storyteller, and mushroom connoisseur, shares his secrets with us, as his father did with him. Mushrooms should be eaten "in the kitchen to bathe in their scent" (41). He continues to ferment cabbage, as his parents did, out of love for sauerkraut which "set on the table elicits silent respect" (20). As for the potato, a staple of his everyday dishes such as stew, soup, pot-au-feu, "a world" without it would be "science fiction"! (33) His Laguiole[10] pocket knife is elevated to the rank of gourmet cutlery since it allows eating without haste, chewing while gazing at the scenery, listening to birds, and especially having one's mouth water. The closing text pays homage to a feeding person; she might have been a relative. A grandmother, dressed in a dark blue apron, spreads "malleable butter" with a knife (91) on slices of bread for snack; she adds, according to the children's tastes, raspberry or blackberry jam, "or better yet, blueberry jam which will leave on lips, teeth and tongue, the blue mark of its delight, ten times sweeter than bitter" (91-92).

Dominique Sylvain rediscovers her youth delicacies in Metz through her son Hugo, who during a city walk tastes all that her mother loved, and in particular "diabolo orgeat"[11] (56) already present at the author's great-grandmother's. This forebear owned a "black furnace" in the "the heart of the home" (93), with "quivering flames of a bright orange" (94). In her "round pots" (93) she prepared rabbit stew and rhubarb jam, and initiated the writer into the magical flavors of her magical dishes, thus making her dread "vulgar flavors" (97).

Before sampling food from elsewhere, Chantal Pelletier saw her taste formed by her parents from Bresse who cooked well: "We have to, her mother used to say, we will not be buying steak every day, at the price it costs" (36). "At

---

10 The **Laguiole knife** is a high-quality traditional Occitan pocketknife, originally produced in the town of Laguiole in the Aveyron region of southern France. http://en.wikipedia.org/wiki/Laguiole_knife. Consulted March 17, 2012.

11 A mixture of soft drink, like Seven-up, and barley syrup.

the table, they used to talk about what they were eating, had eaten, dreamt of eating" (27). Even when exiled in Lyon, they cultivated an allotment garden to eat fresh, and better, and to avoid buying. She remembers the long preparations of her childhood Sunday meals in which fathers and husbands took part cooking frogs, snails, small fried food, chicken, calves' heads, preparing also canned jars for the winter. Her grandmother's soup, called *gaudes*, made from tender corn grilled and ground at the mill to which was added after cooking "a large spoon of butter from the farm, a strong tasting butter smelling of the barn and fresh grass" (41), "was the most beautiful travel" (42) of her childhood.

But in the seventies, Chantal Pelletier betrayed "the dynastic cuisine of Lyon" and its inevitable marker, "His Majesty Béchamel," (13) to succumb to the pleasures of tastes from elsewhere, and dietetics: "I followed the trend and appreciated, over the years, dark chocolate, sushi, olive oil, tea without sugar, and whole wheat bread" (15). This opening was accompanied by royal "black juice," "Shoyu," used all the time. "So I went from white to black" (16), Pelletier confessed humorously, accepting high places of gastronomy eastward, "elsewhere" rhyming with "better" (19).

It is enough for Anne Bragance, born in Morocco, to catch "the smell of coriander" (15) in market-stalls for her past to resurface, and for her "to quiver" (17) with joy. When she was a child, the "miraculous" orange (25) given at Christmas, peeled with patience, divided into quarters, then slowly eaten, taught her the elegance of fine eating. Some goatfish with their "succulent flesh" (33) led her to the "fullness of bliss" (33) in a Palermo "greasy spoon where workers [hung] out" (31). With family and friends, she does not hesitate to get a "bellyful" (41) of cherries under the very trees before canning this "juicy ruby" (41). Anne Bragance is too greedy to enjoy dinner parties where one has "as table companions, boredom, vanity, and frivolity" (57) because she prefers friendly slow food.

Maternal dietary taboos render the child and adult Claude Renaud Pujade curious of everything that is food. As a child, she would have enjoyed the speaking lamb in *Alice in Wonderland* to be presented to her (39). Family expressions like "pommes de terre en robe de chamber"[12] make her regret that there are no studies on family terms pertaining to food (44-45). In spite of its blandness, she likes "Panisse"[13] sold on a Provence market only because of "the word" (97), is fond of Colette's[14] undoable recipes, such as the "kick

---

12 "Potatoes in a dressing gown"

13 A specialty from Southeastern France, It is made with chickpea flour, fried and eaten warm in small cubes.

14 A famous female French writer (1873-1954).

fish" (31). "Words and meals do not always agree," she states when reading cookbooks with delight. Through several culinary metaphors, she points out the difficult relationship she had with her mother: "scrambled eggs" (61), "floating island" (60) "cheese soufflé" (61) evidence their emotional failures. The delicious aroma of quince jelly that she and her mother used to make around Christmas would fade away, leaving her disconsolate. An incident at a children's party made wonders, however, by showing her mother accepting the unforeseen: the young girl had been drinking cider several times and "[sang] out loud" (101) staggering in the subway, but her mother, so strict ("no wine at the table" [102]), proved then indulgent. The final poem (108), in honor of alcoholic beverage, bears the memory of this complicity. With drinking, words of love, at last!

The same experience of childhood drunkenness is to be found with Michèle Gazier, who is immediately deprived of "dinner" and sent to bed (92). With Gazier indeed, showing oneself too greedy or too little famished, leads to being scolded as Olive Oyl: "I was called Olive Oyl, after Popeye's girlfriend's name. (...) Olive is not bright, and much less a beauty. She has pigeon round and stupid eyes, legs like twigs, big feet, no breast and a kind of a shell of black, ridiculous hair. Olive was in my eyes the foil image of femininity..." (65).

This is the nickname given to her by her father that she recounts with self-derision in a text about olives (95-96). The girl's anorexia is scary and upsets the adults who are defenseless in front of "this little girl pale as a Belgian endive and thin as a rake" (29). She takes refuge in small sweet treats: the pink cookie (le petit rose), the bittéroise, a soft bun made with orange blossom and candied fruit, apples from the garden, persimmons and watermelon from Italy. As an adult though, Michèle Gazier will prefer salty gustatory pleasures: salads, the "doll portions" of tapas that invite her to try everything (84). Her kitchen can be the "place where imagination is exercised," where books are invented when "hands are busy peeling or slicing," where she is having fun with leftovers (22) or more often where she experiences "the constant torment of the housewife-mother-cooker—also working outside" (73). She then protests against her daily life akin to that of a convict which makes her choose "easy cooking" (74) whose enchantment is provided by a flavoring, orange blossom water, the miracle that illuminates "a gray Parisian winter" (76).

À ma bouche[15] is the book-title of Martin Winckler, a doctor who defends good food against diets that are just a source of doubtful profits for him: "[Cholesterol] today, he writes, is the universal scarecrow that the industrial world as a whole, puts in front of people in rich countries—including the

---

15 *To my mouth.*

poorest of them—to make them die of fear and gobble ... medical visits, blood tests, medications, liposuction, 0% fat food, omega-3, slimming creams, exercise bikes, spa treatments and more" (95-96).

Thanks to Nelly—his modest mother who served him meals, claiming it was "not much" (38), that she had not had "time to cook"—Martin Winckler has "always loved eating" (37). He fondly remembers some cookies, and his Jewish family feasts characterized by "the pleasure of eating together and talking about what is being eaten, what it reminds of and what it tells" (69)[16]. He pays tribute to her mother by quoting extensively from her book entitled *La cuisine de ma mère racontée à mes enfants*[17] where she describes eggplant caviar, tchoutchouka and coleslaw. And to show that he has kept the message of maternal love (75), he recalls, with some pleasure and complacency, the "tender" and "melting" omelettes he masters for his children (76).

In his book *Mes péchés bretons*, Hubert Michel also presents himself as a father-cook and "gourmet." The taste of vanilla and orange in his pancakes is so exceptional (77) that his daughter Carla, aged five, introduces her friends from kindergarten to them. As time goes on, the author humorously imagines a surge in his culinary reputation among their mothers, to the point of creating a website and writing *My crêpe*, a book in honor of his daughter who alone will be able to follow in his footsteps (82). He includes, besides, a necessary praise for Breton butter, this "creamy gold sufficient to (his) happiness" (19), and oysters too (49). He funnily compares a bakery to a library where "country bread" would be a "regionalist novel," the "crown-shaped bread" a history book, an individual bun a short story" (61).

Denis Grozdanovitch, even if he wonderfully and successfully cooks crêpes on Candlemas, surprises more in *Minuscules extases*[18] by his literary gifts enhancing the richness of moments of pure "gustatory synesthesia," of jubilation when the pleasure of taste is part of a set of memories and sensations he describes with relish:

> What Proust's famous madeleine teaches us, in my
> opinion, is that our past is never really *passed*, that it
> continues to exist underground, constantly on the verge
> of emerging, and that a chance encounter of taste, smell,
> sound, a faint shadow, a fleeting impression is enough for

16 Kaufmann, Jean-Claude: "The dream today is to crystallize the reality of family meals by syncretism, to communicate together through pleasures and shared words." 136.

17 My mother's cooking told to my children. Nelly Zaffran, Pithiviers: 1980.

18 *Tiny Ecstasies*. 19 See also Kaufmann commenting on "gustatory synesthesia," 38-39.

it to reappear like the genius of the fable, and to take us through the labyrinth of sensory connections—in other words, the complex maze of synesthesia (13). [19]

His tea experience echoes his London maternal grandmother's ritual, having her five o'clock tea "in her living room overloaded with ornaments" (27), with days spent "under the spell of (the) vision" of her painter-friend Igor (34). Reading his favorite Chinese poets at home goes together for him with "a few cups of Lapsang Souchong drunk in meditative sips" (29). His pleasures are many and Denis Grozdanovitch delights remembering both potato peeling because it plunges him again in "the profound numbness of family happiness without fuss" (42) and "Bacchic intoxication" shared with companions for a night of carousing, "utter greedy and insatiable urchins, fraternally embraced, luxuriously pampered by the maternal solicitude of the Italian culinary soul" (91). Recreated by his pen, a wine of Saint Estèphe Clos d'Estournel invites him to "the quiet happiness of existence" (111-112). On the island of Cythera, discovering the ruins of an ancient temple, he catches sight of "a splendid fig tree" whose figs with their "sweet taste, enhanced by tender crunchy seeds" are the revelation of "the very essence—secretly ecstatic—of ancient Hellas" (71-72).

This set of self-portraits in food-country gathered by Chantal Pelletier for her collection "Exquis d'écrivains" pays tribute to regional culinary traditions crossbred with a "layering of influences,"[20] as she puts it:

> Our tastes at the table and in the kitchen are
> superimpositions of influences. In what I cook most
> readily, there are traces of Lyon, my hometown, and Bresse
> where my family is from (dumplings, chicken livers,
> roast chicken, soups), of Japan (tofu, gomasio, raw fish,
> soy sauce), of India (ginger, turmeric, curry, tandoori,
> cardamom, all kinds of pepper, cinnamon, nutmeg), of
> North Africa (camoun, semolina, bricks, orange blossom),
> of Southern France (olive oil, ravioli, guinea fowl,
> ratatouille, stuffed vegetables), of Italy (pasta, osso bucco,
> polenta, pesto), of China (rice, sautéed vegetables, soups,
> duck), of South America (chili, ceviche, tacos, tabasco)...

Her cuisine gets enriched from her travels and her adoption of the widest food selection to date from around the world. She refuses diet and fast food

---

19 See also Kaufmann commenting on "gustatory synesthesia," 38-39.
20 Chantal Pelletier's blog <http://chantalpelletier.hautetfort.com/>

dictatorship, favors local markets, places of hope, as opposed to supermarkets, places synonymous with loss of taste, loss of health, and not saving our planet. She must also forget that "nobody cooks like Mom" (idem), preferring creativity to memory, sometimes a cause of malfunction; she needs to have flavors go round, because "if the journey ends, taste dies" (idem). In short, "Eating never is an innocent act,"[21] it produces "social ties and culture as much as it satisfies hunger."[22]

Works Cited

Attali, Jacques. *Dictionnaire du XXIe siècle*. Paris: Fayard, 2000.

Bragance, Anne. *Un goût de soleil*. Paris: Exquis d'écrivains, Nil Editions, 2007.

Gazier, Michèle. *Abécédaire gourmand*, Paris: Exquis d'écrivains, Nil Editions, 2008.

Grozdanovitch, Denis. *Minuscules extases*, Paris: Exquis d'écrivains, Nil Editions, 2009.

Kaufmann, Jean-Claude. *Casseroles, amour et crises, Ce que bien cuisiner veut dire* Paris: Armand Colin, 2005.

Michel, Hubert. *Mes péchés bretons*, Paris: Exquis d'écrivains, Nil Editions, 2008.

Pelot, Pierre. *La croque buissonnière*, Paris: Exquis d'écrivains, Nil Editions, 2008.

Pelletier, Chantal. *Voyages en gourmandise*. Paris: Exquis d'écrivains, Nil Editions, 2007.

Pujade-Renaud, Claude. *Sous les mots les mets*, Paris: Exquis d'écrivains, Nil Editions, 2007.

Reyes, Alina. *Cueillettes*, Paris: Exquis d'écrivains, Nil Editions, 2010.

Sylvain, Dominique. *Régal du Japon et d'ailleurs*, Paris: Exquis d'écrivains, Nil Editions, 2008.

Winckler, Martin. *A ma bouche*, Paris: Exquis d'écrivains, Nil Editions, 2007.

21 Attali, 31.
22 Kaufmann, 29

M.G. Piety

Time Travel

The philosopher Richard Taylor asserts, in his book *Metaphysics*, that the idea of time travel is incoherent. The incoherence, he claims, "is exposed in saying that . . . at a later time—someone finds himself living at an earlier time. To imagine," he continues, "'returning' to an earlier time is merely to imagine the recurrence of events of that time. More precisely, it is to imagine everything, except oneself just as it was then" (73).

I believe he's wrong. I believe time travel is possible, not in the sense, however, of imagining the recurrence of past events just as they were, while remaining oneself unchanged. That, after all, is nothing but reminiscence, perhaps extraordinarily vivid, but reminiscence nonetheless. Time travel, real time travel, I believe, is the reverse of Taylor's description. It is to have everything around one just as it is now, while returning oneself to the way one was at an earlier time. In this sense, it is to be not what one is, as the philosophers say, but what one *was*.

To the extent that most of us go through some kind of moral development as we mature, this may not seem like a desirable project. Moral development is not the only thing we undergo, however; we tend, as we become older, to lose something of the joy and optimism of youth. It ebbs away with the passage of the years, more or less quickly depending on the events of our lives. I lost much of my own joy and optimism, I think, with my parents divorce when I was seventeen. But there were other events, both before and after, that gradually eroded my innocent faith in the benevolence of fate.

One such event was when I gave up my dream of becoming a figure skater. I was forced to confront the fact that my family simply did not have the money to allow me to pursue that particular dream. I don't remember ever dreaming of being in the Olympics or anything like that. I did dream, though, of being good, really good.

I always loved skating. My sisters and I used to pretend to skate on our driveway in the winter. The driveway was behind and slightly lower than the house and when it was covered with snow it looked a lot like a little pond. We would pack the snow down very hard and then slide around on it in shoes with slick soles, pretending we were skating. Sometimes we would dress up. My mother used to take us to the Goodwill store and allow us to pick out cast-off party dresses, or "formals" as we called them, to dress up in. I had a black velvet one with a heavy rolled hem that made it puff out and flare beautifully when I turned. I would wear it and carry a little rabbit fur muff that must also have come from the Goodwill store. I felt like a princess as I glided across the packed snow. We often "skated" in the evening when the light over the garage would illuminate the falling snow and if I looked up toward the night sky, it would seem as if the stars were actually falling softly on me or as if the sky were opening up and I were being carried away into it.

We would "skate" like this until our feet were so cold we had lost all feeling in them and then we would ascend the stairs at the edge of our "pond" that led into the kitchen where my father would be waiting with hot chocolate. My feet used to hurt excruciatingly as they warmed up again, but that never kept me from "skating" if there were sufficient snow.

I think I was ten or eleven years old the first time I went skating for real. I went with my Camp Fire Girl troupe. I don't remember much about that first time except that I greatly admired the skates of one of the other girls. Most of us had to rent skates, but she had her own and they were not brown like the rental skates, but blue with fur at the top.

I must have liked skating that first time because I went back. My sisters and I began to go skating fairly regularly and soon we each had our own pair of beautiful white skates. None of us had had lessons, but we would wear little skating skirts and watch the other better skaters and imitate what they did.

My parents could not really afford to give us lessons, but I pestered them anyway until they finally gave in. My lessons were during the public skating sessions at the local rink on a little portion of the ice that had been sectioned off for that purpose by orange traffic cones. I had one fifteen-minute lesson each week with a second-rate instructor. Eventually, my lessons went to half an hour, not because we could afford it but because, in my mother's words, I had a talent for getting what I wanted, and I wanted to skate.

I was in a Barnes and Noble a few years ago when I ran across something that brought this all back to me. I wandered aimlessly through the magazine section. My eyes fell on a copy of something called *International Figure Skating*. I was curious to see what skating was like these days, so I picked it up and began to leaf thought it. There was a section at the beginning of photos from some gala or other. I flipped quickly past it, but then went back. Perhaps, I thought, perhaps there will be a photo of someone I used to skate with. Some of the people in the photos weren't all that young. I'd assumed I'd have to pore carefully over the several pages of photos before I would find anyone, if I did find anyone, I'd known. But there, in the very first frame, was Lee Anne Miller. And I wondered whether I'd actually registered the picture unconsciously and that that had been why I'd flipped back to look at the photos again. Or perhaps it had been the name I'd registered and that had called me back to the page.

There she was, staring out at me from the glossy pages of a magazine, the little girl I'd so envied. I recognized her. She seemed barely changed. The same delicate features, the same pale brown hair. I can still see that hair pulled into a small dancer's bun, held in place with barrettes that matched the color of her leotards and little wrap-around dancer's skirts. Pink leotard, pink barrettes; blue leotard, blue barrettes. She was like a doll, Lee Anne. Perfectly proportioned, tiny delicate features, dressed like a little ballerina. She looked like one of those dolls that dances in a jewelry box when one opens the lid, but prettier than that really. Lee Anne was the most beautiful thing I had ever seen. Her every movement was like a dancer's, slow and deliberate and graceful. I used to love to watch her skate. There was something swanlike about her.

I was not part of that crowd, the elite skaters, not the first year anyway. I came to skate in Troy, Ohio, in the huge cavernous old Hobart Arena, simply because it was the only rink that was open in the summer. I loved the place. Most skating rinks look like barns, or warehouses, from the outside, but there was something noble about Hobart Arena. It was built of brick and stone in the grand style of the late 1940s. It had been given to the town by the Hobart Electric Manufacturing Co. in 1950 and had clearly been intended to be a showpiece. It was not only the rink, however, that was beautiful. It was in the middle of a park and just behind it was the municipal swimming pool that had a snack bar the skaters used to frequent between skating sessions. There was something almost magical to me about that grand cathedral of winter sport situated in the middle of a verdant summer paradise.

A bunch of us came up from Dayton that first summer. We were out of our league and that was kind of humiliating, but there was also something incredibly exhilarating about being around all that talent and dedication. I was fascinated by the discipline of it and all the esoteric trappings like the harness that hung from the ceiling and that was fastened around the waist of the female when pair skaters practiced overhead lifts. I loved the almost meditative hush of the sessions devoted to school figures, a hush broken only by the soft whir of the scribes, the large aluminum ice compasses, scratching circles on the ice for the skaters to follow, or the occasional muscular, ripping sound of the push of skaters working on backward eights.

We had stroking class for an hour every Thursday evening and that first summer, at least, I spent the entire session in abject fear of being mowed down by the hoards of more powerful skaters. The second year was better, though.

I switched teachers. I got a better teacher, Dick Rimmer's wife, Lynn. They ran that place, Dick and Lynn Rimmer. Dick had been the official coach to the 1972 Olympic team (at least I think that is what it said on the brochure I showed to my parents in an effort to convince them that the program would be worth the expense). I was determined not to remain the worst skater there, so I spent almost a year convincing my parents to secure Lynn Rimmer for me as a teacher. I liked her, she was kind. She told me once, when I was working on a split jump, that I was a "smart skater." That made me happy, though I was never really sure what she had meant.

I did better that second summer. Not only was I not mowed down, I actually kept up, sort of. I got better skates, passed my preliminary figure test and was accepted, finally, into the periphery of the elite group. But then I had to quit skating. I needed a scribe in order to be able to progress to the first figure test. But a scribe cost fifty dollars. That was a lot of money back then and my parents couldn't afford it.

Few middle class families can afford the cost of training a serious competitive skater. Figure skating, according to an article in the *Wall Street Journal* a few years ago, is one of the most expensive sports there is. Skating parents must either have so much money that almost any sum can be spent on their children's hobbies, or they must be willing to sacrifice everything, even their children's education, for art or in the hope that they will "win the lottery."

My parents had neither so much money that they could afford the cost of training a competitive skater, nor the values that would have led them to sacrifice everything else to get the money. I didn't really understand that. All I knew, or thought I knew, at the time was that what I loved most was not important to them.

I didn't even follow skating after that. "Never look back!" It was not just my motto, but my entire personality. I began to dream though, when I was in graduate school and when I first began teaching, about taking up skating again. I had a bad time in graduate school and that dream, distant as it seemed, was one of the things that sustained me through that difficult period.

I bought the magazine with the picture of Lee Anne Miller and decided that I should begin taking skating lessons.

I had intended to take freestyle lessons but my first teacher steered me gradually toward dance, divining, I suspect, that I would be a much better dancer than I would ever be a freestyle skater. Dance is probably better for most adult skaters anyway because there is less chance of serious injury and a much greater chance of gaining something approaching genuine mastery of the sport. There are quite a few adult skaters who are expert dancers. They have become my role models.

I'm never happier these days than when I am skating. Skating is the only thing I do now for no other reason than the joy of it. It will not make me wiser. It will not help my career. Indeed, for an adult to take up figure skating is viewed by many people, including my husband (who, to his credit, has taken it up himself in order to be able to spend more time with me), as somewhat bizarre. Skating is popularly believed to be an activity for children, not for older people, people with brittle bones.

When I'm done skating my session, the "adult session," and the ice has been freshly resurfaced, I will sometimes stay to watch the beginning of the next session when the competitive skaters, one by one, take to the ice like so many seagulls gathering gradually about an invisible school of fish. They glide easily onto the frozen surface. Flying past me, they swoop, they dip, they dive, each listening to his own inner compulsion. There's no effort at coordination, and yet they're a kind of visual symphony, as beautiful as a flock of birds, if not more beautiful, because after all, what birds do is natural to them, whereas what skaters do is natural only to the spirit, not to the body, so to see bodies do it with such effortless grace—well, there's something miraculous in it.

I am filled sometimes, as I watch them, with a terrible aching melancholy at the realization that I will never be one of them. There's a tiny window of time in everyone's life through which he can reach to grasp that sort of dream and mine was closed and locked long ago. Sometimes I can't bear the ache that accompanies the realization that what I once wanted more than anything, I'll never have, that I will have lived and died without ever having realized that dream.

Most of the time, though, I am not unhappy. Most of the time I count myself very lucky. Many competitive skaters give up skating entirely after they stop competing, or after they stop performing (if they are so fortunate as to have had a professional career). Some say they simply don't enjoy skating when they can no longer perform at what was once their peak, others have had all desire to skate extinguished by too many years of too rigorous a training schedule. They accept the diminished vitality that comes with aging as a matter of course. They age, they grow old, they die.

But I'm growing younger. I'm a better skater now than I was when I was a child and I have every reason to believe that my skills will continue to improve for many years to come. Oleg and Ludmila Protopopov, the 1964 and '68 Olympic pair skating champions, still perform and they are in their late seventies. Richard Dwyer still performs and so is he.

I don't know that I'll ever don a little skating skirt again and my dreams, whatever they are, no longer include becoming a competitive skater. When I skate now, though, I feel like a time traveler. Something of the beauty of the slow and paradoxical summers I spent on the ice as a child comes back to me. I sense again the sweet strangeness of crossing the green expanse of park to get ice cream and then returning to the frosty unreality of the rink. When I skate now all the struggles, stresses and disappointments of the years fade away and I am once again the little girl gazing up at the stars falling from the sky.

Don Riggs

An Inadvertent Mentor

I have observed and been shaped by many people in my half century of schooling, and my more than a half century of living and experiencing. I am aware that I have benefitted from friends who needed, or at least took advantage of, someone docile like me to bounce their ideas off of, or to use to practice their lecturing and other teaching skills. The friend I am thinking of particularly as a mentor is Bill. We were classmates in college, and my dorms were always very noisy and distracting—impossible for me to study in—and he lived in a single, in a very civilized co-ed dorm, so I would stop by his room two or three times a week to study. After a couple of hours, we would close our books and he would enthuse to me about...Art History. He had discovered Art History in freshman year, and in our sophomore and junior years, when I would visit him, he was getting increasingly fascinated with how various painters and sculptors had influenced each other, and each course he took—Italian Renaissance, Baroque, Romanticism, Modernism, etc.—he made up a 3"x5" index card for each artist they studied, with various biographical and artistic facts listed there, then as the semester progressed, he would make up large charts with a box representing each artist, a different color for each nationality, and lines drawn from the earlier artist to the later one in cases of influence. For example, in his Baroque semester, he drew a line from the green box marked "Caravaggio" to the red box marked "Rembrandt," showing that the Italian painter Michelangelo Merisi da Caravaggio, with his stark light-dark, or *chiaroscuro*, contrasts and use of common people as subjects, had influenced the Dutch painter Rembrandt van Rijn, whose career shifted from that of a successful painter of individual and group portraits with adequate lighting to a devastatingly brilliant painter of portraits of great psychological and emotional depth plunged in a "rich gravy" of shadow.

Bill's enthusiasm was what he communicated to me, although what I was consciously aware of were the facts, the connections, the biographical anecdotes, and the paradigm shifts that painters, sculptors, and architects made over the centuries in the depiction of three dimensions—though on a two-dimensional paper or canvas—of life—though with unmoving stone and dried oils—and the shaping of people's perceptions as they entered a building, walked through it, experienced it. He practiced his teaching style on me, and I modeled my teaching style, a number of years later, on his.

Another thing that Bill taught me by example was the persistent pursuit of a dream, once that dream has become clear to the dreamer. Because of falling in love with Art History, Bill took his senior year abroad, going to Italy with the juniors who were following the more traditional schedule. This was so he could learn Italian by immersion, and in addition could see for himself the frescoes, statues, and churches that he had studied in books. After our senior year, while we were waiting to go to grad school, Bill got a summer job as a guide at the National Gallery of Art in Washington, D.C., where I visited him. His wife Beth and I together went on his first tour, and I still remember him showing a Constable painting of the harbor of Venice; there is a smudge on the surface of the water that he said he couldn't help but think was a space capsule, like the early Mercury space capsules that floated on the surface of the ocean when they returned to Earth. It was a joke, and everybody chuckled, but it showed that he was comfortable enough with the art, and also with the audience, that he could tease them a little, and point out something a little odd in a nineteenth-century work.

I didn't see Bill for many years—in fact, I still haven't—but when I was teaching at a community college and they found me useful—as I had a Ph.D., though in Comparative Literature—to teach art, I took a graduate course in Michelangelo, Caravaggio, and Bernini to help secure me more Art History courses. I decided to write a term paper on Michelangelo's natal horoscope, as it would have been interpreted at the time, and wrote Bill to ask if Michelangelo's exact birth time were known. He referred me to an article that definitively established his exact birthdate and his birth time to within an hour, and after I'd sent him my "A" paper at the end of the term, he wrote back that he hoped I'd pursue it to publication. I researched and expanded the paper, and he sent it back to me time and again with extensive comments and corrections—he made vicious fun of a certain turn of phrase, for example: I had written that a sculpture dedicated at just the right moment would be imbued with the "essence of Mars," meaning the essential energy or *anima* connected with that planet; next to this phrase he wrote, "Is this like Oil of Olay? Powder of Pudenda?" The last time I sent it to him, he replied that he had forwarded it to the editor of the *Sixteenth Century Journal*, where it was ultimately published. He never told me what to write; he just told me where I needed improvement and gave suggestions of better, more authoritative, and more recent sources, but his initial enthusing to me about his coursework in his dorm room had evolved into truly teaching me how to whip a paper into shape in a discipline where I had never published before.

To bring this analysis somewhat up to date, the entry for Bill on <ratemyprofessors.com> has eight entries from 2004-2009. Seven of these rate him at "Good Quality" while one rates him at "Poor Quality." Among the comments, the most recent says, "PROFESSOR WALLACE IS AN ART HISTORICAL GOD!" (sic)—surely relevant to the original Greek conception of enthusiasm as *entheos* or divinely inspired. Other comments include: "Very entertaining. Makes art history fun and interesting" and "Excellent teacher, totally changed my feeling about renaissance art...used to be completely uninterested now I'm hooked." One of the most intriguing comments comes from the one "Poor Quality" rating: "Can be boring or very entertaining to listen to. Tests easy, papers hard." What strikes me about that comment is that, though I have never taken one of Bill's tests, I did go through the rigors of his critiquing my paper, which resulted in publication. As a result, I feel that the "papers hard" comment is absolutely true—but worth the trouble.

Epilogue

Last October, I went to the Washington, D.C. area for my fortieth high school class reunion. I was three hours early for my train back to Philadelphia at Union Station, so I walked the twenty minutes to the National Gallery of Art. I had a hunch...so I went to the bookstore, to the Italian Renaissance section, and...there it was: *Michelangelo: The Artist, the Man, and His Times* by William E. Wallace (Cambridge University Press: 2010). Bill's life of Michelangelo had just come out! When I saw that a section of chapter two was titled "Born under a Fateful Star" (29), I flipped to that section, and saw my article referred to, not in the body of the text, but in an endnote—n. 6, page 346, along with the article that Bill had originally referred me to. He doesn't mention the content in the text, as it's a rather minor point to most people, but he at least gives those who are interested the specific reference needed to see...well, I will let those of you who want to know what that point is, to find my article yourselves!

Works Cited

Lippincott, Kristin. "When Was Michelangelo Born?" *Journal of the Warburg and Courtauldt Institutes* 25 (1989) 228-32.

Riggs, Don. "Was Michelangelo Born under Saturn?" *The Sixteenth Century Journal* 26 (1995) 99-121.

Wallace, William E. *Michelangelo: The Artist, the Man, and His Times*. Cambridge: 2010.

Gail D. Rosen

Worthwhile *Waiting for Superman* Doesn't Explore Reasons for Failing Schools

In *Waiting for Superman*, Davis Guggenheim takes on the public education system in the United States, in much the same way he took on global warming in his 2006 *An Inconvenient Truth*. But the villains here are not so clear. *Waiting for Superman* has attracted the attention of both *Time* magazine and Oprah, and the education problem certainly merits the attention. This documentary has plenty of drama and shocking information, but Guggenheim grossly oversimplifies this complex problem. In spite of this, it is a film well worth seeing.

The film follows five children and their families as they strive to find a better education, pinning their last hopes on a lottery that would allow them to go to a successful charter school. At the end of the film we see these lotteries. The film alternates the stories of these children with scenes of founders (Geoffrey Canada and others) of high-performing charter schools. The film also features Michelle Rhee, the controversial chancellor of the D.C. public schools, who fired thousands of teachers and principals, including the principal of her own child's school, in an attempt to shake up the failing D.C. public school system. Randi Weingarten, the president of the American Federation of Teachers, also gives her opinion of Rhee's ideas. Guggenheim provides voiceover narration, reciting disturbing statistics and providing commentary.

The strongest parts of the film involve the drama surrounding the children trying to win the lottery. They want to attend charter schools that have a very small number of places and a ridiculously large number of applicants. The five children all have compelling stories, and it is impossible not to root for them, and to be moved by their tears. The film also features interviews with charismatic reformers like Geoffrey Canada and others who have achieved wonderfully impressive results with their charter schools. When the film recites statistics like the one showing that of thirty developed countries, the United States is ranked 25th in math, 21st in science and 1st in confidence, it is hard not to be alarmed. Guggenheim rightfully makes a convincing case for the dire need for education reform and the devastating effects for kids and adults of failing public schools.

The problem is clearly stated in this film, but I wish that the filmmakers had explored the many reasons for failing schools. Instead, *Waiting for Superman* lays all of the blame at the feet of teachers. According to the film, ineffective teachers and the difficulty of firing ineffective teachers are the reason for failing schools. Guggenheim cites union rules that make it very difficult to fire teachers. It is clear that the filmmakers side with controversial Chancellor Michelle Rhee and her attempts to demonize the teachers and their union. Rhee and many others feel the solution is to evaluate teachers and reward the effective ones with higher salaries and terminate the ineffective teachers. But no mention is made of the possible problems with this kind of evaluation or how it may be detrimental to actual education. There is much talk in this film about good and bad teachers, but no clear guidelines about how to determine this. Moreover, the children featured in the film all have at least one committed parent or guardian; no mention is made of the difficulties of teaching children who are in family situations without such a parent or guardian. The film never mentions the difficulties faced by teachers in some of the low-performing schools in high-crime neighborhoods, including the risk to their personal safety. No mention is made of the difficulty of teaching in a classroom where violence might erupt. In fact, someone in the film suggests that the failing schools are responsible for the failing neighborhoods.

To his credit, Guggenheim admits that he and actress wife Elizabeth Shue send their children to private school instead of the public school in their neighborhood. In the film and in the Q&A after the preview screening, he talked about the need to do what is right for his children while still caring about other people's children. He said he has been hearing arguments to his ideas at these Q&A's, but he is fine with that, as long as people are talking about the problem. *Waiting for Superman* will certainly inspire heated discussion and perhaps that is the film's purpose.

Donald Rutberg

Home of the Road Warriors

Before the 2006 season, the Atlantic League was missing one of its baseball teams. It had seven teams ready to go but needed an eighth to step up to the plate and smooth out the schedule. So it filled the need by creating a ephemeral team called the Road Warriors. The team, administered by the league, plays all of its games on the road (as per everyone's expectations) and has no home, no future and no fans, except for those they can convert in strange cities.

It's difficult to inspire devotion in fans who live minutes from the other team's ballpark; who shop, eat and vote with the local players and who babysit the local players' children. It's not easy to earn love and respect in places like Camden, Newark, or Atlantic City, NJ—*ever*, especially when you're an outsider trying to spoil the local squad's home stand. It's similar to trying to steal the local prized farm animal. If you think it's no big deal to play under those circumstances, then you must think it's easy for the Boston Red Sox to venture into Yankee Stadium and inspire New York fans to root for them instead of the Yankees. (If you have the option, go for the prized pig.)

How did I get drawn into this dramedy? I attended a Camden Riversharks' game at Campbell's Field recently and noticed that the Road Warriors were coming to town.

"Who roots for them?" my wife asked as she went spinning around on a carousel in the children's play area behind third base.

"People who don't like their hometown teams," I guessed.

The carousel was halfway through its cycle. I had a moment to think.

"Champions of the underdog, maybe?"

I didn't have a clue ... yet I was intrigued. I wondered if the team lived near the railroad tracks and, like outcasts in a Charlie Daniels' song, ate muskrat barbeque. Was there a Road Warrior's fan club out there? If I wanted to pay $10 to join, where would I send the check—to a bus on the Pennsylvania Turnpike or a tree stump near the Pine Barrens? Did they even bother designing a logo and color schemes? What was their theme song: "Hit The Road, Jack"?

Everyone who has played sports, even kids in schoolyards and sandlots, knows that all teams have home fields. For example, when I was a kid playing street hockey, we used to play home games at Moore school, right in the middle of our neighborhood. If we went to play at Farrell school, it was a road test and we knew we'd be facing unknown obstacles. At Moore school, we had all the intangibles working for us. We knew the monkey bars better than anyone. We knew where the fences were forgiving and where the brick walls were not. We always went downhill and shot at the bigger net in the third period. Besides, that was our practice court. Where did the Road Warriors practice?

Mike Miller, an Atlantic League official, said that the Road Warriors practice wherever they happen to be that day and serve as a farm system for the rest of the league.

"They work really hard," Mike said (for an average salary of only $10,000-$12,000 per season). "And people do root for them, even though they have no home base and will be disbanded after this year."

Homeless and facing extinction? Why *not* root for them? I mean, who are they going to threaten, especially with a winning percentage under 400?

Mike and I entered the visitor's clubhouse and sat with the Road Warriors manager, former major league pitcher Jeff Scott. Jeff is a stocky fellow with a thick head of gray hair and gentle personality. If you called Hollywood casting agents and asked them to send someone who looked and spoke like a baseball lifer, they'd send Jeff.

"What's it like not having a home?" I asked.

"It's really not that big a deal," he answered, "other than picking up and moving every three days. You kinda get used to it."

I've picked myself up every three days, too—to see family near San Francisco, to meet with producers in L.A., then to visit Las Vegas for ... well, what happens there has to stay there (one of the few rules we all seem to respect).

"But," I explained to Jeff, "after three cities in nine days, I flew home. Where is your base?"

"Our base is our clubhouse everywhere," Jeff explained. "Our players probably spend more time in the clubhouse than all the other teams because they get tired of staying at the hotel."

"So it's good for camaraderie?" I asked.

"Well, it can be. It can be bad, too. We see each other all the time, probably get a little tired of looking at some people but ... we haven't had much of a problem. Some guys have wives in the area. We accommodate; try to make it as easy as we can."

Some of the players, though, have wives in distant cities and don't see their families for 5-6 months.

"That's what happens, unless they come to visit the players and follow us around on the road," Jeff said. "There's a trade-off. The players don't have to pay any rent or utilities, don't have to put any gas in their car. If they played in Camden, they'd be home for a week...they'd have to pay for all those things. Here, everything is taken care of, and they get meal money every day."

"Every day?" I asked, trying to block out the image of a player sitting by the railroad tracks, eating from a bag that read, "Muskrat King."

"Well, every three days. They're always asking, 'Is it here yet?' First thing they do is ask for the meal money, not for their love letters. Not much mail floats around these days, not with cell phones and the Internet. A lot of the guys are single, still live with their parents."

The lifestyle was conducive to a single, bachelor lifestyle. All meals, hotel rooms and van rides were paid for during the season. Players only needed rent money and car insurance for half the year. Young girls often showed up to cheer for them. It wasn't sounding too bad.

"Some wives or girlfriends visit," Jeff continued. "We try to put a guy in a single room and put his roommate in another room for that night."

I thought about what could happen if a player, a young man, came to bat with the bases loaded in the 9th inning. Would he be thinking, "Look for the fastball, up high and in tight" or would he be thinking of ways to clear his roomie out of his hotel room that night?

"We don't do it quite that way. They tell me in advance," Jeff said, and I realized I had wondered those thoughts aloud. "I try to arrange things. I'm a good traveling secretary. I've got a van. I carry the baseball equipment. Travel between each city is different. Between Camden and Atlantic City, we use a van service: two 15-passenger vans. And they carry the kids' personal luggage in a trailer behind the vans. We use the most economical way possible."

No one walks around thinking, "What will I wear next game?" The team doesn't need two uniforms, one for home and one for the road.

"We just wear the grays," Jeff said.

So, they're homeless, facing extinction and have only one suit to wear to work ...and the color of that suit is a drab gray.

I asked Jeff, "Any chance that, by next year, your team will morph into a new team and play in York, PA or become the Southern Maryland Blue Crabs?"

"No," Jeff told me. "This franchise won't be transferred anywhere. It is totally run by the league. It's a made-up franchise."

"But, there was a Road Warriors team a few years ago—they became the Lancaster Barnstormers...weren't they made up?"

"No," Jeff said. "They were set to become the Lancaster team. I was the pitching coach for that team two years ago."

"Were you a pitcher?"

"Yeah. With the Texas Rangers. That team wasn't very good. I had a cup of coffee with the Rangers, then I pitched at Triple A, then I blew my arm out, became a pitching coach."

I asked Jeff if he hoped to get back to the major leagues as a coach or manager. His answer surprised me.

"Oh no, I don't have any desire. I've been away from the field for a long time. I'm 52. I've managed and coached in the minor leagues back in the '70s and '80s and since then I've been scouting. I much prefer to scout in the big leagues or scout amateur players."

"So you won't be the manager of either expansion team next year?"

"I don't intend to be, no."

"So, conceivably, *no one* here could be associated with the new, 8th team (in Southern Maryland or York, PA) that joins the league next year."

"That's right," Jeff said. "Some players here will be with other teams in the league next year. Some will get signed by major league clubs."

I asked if he thought any of his current players were destined for the majors.

"Uh, no. I don't think we have anyone ... but they'll wind up in Double A or Triple A. There's a handful and a half who will want to come back next year and if they keep performing well, the other teams in this league will have interest. Most of these guys were signed off the scrap heap, so to speak, and they have some ability."

To recap, the players were signed off the scrap heap to play for a team that has no home and is rapidly moving toward the final reel; i.e., "I'm ready for my close up, Mr. DeMille/The End." Is there anything else working against them?

"We've got 15 Latinos, from Puerto Rico and the Dominican Republic. We've got a couple guys who don't understand English 100% of the time but they can all get by and go places."

In other words, "Yes," these homeless, nearly extinct, scrap heap kids in drab, gray uniforms have a language barrier to overcome, as well.

"Remember Fernando-mania?" I asked Jeff. "In Los Angeles, in the 1980s, Fernando Valenzuela said he didn't understand English so he didn't have to do interviews."

"Fernando spoke good English. He played it to the hilt," Jeff said. "I know guys who played with him and they said it was all a charade—to avoid doing things he didn't want to do."

Ah, we were all like that in L.A. in the 1980s. Fernando, a kid named Magic Johnson, a bunch of Russian teens who defected during the Olympics, myself... we were all confused. We all missed our families.

Jeff added, "For a lot of these guys, being away from family is the hardest part."

I got the feeling that Jeff basically told his players, "Concentrate on baseball for six months and don't complain. It's not the worst thing in the world for someone pursuing a pro career."

"I've been in professional baseball for 35 years and I've had seasons where I lived out of a hotel for 300 days a year, so for me personally, this is a piece of cake. I mean, guys go off to war and they don't see anybody for a year ... people work other jobs and they go away from home for extended periods. I don't view it as that hard a thing. If they want to play, they have to do it.

"But the biggest hassle for us is that we never get to hit in the bottom of the ninth. It can be a tie game and we still get the same chances but the other team always gets to hit last."

This is a team—one of the very, very few teams in the history of baseball and the world as we know it—whose players *can't* dream about hitting a walk-off home run in the bottom of the ninth inning. That's uncivilized. That's worse than playing a street hockey double-header at Farrell School.

"So what do you do?" I asked. "Go to the whip early, try to get a lead and hold on?"

"Only if you're fortunate enough to have a great closer. We really don't have one now," Jeff admitted, "but even if we did, using them is always difficult. Oftentimes, if I don't use them in the eighth inning … it might be too late."

I asked Jeff about his team's fans.

"People send letters, asking for schedules and where to buy our shirts. There are a couple older ladies in Bridgeport, they sit behind the dugout and root for us. They wear our jerseys, too."

Mike Miller reminded Jeff that many of the Road Warriors jerseys (their gray *road* jerseys, in case you're wondering) were sold at the recent Camden games.

"Maybe I can go to a fancy restaurant with the profit," Jeff joked.

It shouldn't surprise anyone that the Road Warriors are sentimental favorites in the Atlantic League. They're always itinerant, removed from their families, worried about job security. They never get a chance to bat in the bottom of the ninth … I mean, they can't even have great rivalries. When they say, "Judge me by my rivals," they're talking about gridlock or the busted traffic light at 4th and Broadway in Camden. That's not very romantic. I couldn't write a poem about that. Believe me, I tried.

I asked Jeff, "Besides those ladies in Bridgeport, who roots for you?"

He replied, "You end up rooting for yourself. That's what you gotta do. You play as hard as you can, as quick as you can, and then go to the next city."

I thanked Jeff for sharing his thoughts and headed up to the stands in Camden's Campbell's Field. I noticed a doctor from Cooper Hospital who had walked in and, like a line drive, headed straight for the ATM machine. From there, he walked to the table display of Road Warriors' jerseys and started counting his money. (The official nylon game jerseys sold for $75 a pop.)

"Why buy this team's jersey?" I asked.

He answered, "They're going out of business next year, aren't they?"

So, there was proof that the Road Warriors attract faithful followers because the team is an endangered species and because human nature tends to side with the underdog.

I say let them charge $75 for a drab, gray nylon shirt and let them take our prized pig ... and let them cook it out on the scrap heap by the railroad tracks. After all, they've taught us an important lesson in life: "You play as hard as you can ... and then go to the next city."

Sheila Sandapen

The Spider Princess

Once there was a princess who lived in a steel tower in the middle of a thick forest at the furthest end of the kingdom. Her mother had shut her in the tower when she was still a small child. There was no way for the princess to come down and there was no way for anyone to go up to the princess. Time passed and people began to forget about the princess.

The princess spent her days singing, spinning and reading. As the days dawned and set, the princess grew into a lovely young woman.

One day a young man was hunting in the forest and came upon the tower. He could hear the princess singing and looked up. He immediately lost all reason to love. There he stood, gazing at her lovely face and despairing that he'd never get to be near his beloved.

A witch who lived in the forest took pity on the young man and offered to help him by turning him into a fly. He agreed, and the young man-fly eagerly flew upward and landed on the ledge of the princess's prison.

The princess turned and smiled lovingly at the young man-fly. She gently moved forward, her ruby red lips parted, a forked tongue darted forth and she swallowed him whole.

"Thank you, dearest godmother," the princess called down to the witch. "That was the best one yet." And the spider princess went back to spinning her web, humming softly under her breath.

Myrna Shure

Anger: *Oh, Those Tantrums!*

You're in the grocery store with your three-year-old when he spots a box of cereal he wants. He reaches for it hungrily, but you tell him that you don't want to buy it—it's too sweet—and you select a brand with less sugar. Angry, he strains against the cart, trying to stand up in the seat. Growing agitated, he flails his arms, his face turns red—and you get that awful, sinking feeling in the pit of your stomach. He's going to have another temper tantrum. He had one just the other day when you were visiting your mother. They always come at the worst possible time.

By now your son is screaming and you have to figure out what to do.

You can plead with him to stop crying but he won't hear you.

You can threaten that you won't take him to the playground when you're done, as you promised—but that doesn't faze him.

You can ignore it and hope it will go away, but you know it won't.

You can give in and put the box of cereal in your cart, but you don't want him to grow up thinking that he'll get his way if he cries hard enough.

You can get angry in turn—raise your voice, grab the box out of his hands—but how can you expect your child to learn about controlling his temper if you don't control yours?

Unfortunately, none of these possibilities sounds appealing—or effective. There's no perfect way to deal with a temper tantrum. But there is a way to avoid tantrums—to stop them before they begin.

You can do it by playing "The Same and Different" game with your child.

One afternoon, when you and your child are feeling relaxed and enjoying each other's company, tell your child to watch what you do with your arms. First, make big circles with your outstretched arms. Then, clap your hands. Now ask your child, "Did I just do the *same* thing or something *different*?"

When your child replies, "Different," think of two different things you can do with your feet so that she gets the answer right again. Then ask her to make up two body motions, and to ask you if she's doing the same thing or something different.

You can also play this game in the playground. "Look at those two kids," you can say. "Is their shirt the *same* color, or *different*?"

Play it when you watch television, take a car ride, or walk to a friend's house. The goal is to teach him about the words "same" and "different."

How does this relate to temper tantrums? The next time you're in the store, or at your mother's, and you sense that your child is heading for a tantrum, you can calmly say to him, "Let's play the 'Same and Different' game." Can you think of a *different* way to tell me how you're feeling right now?"

One three-year-old stopped crying the moment her mother asked her the question. She remembered playing the game with her mother, laughed, and said, "Yeah, I can make circles with my arms." Her tantrum was history.

Another child, four years old, was on the verge of blossoming into a tantrum in the playground when her mother asked, "Can you think of a *different* way to tell me how you feel?"

The girl recognized the word "different," paused, smirked for a moment, and calmed down. A five-year-old girl screaming for some ice cream stopped yelling when her mother asked her the same question and said, deadpan, "But ice cream will help me grow." Mom couldn't keep from laughing. Although she had to muster all her resolve to keep from giving in, she held her ground. Within a minute, her child's cries turned to laughter as well.

Turn temper tantrums into an opportunity to teach your child that he has a choice—that he can choose among a wide spectrum of possibilities to express how he is feeling. That way, you'll both stay more in control.

Kathleen Volk Miller

Too Close for Comfort

My 20-year-old daughter, Allison, who has her own apartment in Philadelphia, sent me a text the other day: "I need socks and dandruff shampoo." I laughed aloud and texted back, "I need deodorant and coffee filters."

I had a fleeting thought that she was actually asking me to pick up those items for her, but I preferred to think we were playing a cellphone game. I try not to be a helicopter parent. Experience as a mother and professor has taught me how badly that can backfire.

Instead, I prefer a more hands-off approach, which came naturally. From the time Allison turned 18 something kicked in, and I simply no longer had any desire to know her work schedule or pick up her tampons. I remember wondering if this was as instinctual as nursing her or bundling her up when she was a baby. But that's not what I see at Drexel University, where I teach and where my daughters go to school. The vast majority of my students talk to their parents three times a day or more. One student's mother called when she didn't hear from him for a few days. He picked up the phone, but he was in the library and so he whispered "hello." She accused him of being hung over or drunk, even though it was about 10 a.m. on a Tuesday. He tried to convince her, avoiding eye contact with those library patrons giving him exasperated looks, but she insisted that he take a picture of himself, in the library, *holding a newspaper with that day's date*, and send it to her. I cannot shake how similar that is to a hostage situation.

As a professor, I've always treated my students as autonomous beings, telling them on the first day of class that I will not follow up with them on missed classes or assignments as other instructors might. It's my tough love way of getting them to become independent thinkers and to do for themselves.

But I can't help contrasting that to the way their parents treat them. In Allison's senior year of high school, parents rolled their eyes over filling out their sons' and daughters' college applications, expecting commiseration from me. I smiled and nodded and hoped my face didn't show the absolute incredulity I felt. Didn't they see the disservice they were doing their children? Two years later when my daughter Hayley graduated, the situation was worse. Parents would use the word "we"—as in, "We're looking at Rutgers," or "We're thinking he should take a year at community college until we figure out what he should focus on." My parents didn't see my college campus until they came to visit. My roommate and I drove ourselves to orientation, and we still laugh remembering how we ended up a state further south, forced to ask a toothless gas station attendant in Virginia where we were.

College is a perfect middle ground for this age group: Students are forced to make their own choices and take responsibility for them, but help and guidance are there if they need it. What I see, though, is that the self-reliance they should be developing is thwarted by parental involvement. An academic advisor at Drexel told me the other day what she is most surprised by is how students "tolerate parental interference." Even worse, "They want and ask their parents to come to advising meetings." I know a mother who watches the surveillance cams at her child's school, for hours, hoping he will randomly walk past the camera's corner. I know a mother who requests her college-age children's syllabuses, puts exam and project dates in her own calendar, and sends her children reminders. I know a mother who checks her kid's debit card daily, and then calls him and questions 3 a.m. pizza purchases. My daughters are on the same campus as me, and I don't even know what classes they are taking. But so far, they come to me with the stuff that's more important than any 3 a.m. pizza purchase or chem quiz, and I think they do because I give them space. I let them make that choice.

I wonder if the parents so anxiously hovering, just trying to do their best, understand the twisty ways their students hide from them. Many students tell me they have fake Facebook pages, ones they use only for their parents, and "real ones" for their friends. The decision over whether to "friend" a parent is a never-ending source of antagonism. The stories of kids getting "busted" in red cup photos are far too numerous to reiterate.

As much as parents use technology to peek in on their young adult children's lives, students also use technology to remain dependent on their parents and avoid the hard work and sacrifice of growing up. They tell me about texting their parents with requests for cash, and parents using online banking to make the transfer. One student was proud that he conducted this whole text conversation as he walked to the bar where he intended on spending the deposit. His mother texted back "done" when the transaction was complete, just as he opened the door to the bar.

Parents have a view into their children's lives that was not possible in the past. That makes letting go virtually impossible, forgive the pun. I spoke with a mother recently who said if it were not for Twitter, she wouldn't know if her college junior son was dead or alive. He is at Penn State, and in his freshman year, a fellow student was found in a stairwell, dead from alcohol poisoning. He had been dead for almost two days. She thinks this made her extra leery, and on the day we spoke he had been diagnosed with strep throat but hadn't responded to any of her texts, so she found herself obsessively checking her Twitter feed, only able to relax and focus on her work when she saw he had put up a post.

I'm not immune to this, either. The other night I was wondering about the whereabouts of my own college freshman and willing myself not to text her. I picked up my phone when I heard a buzz, and lo, Hayley had checked into a restaurant on 4Square. Phew. But I am doing my best to maintain balance.

Trying to think of a new metaphor for my ideal style of parenting, I decided I want to be one of those guys on the landing strips at the airport, with the flags. I am on the ground, and my kids come see me when they need something and I direct them, but they are still operating the plane. I also decided that was a lot of words and I needed to find out what those people in the bright jumpsuits are called. After much unproductive googling, I contacted my air traffic controller cousin and this is what he wrote back:

"That position is called a 'Ramp Agent.' They do everything from guiding the plane into its gate, loading and unloading bags, cleaning the inside of the cabin, and just about anything else needed to get a plane 'turned around' and ready for its next flight."

Perfect.

The code I have developed with my own daughter is this: If I haven't heard from her in a few days, or if I just have an ache for her, I will send her a text that says, "Say 'hi.'" She will respond with those two letters and it is astounding, really, how much better I feel.

I think we're all more afraid in 2012, and that technology can both relieve and feed those fears. I'm not accusing anyone of being a bad parent. The only reason we panic when we haven't heard from our child for three days is because we can, and often do, hear from him or her nearly constantly. But learning to respect boundaries is part of this process, and we have to do it, even when technology has erased the lines. This is the same moderation and balance we want our kids to learn as they navigate the bumpy freedoms of adulthood. Just because you have access to all the alcohol you can drink doesn't mean you should. Just because you can shut off your alarm and roll over without any immediate ramifications doesn't mean you should.

That's the lesson we parents have to learn. Just because we can peek in on our children, doesn't mean that we should. Just because you can see that your child has not swiped in at the Dining Center but instead bought $12 worth of snacks at the campus bodega, do you need to know that information? Would you tell your vegan friend that you polished off a family-size bag of Doritos last night, texting her that information as soon as you sucked the orange dust off your fingertips? I am going to do my best to stay a ramp agent and try not to helicopter, waving my flags on the tarmac—even if sometimes that waving gets frantic.

Scott Warnock

Warning: Your Child May be a Carrier of Adverbs

Maybe I'm just a linguistic sponge, but I find myself falling into the discourse of those around me. A Northeastern boy, I've felt that if I moved to say, the South, that I'd pick up not only the vernacular but the accent within weeks.

This brings me to adverbs.

You know these words, which serve as modifiers or intensifiers. They often end in –ly. They are words like really and very or words answering questions like *How? In what way? To what extent?* Your knowledge may consist of information from the "Lolly, Lolly, Lolly, Get Your Adverbs Here" *Schoolhouse Rock!* song (which you can find easily on YouTube).

That song shows a store dealing in adverbs. But while everything else in our culture—except maybe fast food—has become more expensive, adverbs are cheaper than ever. The "Lolly" song—and with its catchy tune, how could it be wrong?—comforts us that "anything that can be described can be described some more," so pile those adverbs on.

Adverbs do have their place, but these words, particularly ones that end in –ly or words like *really* and *very*, can spread like kudzu throughout your communications. By making everything "really great" or "very important," we make nothing great or important. In extreme cases (see below), adverbs might make you seem like a pompous, condescending jerk.

Good communicators avoid overusing adverbs (a search of [avoid adverbs] results in hundreds of anti-adverb sites). I heard a story, probably apocryphal, about a budding writer who sent a manuscript to a famous author. All the famous person did was blacken out the adverbs with a marker and send the manuscript back: *There's* your writing lesson.

What does this have to do with my linguistic sponginess? I realized adverbs are popping up everywhere in my language, in *our* adult discourse, and I'm blaming the kids. Like mosquitoes are vectors of West Nile virus, kids are vectors for adverbs. Spend enough time with the sub-ten-year-old set, and you will find yourself modifying everything.

Not that these little words don't fit, well, *perfectly* sometimes, and not that kids have a monopoly on adverb use. (One dear friend of mine uses the word "frankly" as a warning that he is about to tell you a lie.) But the epidemiological examination of adverbs reveals they emanate from children, perhaps stemming from a child-like desire to exaggerate or just from a linguistic reflection of the struggle to express intensity for first-time life experiences, no matter how minor: "This new cereal is *completely* awesome!"

There was a time when the kids had us *totallying* everything: "Totally this" or "Totally that." They have given us the bauble very: "She is very honest." "This is *very* valuable." "He is *very, very* tired." Now we are awash in *really*, not just as a worthless modifier like very but often as a one-word question indicating disgust-laden disbelief. You know that cell phone ad campaign in which people are amazed at how fixated their friends are on their cell phones (including one guy who fishes a dropped phone out of a urinal)? "Really?" is cemented into our culture as a way of saying, "Are you that stupid?"

Because I spend time with these little spouters of adverbs, I knew I was infected, but I thought I was aware of the extent. Then I was shocked to discover a new vocabularic virus had embedded itself in my discourse. When I looked, it was everywhere.

The word? *Actually.*

I realized my little son has filled my house with a cloud of *actually*. Worse, what he is saying through this onslaught of *actually* is "as a matter of fact, dear father, *this* is the reality, not the one you are proposing." As I noted that these *actuallys* left the house with me, I began observing his subversive linguistic behavior. When I asked him something, I learned that 94% of his responses begin with *actually*. (Further, of that 94%, 81% are accompanied by his raising an index finger, as if to emphasize his superior view.) We have conversations like the following:

"Stay out of that freezer! You know you can't have dessert until you finish your dinner." "*Actually*, Mommy said I did finish eating."

"I want those Legos picked up." "Actually, [some other guilty party, normally a sibling] left them there."

"Why are you still wandering around the house? We put you to bed an hour ago." "Actually, I go to bed at 1:00 a.m. now that I've turned seven."

Method of transmission? Brute repetition. I half-heartedly engaged in the task of disciplining myself to eliminate *actually* until a colleague of mine called me out. We were brainstorming about a project, and I responded to one of her comments by saying, "*Actually*, that's a good idea." She laughed at my use of actually, and I then understood how I sounded. In "*Actually*, that's a good idea," *actually* serves as a condescending head pat. I might as well have said, "While I didn't expect the nonsense you were spouting to be a good idea, I now find myself surprised to find that it is."

So I accelerated my mission of linguistic cleansing. I have asked friends, colleagues, family, and students to point out my adverbial excesses. But the vectors, while they pretend to assist, are crafty. Just the other day, my innocent little diseaser of diction "helped" me, catching a stray actually I had uttered by saying, "*Actually*, Daddy, you just used the word 'actually' again."

Contributors

Scott Barclay is a professor and department head in the Department of History and Politics at Drexel University.

Genevieve Betts is an instructor for the Department of English and Philosophy. Her most recent work is forthcoming or appears in *Clockhouse Review, Buddhist Poetry Review, Poetry Quarterly*, and *Nano Fiction*.

Zach Blackwood is from Winter Park, Florida and is majoring in entertainment and arts management at Drexel University. Since beginning his poetry endeavor in spring of 2011, he has been published in *Maya* as well as *The 33rd*.

Christa Blumenthal is a freshman business major with a passion for food. She frequently updates her food blog with her latest culinary escapades, and hopes to frequent as many Philadelphia restaurants and food trucks as possible before graduating from her five-year program. She envisions a food-related entrepreneurship venture in her future.

Taylor Bush is a sophomore creative writing major from Pottstown, Pennsylvania—his faithful muse. He plans to become an author after graduation. His favorite things to write about are memory, fantasy, music, and '90s culture.

Paula Marantz Cohen is Distinguished Professor of English at Drexel University. She is the host of *The Drexel InterView*, an award-winning television series that premiered in 2004 and is now broadcast on over 350 public television and university-affiliated stations throughout the country. She is the author of eight books, is a co-editor of the *Journal of Modern Literature*, writes a weekly blog, "Class Notes," for TheAmericanScholar.org, and is a regular contributor on books and movies to the *Times Literary Supplement*, the *Philadelphia Inquirer*, and TheSmartSet.com.

Casey Condon is a freshman game art and production major from Scranton, Pennsylvania, who hopes to one day direct or produce video games. He wants to continue to write throughout his life and to teach college students game design. He enjoys helping others and is excited to work both as a resident assistant and in the Drexel Writing Center as a peer reviewer. He is also a brother of the Pi Kappa Alpha fraternity, a runner, and a student ambassador.

Ingrid G. Daemmrich teaches writing and literature in the Department of English and Philosophy at Drexel. Her textbook, *The Changing Seasons of Humor in Literature*, now in its seventh, web-friendly edition, aligns humorous literature with the seasons in moving from springtime hilarity to winter grim absurdity. She is currently exploring how traditional literary genres such as parody interact with current forms of social media and finds that "the more things change, the more they stay the same."

Kelly Davis is a freshman Communications major. She works as an A&E correspondent for the *Triangle*, and aspires to one day write a story which does not involve a plot twist.

Richardson Dilworth is Associate Professor of Political Science and Director of the Center for Public Policy at Drexel University. He is the author of *The Urban Origins of Suburban Autonomy* (2005) and the editor of three books, most recently *Cities in American Political History* (2011). He has held visiting positions at the Academy of Natural Sciences of Philadelphia and the Pennsylvania House of Representatives, and in 2008 he was appointed by Mayor Michael Nutter to serve on the Philadelphia Historical Commission, where he is chair of the Historic Designation Committee.

Alexander Fatemi-Badi is a freshman majoring in game art and design. He currently resides in Philadelphia, but has also lived in Riyadh, Saudi Arabia and Dubai in the United Arab Emirates. Though his current focus is on 3D modeling, Alex also wants to pursue the story-writing side of video game development.

Dana Formon is a junior psychology student, distance running and dancing professionally in her spare time. She is a freelance writer and the author behind TheEvolutionaryFoodie blog (evolutionaryfoodie.wordpress.com). Currently, she is working on her undergraduate thesis covering the effects of incarceration on mental illness stigma, and is also working on a review of the ethical challenges in forensic psychology research. She plans on attending a Ph.D. program post-graduation and studying offender and prisoner populations.

Valerie Fox's most recent collection of poetry is *The Glass Book* (2010, Texture Press). Her poetry has appeared in numerous journals, including *Hanging Loose, Sentence, Ping Pong, West Branch, Feminist Studies,* and *Six Little Things*. She is a founding co-editor of *Press 1*, a magazine that features fiction, opinion, photography, and poetry.

Eric Friedensohn is a senior graphic design/product design student who takes every opportunity to make great things happen. Recently, he organized, co-hosted and designed for the first ever TEDx conference at Drexel University, and he is very excited to graduate.

Liz Galib is a sophomore at Drexel University and enjoys music, music composition, singing, piano, guitar, filmmaking, theatre, all sports, baking, bodybuilding, creative writing, poetry and songwriting, photography, moon walking, collecting shoes, perfumes, make up and jewelry, as well as anything pink.

Abigail Harris is a biology major with a concentration in biochemistry, and a nutrition minor. She hopes to study nutrition science in graduate school, which has been her plan since sixth grade. She is a member of the Honors Program, a STAR scholar, and a volunteer at The Caring Center..

Aaron Hartmann is a freshman in the LeBow College of Business studying economics and finance.

James D. Herbert is Professor and Head of the Department of Psychology at Drexel University, and Director of Drexel's Anxiety Treatment and Research Program. Research interests include the assessment and treatment of anxiety disorders (with particular emphasis on evaluating the effectiveness and mechanisms of action underlying new acceptance-based models of behavior therapy); remote Internet-based treatment, and the promotion of evidence-based practice in mental health. He has published over 125 papers and book chapters on these and other topics, including a recent book on mindfulness and psychological acceptance in cognitive behavior therapy.

Laurel Hostak is a junior screenwriting and playwriting major. She serves as president of the Drexel Players and participates in theatre on campus and in the Philadelphia community in various capacities. Her writing has been published in *Maya* literary magazine and *The 33rd* (2009).

Devon Ikeler is a transfer student from the College of Charleston and is currently a pre-junior in fashion design and merchandising at Drexel. She is extremely involved in Greek life on campus as a sister of Phi Mu Fraternity and a part of the Panhellenic Council as a social chairman and as a recruitment counselor. Devon aspires to be the next Betsey Johnson meets Lilly Pulitzer designer but, if all else fails, she would love to have her own bakery one day.

Henry Israeli is an assistant teaching professor in the Department of English and Philosophy at Drexel University. He is the founder and editor of Saturnalia Books and writes poetry.

Siara Johnson is originally from San Antonio, Texas, and has spent the past eight years in Hershey, Pennsylvania before coming to Philadelphia to study psychology at Drexel University. She wants to be a positive influence in people's emotional lives and aims to earn—at minimum—a master's degree in the field of child and adolescent psychology. Siara ultimately endeavors to become a psychologist who specializes in working with abused individuals.

Miriam N. Kotzin, Professor of English at Drexel University, co-directs the Certificate Program in Writing and Publishing and teaches creative writing and literature. She is a contributing editor of *Boulevard* and a founding editor of *Per Contra*. She is the author of a collection of flash fiction, *Just Desserts* (Star Cloud Press, 2010) and four collections of poetry: *Reclaiming the Dead* (New American Press, 2008), *Weights & Measures* (Star Cloud Press, 2009), *Taking Stock* (Star Cloud Press, 2011), and *The Body's Bride* (David Robert Books, forthcoming 2013). Her satiric novel *The Real Deal* will be published this fall by BrickHouse Books/Stonewall Press.

Michael Leone is an adjunct professor of English at Drexel University. His work has been published in *Hayden's Ferry Review*, the *Southern Review*, the *North Atlantic Review*, the *Indiana Review*, and other literary journals. He lives in New Jersey.

Lynn Levin is an adjunct associate professor of English at Drexel and producer of the TV show, *The Drexel InterView*. A poet, writer, and translator, she is the author of three collections of poems, most recently *Fair Creatures of an Hour* (2009), a Next Generation Indie Book Awards finalist in poetry, and *Imaginarium* (2005), a finalist for *ForeWord* Magazine's Book of the Year Award. She holds a BA from Northwestern University and an MFA in writing from Vermont College.

Joanna Lyskowicz, originally from Poland, has been a Spanish Instructor at the Modern Language Program at Drexel for the past eight years. Although her primary subject taught is Spanish, in the past she taught a few others, as she speaks several languages, the fact that influenced her major research interest: comparative linguistics. She hopes to make the language learning process easier for students.

Colleen McLaughlin grew up in Nanuet, New York. She will graduate from Drexel in 2014 with a BS in film/video production, and a minor in dance. She hopes to enter the film industry and work in post-production as an editor.

Ian Micir graduated from Drexel in 2012 with a BA in English. He plans to attend graduate school in the fall of 2013 to earn his MFA in Creative Writing, and looks forward to a successful career as an author.

Ryan Nasino is a third-year business student from Ridley, PA. He is the president of Drexel Mock Trial, and plans on attending law school after graduation. He cites Taylor Mali as his largest poetic influence.

Anne-Marie Obajtek-Kirkwood is an associate professor of French at Drexel. She co-edited *Signs of War: From Patriotism to Dissent* (Palgrave Macmillan, 2007) and has published extensively on French authors like Simone de Beauvoir, Patrick Modiano, Marguerite Duras, Sophie Calle, Viviane Forrester, and 21st-century writers. She holds an MA in Elizabethan and Jacobean

Comedy from the University of Lille III, France and a Ph.D. in 20th Century French Literature from the University of Pennsylvania.

M.G. Piety is an associate professor of philosophy at Drexel University.

Ariel Pollak is a freshman psychology major who plans to pursue a research career in language acquisition. She is a staff member at *Maya* (Drexel's undergraduate literary magazine), where her work has appeared. In every possible future she can imagine, she continues to write.

John Quagliariello is a freshman student-athlete at Drexel. Majoring in sport management, John also competes for the Division I Swimming and Diving Team. In his free time, he enjoys watching television and hanging out with friends.

Richard E. Redding is Professor and Associate Dean for Academic Affairs in the College of Law at Chapman University. His research interests include forensic issues in criminal law; juvenile justice; the use of social science research in law and public policy; and the ways in which social and political attitudes influence how science is used in policy making.

Sarah Rettew is a sophomore majoring in biological sciences. She is from Denver, Pennsylvania and aspires to become a forensic pathologist after completing medical school here at Drexel.

Don Riggs writes 140 syllables every morning, as obsessively as the Hunger Artist fasts. He also teaches freshman writing, science fiction, and Tolkien here at Drexel.

George Risi, Jr. was born and raised in a suburb of Washington, DC. He is a freshman mechanical engineering student at Drexel. His passion continues to be engineering the future, but he has also chosen to put a heavy emphasis on writing, as it is an essential skill in the professional world.

Justin Roczniak is a civil engineering major at Drexel University.

Marina Roscot is an international student from Moldova who transferred to Drexel from Bucks County Community College. She is a senior majoring in accounting and is passionate about math and research work. Upon her graduation she is planning to obtain her CPA license and seek employment with one of the Big Four accounting firms.

Gail D. Rosen teaches English at Drexel. She holds a BA from Temple University and a JD from Temple University School of Law. She has written weekly film reviews for *When Falls the Coliseum*.

Arhama Rushdi is a political science major in her third year of the BS/ JD program. She is the Secretary-General of Drexel Model United Nations, director of academic affairs for the Honors Student Advisory Committee, as well as co-founder of Dragons for Palestine. After completing law school she plans on working for the United Nations.

Don Rutberg has a master of fine arts degree from the University of Southern California and is a published author of books, children's books, stage plays, comic books, and magazine articles. His book, *A Writer's First Aid Kit* (Pale Horse Publishing), is a proactive approach to writing and selling books and scripts. He is researching a stage play about pioneering female jockeys, circa 1970. Don is an adjunct professor at Drexel University (communication) and Community College of Philadelphia (writing).

Sheila Sandapen is an assistant teaching professor in the Department of English and Philosophy. She also serves as a faculty fellow in the Drexel Writing Center. Reflecting her eclectic interests in cultural studies, women's studies, history, and film, her publications include book and film reviews and articles on World War I Aviation, Jane Austen, and British Cinema.

Sonia Shah is a senior biology major, with a minor in philosophy, from North Wales, PA. She will be conducting stem cell research at the National Institute of Health after graduating, and plans to attend medical school in the future.

Myrna B. Shure is a developmental psychologist at Drexel University. Her research interests include social and emotional development in children, and her programs *I Can Problem Solve* for schools and *Raising a Thinking Child* for families have been recognized as evidence-based by the Office of Juvenile Justice and Delinquency Prevention, among others. She is also the author of three trade books for parents, her most recent being *Thinking Parent, Thinking Child*, which helps families turn their most challenging problems into solutions.

Kerri Sullivan is a senior in the film/video program. During her time at Drexel, she was editor-in-chief of *Maya* (Drexel's undergraduate literary magazine), did her co-op for the Department of Photographs at the Metropolitan Museum of Art, and wrote/shot/edited a senior thesis film about a school shooting. She plans to go to graduate school for library science and concentrate on archival work. She will always continue to write and make photographs.

Shelby Vittek is a liberal studies major pursuing her love for food and traveling through writing. She writes a biweekly column for the *Triangle*. Her writing has appeared in the *Washington Post*. After graduation she wants to attend graduate school for journalism.

Kathleen Volk Miller is co-editor of *Painted Bride Quarterly*, co-director of the Drexel Publishing Group, and an associate teaching professor at Drexel University. She is a weekly blogger (Thursdays) for *Philadelphia Magazine*'s Philly Post and is currently working on a collection of essays.

Scott Warnock is an associate professor of English and Director of the Writing Center and Writing Across the Curriculum. He writes "Virtual Children," a bi-weekly column/blog, for the site *When Falls the Coliseum*.

Matt Whitworth is a junior pursuing a double major in international area studies and philosophy. He fully anticipates writing, reading, traveling, and thinking throughout his entire life.

Kenneth Wittwer is a freshman sociology major in the College of Arts and Sciences and the Pennoni Honors College, and is pursuing a Certificate in Writing and Publishing through the Department of English and Philosophy. He has a work-study position as an intercultural advocate in the Office of Multicultural Programs, and has been a museum educator at the Franklin Institute for the past two years. He is very active in FUSE (Foundation of Undergraduates for Sexual Equality) and the LGBTQ rights movement. He has always lived in the Philadelphia area and is very passionate about music, writing, education, and being an active community member.

Stephen Zachariah is a first-year biomedical engineering major from Succasunna, New Jersey. He attended Roxbury High School, where he graduated in the top 1% of his class and was heavily involved in the instrumental and vocal music department, most notably singing in the 2010 New Jersey All-State Chorus. Stephen plays tennis and also enjoys playing the guitar and piano. He is currently involved in Drexel's auditioned University Chorus and was selected for Drexel's 2012 STAR summer research program. In the future, he hopes to pursue a career in the field of medicine.